# THE TALMUD
# A BIOGRAPHY

# The Talmud
# A Biography

*Banned, Censored and Burned.*
*The book they couldn't suppress*

Harry Freedman

BLOOMSBURY
LONDON • NEW DELHI • NEW YORK • SYDNEY

First published in Great Britain 2014

Copyright © Harry Freedman, 2014

The moral right of the author has been asserted

A Continuum book

Bloomsbury Publishing Plc
50 Bedford Square
London WC1B 3DP

www.bloomsbury.com

Bloomsbury is a registered trademark of Bloomsbury Publishing Plc

Bloomsbury Publishing, London, New Delhi, New York and Sydney

A CIP record for this book is available from the British Library.

ISBN 978-1-4729-0594-9

10 9 8 7 6 5 4 3

Typeset by Fakenham Prepress Solutions, Fakenham, Norfolk NR21 8NN

Printed and bound in the U.S.A. by Thomson-Shore Inc., Dexter, Michigan

# Contents

# About the Author

Harry Freedman has a doctorate in the ancient Aramaic translation of the Bible. His previous books include *The Gospels' Veiled Agenda: Revolution, Priesthood and the Holy Grail.* He lives in London with his wife Karen.

You can read more about the Talmud, including selected passages, at www.talmudbiography.com.

# Preface

This is the story of a book. A book which defines the religion of the Jews. A book which, arguably, defines the Jews themselves.

Most books don't have their own story, at best they have a narrative about their publishing history and subsequent reception by the public. But the Talmud has more than just a story, it has a turbulent history. One which, in many ways, parallels the history of the Jewish people.

The Talmud was composed as a record of discussions amongst scholars and sages in the ancient Jewish diaspora, in towns and villages close to Baghdad. As the Jews dispersed across the world, the Talmud went with them, travelling along trade and migratory routes into the Maghreb, Europe, Arabia and the East. It became the foundation of the Jewish legal system, the bedrock of the Jewish faith. It became more important to the Jews than the Bible itself.

The Jews dwelt amongst many cultures. They exchanged perspectives and ideas with their neighbours. Early contacts between Judaism and Islam produced an intense, intellectual cross-fertilization, the effects of which can still be discerned in Talmudic and Islamic law. The medieval encounter between the Jews and Christianity was less benign, the Church regarded the Talmud as the obstacle which prevented them from converting the Jews. Their response was to challenge, burn, ban and censor it.

Later generations, particularly in Protestant Europe, although just as intent on converting the Jews nevertheless explored the Talmud for ideas. We find philosophers and poets, republicans and kings, priests and professors all probing the Talmud, seeking inspiration, support or validation for their particular points of view.

The most intractable of the Talmud's challenges came from the Jews themselves. Rejectionists, messianic pretenders and savants vilified it, seeking to delegitimize or at the very least to minimize its influence. But like the Jews themselves, the Talmud's capacity for survival is boundless. Today it is studied by more people than at any time in its history.

From one perspective the Talmud's story is a history of the Jews. From another, it is a window onto the development of world civilization. The history of the Talmud is a testament to what can happen, for better and for worse, when the literature of one culture comes into contact, or conflict, with the beliefs and values of another. Conversely, it illustrates the consequences for a self-contained, inward-looking society when its defining texts are confronted by new ideas from the outside.

The Talmud is a classic of world literature. It's a massive, ancient and seemingly impenetrable work. People devote their lives to studying it. But you are not reading a book about what is *in* the Talmud. This is the story of what *happened* to the Talmud, and the role it has played in world history, religion and culture. It's not a book for experts, or for specialists. It's a book for anyone who wants to know the story of one of the great classics of ancient literature, albeit one which is far less heavily thumbed, outside of Jewish circles, than Homer, Chaucer or Ovid. The content of the Talmud may be esoteric. But its history belongs to us all. For there is scarcely a square inch of the world's surface upon which its story was not, at some time, acted out.

# *Introduction*

## What is The Talmud?

Every nation has its laws. Few nations systematically record the process, the philosophical discussions and legal arguments, which led to those laws. Everybody knows the laws are there for a reason. But the reasons don't make much difference to the everyday life of most people.

The Jews are different. As much value is attached to studying the process by which their laws emerged as to an awareness of the laws themselves. Indeed, studying them is said to be more important than keeping them. Because studying them leads to keeping them.[1]

The Jews are known as the People of the Book.[2] But actually they are the people of the Two Books. The earlier book, the Hebrew Bible is considered the sacred, revealed word of God. But the later book, the man-made Talmud, is the more significant for understanding Judaism.

The Hebrew Bible, or Old Testament, is the foundation of the Jewish religion. It is the basis of Jewish belief and the origin of its ethics, rituals and social legislation. But the Bible deals in concepts, principles and generalities; it rarely pronounces upon its injunctions in detail. The Talmud is a record of the discussions that took place over several centuries, which took the principles laid down in the Bible and gave the religion its form and shape.

There is much in the Bible that has been irrelevant to religious practice for at least two thousand years. Including the system of sacrifices, the treatment of an unknown illness incorrectly referred to as leprosy and many of the agricultural

---

[1] Sifre Deuteronomy 41, Kiddushin 40b.
[2] People of the Book is a term that was first introduced in the Qu'ran to describe a faith, other than Islam, which has a sacred text.

laws. Conversely, the Talmud contains vast amounts of material that may be based on the Bible but is not immediately evident in it. Including discussions on the governance and regulation of society, the practical performance of religious rituals, family relationships and contract and monetary law. It also contains much that is not in the Bible. Medicine, astronomy, folklore, magic, sex and humour, to mention just a few.

The Talmud (the word means study, or teaching) defines the Jewish religion. Adin Steinsaltz, perhaps the greatest commentator on the Talmud of our age, describes it as 'the central pillar supporting the entire spiritual and intellectual edifice of Jewish life'.[3] It's not an easy book. It is an exquisitely complex, highly logical and frequently impenetrable work. For most of its history studying the Talmud has been regarded by the Jews as an intellectual exercise in its own right. An exercise which, since it leads the student to the essence of human knowledge and experience, confers profound spiritual benefit.

The Talmud is a massive work. It contains one million, eight hundred thousand words spanning thirty seven volumes. Although it is concerned with law, it is not a law code. It is a record of discussions that took place in academies in Babylon between the third and fifth centuries, discussions that were based on a book called the Mishnah, a second to third-century codification of Jewish law.

The Talmud was not written as a book, the people whose discussions it preserves had no idea that someone would come along generations later and edit them into a coherent work. A characteristic Talmudic discussion contains the opinions of people, who may have lived centuries apart, woven together to sound as if they are having an actual conversation.

Modern editions of the Talmud are printed with dozens of commentaries, a typical edition takes up as much space on a bookshelf as a good encyclopedia. It is arcane and obscure, written as free flowing prose, with no punctuation, in two languages with traces of others which it mixes together and switches between unselfconsciously. Its logic is dense yet immaculate, it is more interested in the analysis of a problem than the outcome, it frequently refrains from reaching a conclusion, and even when it does convey a decision it can be hard to understand. The Talmud does have an overall structure, as does each of the topics it discusses. But its structures can be hard to discern and the Talmud is capable

---

[3] Steinsaltz, 1989.

of shooting off at tangents for pages on end before returning, sometimes, to the original topic.

A traditional Talmud page doesn't look like the sort of book you are reading now. It's written in three main columns, with additional material in both the left and right margins. The central column which is in a bold typeface contains the Talmud text itself. This column typically includes a few lines from the Mishnah, on which the Talmud is commenting, followed by the Talmud itself.

Of the three main columns, the one on the inside, closest to the binding, contains the commentary of Rashi, the great eleventh-century French commentator. We will meet him in due course. The outside column contains another, slightly later, French commentary, that of the *tosafists*. Both commentaries are written in a cursive script. It's known as Rashi script, not because Rashi wrote in it but because it is the typeface the early Venetian printers used for his commentary and has remained a favourite ever since.

The three columns do not always run in parallel from the top to the bottom of the page. The printers needed to synchronize the main Talmud text with the commentaries, to make it easier for the reader to read the commentary and main text as a single unit. So often one of the columns finishes part way down the page and an adjacent column wraps above and beneath it, the result is that the main text is surrounded by commentary. The margins contain other commentaries or cross references to passages from the Bible and elsewhere in the Talmud that are cited in the text.[4]

The Talmud may be the central pillar of Jewish life, studying it may confer profound spiritual benefit, but most Jews have never picked up a volume, let alone studied it. Serious Talmud study is an esoteric activity, for people with scholarly or religious interest, a certain sort of mind and great powers of concentration. But just because few people have studied it, doesn't mean that if they hear a sentence beginning with the words 'the Talmud says …', they won't prick up their ears. There may be no desire or opportunity to study it, but people want to know what it says. It's that sort of book.

---

[4] There are many examples of a Talmud page on the internet. A good resource is that posted by Eliezer Segal, http://people.ucalgary.ca/~elsegal/TalmudPage.html

## The Talmud's Story

Nineteen hundred years of history (if we include the period during which the Talmud was being composed) is a lot to put into one book. If all the events and personalities in the Talmud's history were included it would end up as an encyclopedia. My purpose in writing this biography is to provide a sense of the Talmud's vast and extensive history, not to distil everything that happened into a single tome. The result is that some of the key events and locations have been covered in greater detail than others, a few important places and, unfortunately, many important people have not been mentioned at all. My aim was to keep the story interesting and informative, even at the expense of comprehensiveness.

A similar disclaimer applies to the scholars whom I have quoted and their research. There is much about the Talmud's history that scholars dispute: particularly the questions of who edited it and when; whether it was edited in its oral or written form; how it evolved from an oral composition to a written text and just how fluid the content was whilst it was being transmitted. I haven't tried to present the views of every scholar, nor necessarily to follow the opinions of the greatest authorities in the field. I have tended to follow the research that best fits with the story I am telling, provided always that the research is credible and respected in academic circles. The fact that I have cited some scholars and sources and not mentioned others does not reflect any particular preference or approval, it is simply the consequence of trying to distil such a large amount of history into a readable work.

Much of what I have written will not be well received in traditional Talmudic circles. I have approached the Talmud as world literature, not as the exclusive property of the *yeshiva*. This is not a book for the Talmud scholar, unless they are interested in the events surrounding the opus to which they have devoted their life. It is a book for those who want to know what the Talmud is, and why the world would be a greatly impoverished place without it.

I have tried to keep things as simple as possible in order that the story flows. So although this is a biography of the Babylonian Talmud I have, all the way through, referred to it simply as the Talmud. There is of course another Talmud, the *Yerushalmi* or Jerusalem Talmud, and I do touch on it from time to time. But for over a thousand years the Babylonian Talmud has been dominant and conventionally that is the one nearly everyone means when they talk about the Talmud.

I have tried to minimize the use of non-English words. This hasn't always been possible, particularly when referring to technical concepts, or things that would require a full sentence to translate. The glossary at the back will help.

A word on terminology. The main body of the Talmud, that part which comments on the Mishnah is also known as the *gemara*, an Aramaic word meaning 'teaching'. The words Talmud and *gemara* are synonymous and many people prefer the latter term. The designation *gemara* was introduced by medieval printers because the Church censors had banned the use of the word Talmud. For simplicity I have used the word Talmud throughout this book. References to the Babylonian Talmud are tractate and page only, the prefixes M and J before a tractate name refer to the Mishnah and Jerusalem Talmud respectively.

A man asked a rabbi to teach him something of the Talmud. The rabbi refused. 'You haven't got a head for Talmud.' The man persisted. So the rabbi asked him the following question.

'Two men fell down the same chimney. One came out clean the other came out dirty. Which one went to wash?'

'The dirty one of course' replied the man.

'No!' said the rabbi. 'I knew you didn't have a head for Talmud. Now go away and leave me alone.'

'Try me once more' pleaded the man.

'Just once more then. Two men fell down the same chimney. One came out clean the other came out dirty. Which one went to wash?'

The man thought for a moment then grinned. 'The clean one. He looks at the dirty one and thinks he must be dirty too.'

'Idiot. You have no head for Talmud. Leave me alone.'

The man was crestfallen. 'Try me one last time. Please.'

'One last time then. Two men fell down a chimney. One came out clean the other came out dirty. Which one went to wash?'

He pondered hard. 'The clean one looks at the dirty one. He's looking at me, he thinks, and he's not washing, so he must think he's clean. So I must be clean. So, neither of them wash!'

'Moron!' yelled the rabbi. 'How can you imagine that two men can fall down the same chimney, and one come out clean and the other dirty!'

PART I

*The Talmud in its World*

# 1

## *In the beginning*

Why does every volume of the Talmud begin with page 2 and not page 1? To teach us that no matter how much we learn, we have not yet reached the first page!

R. Levi Yitzhok of Berditchev

### White fire upon black fire

Round about three and a half thousand years ago, according to the book of Exodus, Moses descended from Mount Sinai carrying two tablets of stone. On it were engraved ten commandments. According to one legend the commandments were written in white fire, against a background of black fire. Another legend has it that the words were engraved right through the rock, yet the centres of the round letters, which by rights should have fallen out, remained miraculously in place and the writing was legible from each side.

These Ten Commandments were to become the centrepiece of the five books which Moses wrote during the forty years that the Israelites wandered through the wilderness. The books became known as the Torah, or Teaching.

The Five Books of Moses are amongst the most exalted works of world literature. They contain stories that have inspired generations, proclaim religious and ethical teachings which spawned three great faiths and lay out a complex system of legislation which was designed to animate the lives of the Israelite tribes for all eternity.

But for all their grandeur they are not easy books. The chronology can be confused, sometimes it is hard to fathom out the sequence in which events occurred. Most of the laws and regulations seem to be hazy, invariably they are not spelled out in enough detail. Several teachings appear distinctly cruel, even unethical to modern minds. Inspirational it may be. But the Torah often leaves its readers with more questions than answers.

For example, the Torah instructs the Israelites to keep the Sabbath. But nowhere does it explicitly say how this is to be done. It speaks of husbands and wives, but it does not detail how a marriage ceremony is to be conducted; or indeed, if one is needed at all. It explains that the Israelites are merely lease-holders in the Promised Land; that the earth is God's and every fifty years all property is to be returned to the families to whom it was originally given. But it offers no guidance on how the inevitable property disputes are to be resolved.

Many modern scholars do not believe the Mount Sinai story. Nor do they believe that Moses was the author of the Torah. Literary analysis of the text of Torah suggests it was composed about two and a half to three thousand years ago, with material from several different sources woven into a more or less coherent whole. If that's so, it's not surprising that the book contains contra-dictions and repetitions. It's what one would expect from documents stitched together by ancient editors.

But the origins of the Torah needn't concern us right now. For most of its history, until the nineteenth century in fact, nobody doubted that the Torah was written by Moses in the wilderness (apart perhaps from the last few verses relating his death). If there were any suspicions at all about its composition, it was whether God had dictated the Torah for Moses to write down, or whether the Israelite leader had made it up.[1]

The Jews, without exception, held the first view. The Torah was the word of God, prescribing the way they were to live their lives. Every single letter was significant; the Torah contained all the secrets of the universe. More than that even, according to some it was the blueprint for the creation of the world. The mystics went as far as to claim that the Torah existed before the Creation, that God consulted it when he formed the heavens and the earth.

People likened the Torah to water. It was the source of life, it flowed every-where, no earthly force could hold it back. And just as the flood covers the dry land beneath, so too the Torah conceals hidden depths, of knowledge, wisdom and understanding.

This meant that its inconsistencies and confusing passages would need to be resolved. People could only obey the frequent exhortations in the Torah that they live by its commandments, if they knew what this entailed. It stood

---

[1] This question was being discussed at least as long ago as the second century. When the Mishnah in Sanhedrin 12.1 proclaims that someone who denies that the Torah comes from heaven has no portion in the world to come, it is referring to those who argued that the Torah was Moses' own creation.

to reason that there had to be a system that would enable them to plumb the depths of the text, harmonize its wisdom and fathom its contradictions.

## The interpretative tradition

To the believer, Moses' lack of detail is deliberate. The Torah is perfect by definition, it's inconceivable that it could be incomplete, or lack key information. The reason why parts of it are hard to understand must be that the Torah deliberately challenges its readers to enquire more deeply, to reveal its concealed meaning, to use their God-given power of human knowledge and learning to decode the God-given text.

So people began to study the Torah, seeking to uncover its hidden layers trying to understand what God really wanted from them. It wasn't just a question of understanding the laws, they hoped to become wiser and elevate themselves spiritually, to become closer to their Creator and discover eternal Truth.[2]

The process of interpreting the Torah is one of the longest continuous fields of human scholarly activity. It has been going on for thousands of years. It has spawned a vast literary corpus and a curriculum of study that is virtually unbounded.

At the heart of this curriculum lies the Babylonian Talmud, a multi-volume compendium as big as an encyclopedia, covering topics as diverse as law, faith, spirituality, folklore, medicine, magic, ethics, sex, relationships, humour and prayer. It's called Babylonian because it was composed in Babylon, part of modern-day Iraq, between the third and sixth centuries.

The Babylonian Talmud has a lesser-known, slightly older cousin, the Jerusalem Talmud, which hailed from Roman-occupied Israel. Generally when we talk about the Talmud, we mean the Babylonian version.

The Talmud might look like a book. But it is far more than that. It's an institution. People devote their lives to studying it. No other book in history has made such demands of its readers. Its raison d'être is to explain the Torah.

---

[2] Bible study begins even in the Bible itself. Many of the psalms, which were written after the Torah, add detail and explanations to events first recorded in the Torah. Psalm 29, for example, is an expansion of the events at Mount Sinai and Psalm 104 is a poetic description of the Creation. Many of the psalms are in effect the earliest layer of interpretation of the Torah.

But its explanations only raise more questions. It is not a linear work; it doesn't start with an introduction and build to a conclusion. You can open it anywhere and you rarely have to turn back to find out what's been going on. It's often referred to as the Sea of Talmud, possibly because wherever you dive in, you're swimming.

The Talmud is arcane and obscure. The Babylonian version is written in two languages, which it mixes together and moves between, seamlessly. Its logic is dense, the arguments it puts forward are often perplexing. It presents arguments but it is not preoccupied with finding solutions. Equally, it's quite happy for a problem to have multiple solutions, 'these and these are the words of the living God'.[3] If the Torah raised questions, the Talmud raises questions about questions.

And yet for all that, or perhaps because of it, no other book in the world has had a comparable history. A history that's not always been happy. But a history which leaves us wondering almost as much about the book itself as the material it contains. It's more of a biography than a history, really. Not so much the story of a book as the story of a life.

**The Oral Law**

Most of the Talmud is based on a record of discussions held in the rabbinic academies in Babylon between the years 230 and 500 CE. Perhaps calling it a record is a bit misleading because the discussions are not set out formally, subject by subject, speaker by speaker. It's nothing like Hansard or the Congressional Record, which give precise accounts of who said what, and when, in a debate.

Instead, the Talmud tends to weave several topics together, skipping seamlessly from one to the other, creating conversations between people who lived generations apart, switching languages as it goes; from Hebrew to Aramaic and back again with a few Greek words thrown in, fabricating a complex web of hypothesis, rejection, argument and counter-argument. It is a perplexing, confusing, and rigorously logical work. It takes nothing for granted and is not satisfied with anything less than absolute certainty.[4]

---

[3] Eruvin 13b.
[4] Steinsaltz, 1989, p. 3.

At the heart of the Talmud is an earlier work known as the *Mishnah*. Mishnah literally means repetition, both because it was taught through verbal repetition and because it repeats and explains the laws in the Torah.

The Mishnah sorts the laws in the Torah into topics and clarifies them, generally by giving short, practical examples. The book we call the Talmud is made up of short snatches from the Mishnah, with commentary in between. The commentary can be quite lengthy and shoots off at all sorts of tangents, making it easy to forget what was being commented on in the first place.

One of the sections of the Mishnah is called Chapters of the Fathers. It's an unusual title; there are sixty three sections in the Mishnah and apart from this one they are all named after legal or religious topics, like Betrothals, Vows or Blessings.

But Chapters of the Fathers is not about legal matters at all, in fact it's not really clear why it was included in the Mishnah. It's a collection of motivational statements, ethical urgings and life advice from rabbis who lived during the first and second centuries. In modern terms, it's like a collection of sound bites from leading business gurus, political orators, celebrity preachers and media personalities.

Chapters of the Fathers begins like this:

> Moses received the Torah on Mount Sinai and transmitted it to Joshua; Joshua to the elders; the elders to the prophets; and the prophets handed it down to the men of the Great Assembly.[5]

It's a simple statement and its meaning is quite obvious. The trouble is, it doesn't fit with what the Torah itself says. The Torah is a text for the people, it says so quite clearly.[6] Moses was instructed to teach the Torah to the Children of Israel.[7] It's a public document, the heritage of every Israelite. It's not some arcane knowledge to be handed down in secret across the generations, through a succession of dignitaries to the men of the Great Assembly, whoever they were.

And this is where the story of the Talmud has its first encounter with politics. Because the Torah that Moses transmitted to Joshua and so on is not the Torah that God instructed Moses to write in the wilderness, the Torah that contains

---

[5] M. Avot 1.1.
[6] Deuteronomy 33.4: 'Moses commanded the Torah to us; an inheritance to the congregation of Jacob'.
[7] Deuteronomy 31.9–19.

the Ten Commandments. It's another Torah altogether. It is in fact a Torah which explains the other Torah. It's enough to make your head spin, isn't it?

According to Jewish belief there are two Torahs, not one. One was dictated by God to Moses in the wilderness, placed into a wooden chest overlaid with gold in the sacred Tabernacle in the wilderness, transferred in due course to the Jerusalem Temple and copied by scribes onto parchment scrolls that today reside in places of worship. When people talk about the Torah that's the one they mean.

But the other Torah wasn't written down. It was delivered verbally to Moses by God, for him to transmit by word of mouth to his successor, Joshua, who in turn would pass it on, just as it says in Chapters of the Fathers. This second, unwritten Torah explains and clarifies the public Torah which God dictated to Moses.

It still sounds a bit like a power-play, doesn't it? Moses is given some arcane knowledge which only the leaders of the people have access to. Whoever has it passes it to his successor (all the leaders were men). We don't hear of anyone disclosing it to the ordinary people; in the sections of the Bible that follow the Five Books of Moses, which covers centuries of Israelite history, there is no mention of it. The first we hear of it is in Chapters of the Fathers about a thousand years after Moses received it,

It's the stuff of blockbuster movies, the secrets of power, handed down directly by the All-Powerful to His representatives on earth, to be used to interpret the law to suit the needs of a powerful elite.

But it doesn't mean that at all. The very fact that the Chapters of the Fathers mentions the transmission of this Torah, the Oral Torah as it became known, confirms that its existence was not meant to be secret. On the contrary, the verbally communicated Torah is as public as the written Torah, it was simply entrusted to the leaders of the people to ensure it was handed down and not forgotten. It was essential that it didn't become lost; it was the key to the written Torah. It was needed to decode all the written Torah's apparent contradictions and inconsistencies.

The Oral Torah is the guide to the written Torah, and it was the duty of the leaders to preserve and transmit it. But to ensure that ordinary people were aware of its importance, its existence was publicized in Chapters of the Fathers.

That at least is the religious view. It's not the only one.

To understand the politics of this we have to go back to the period, roughly 100 BCE to 100 CE. The world was rapidly modernizing. New trade routes were opening up, the Roman Empire was facilitating communication between remote places; merchants, armies and civil administrators were coming and going. Change was in the air. New ideas were beginning to circulate, the world was becoming globally connected, in an ancient sort of way.

Like many Mediterranean lands, the Israelite nation was under Roman rule. Life was hard, people were poor (apart from the ruling elite) and generally demoralized. Bands of partisans would spring up from time to time roaming the countryside and launching occasional attacks on the Romans, but most people were too busy trying to scrape a meagre existence together to bother to become heroes.

Jerusalem was the religious and political capital of the Jewish nation. Power resided in its Temple, which the Roman puppet-king Herod was restoring to undreamed of magnificence. But the priests who ran the Temple, and most of the judges who sat in the Sanhedrin, which was both the Supreme Court and the legislature, were part of a patrician sect in Jewish society known as the Sadducees.

The Sadducees had done well under Roman occupation, and many of the ordinary people resented their wealth and privilege. The people found they had much more in common with a group of pious scholars who observed conditions of strict ritual purity, abstaining from forbidden foods and distancing themselves from objects that Moses had declared impure because they carried a taint of death or decay. They called themselves Pharisees, or Separatists. In due course their leaders would go by the title rabbi, or teacher.

As their support grew amongst the working classes the scholars found their political voice. Their leaders started to vie for influence in the Temple and the Sanhedrin. Their numbers and popularity grew and the ruling classes could no longer ignore them.[8]

The Pharisees saw things very differently from the Sadducees. The written Torah had given the priests privileges which had enabled many of them to grow wealthy and complacent. The Pharisees argued that these privileges were being abused, that the written Torah had been misinterpreted. They quoted teachings

---

[8] Freedman, 2009. Nor could they ignore another popular movement led by Jesus of Nazareth, but events led his followers off in a different direction and for now they only touch lightly on our story. The reason why Matthew rails so strongly against the Pharisees is that they rivalled the early Christians for political power. However, the political vision of the early Christians was centred on reforming the Temple. When it was destroyed they disappeared from the political scene and concentrated solely on their universalist religious mission, under Paul's leadership.

that had been handed down by word of mouth, teachings that regulated the power of the priests, teachings to which the Sadducees paid no attention. The Pharisees argued that these word-of-mouth traditions had the full authority of law, that they were in fact an unwritten Oral Torah.

It is not clear whether the Pharisees had always believed that their oral traditions were given to Moses on Mount Sinai, or whether this was a later idea which gained currency because it gave their position more legitimacy. The historical view is that the Oral Torah developed organically through family and social traditions, and connecting it with Moses was just a device to give it authority. The religious view is that it was divinely transmitted from Mount Sinai through Moses and the prophets to the leaders of later generations.

Either way, the Pharisees considered the Oral Torah to be the key to interpreting the written law. The Sadducees denied its existence altogether. The battle for religious and legal power was on.[9]

---

[9] Although belief in the Oral Torah goes back at least 2,000 years we are only now beginning to understand the process through which the verbal traditions were handed down. In the 1930s Millman Parry, a scholar of oral literature showed that Homer's great epic poetry relied on recurring phrases, metre and verse to be memoried (Parry, 1928). Elizabeth Shanks Alexander (Alexander, E. S., 1999) has shown that a similar process of 'building blocks' allowed the Oral Law to be memorized and transmitted. She gives an example from the laws of oaths:

> [If a person took] an oath, [saying 'I swear] I will not eat,' and then he ate wheat bread, barley bread, and spelt bread—he is only liable [to bring a sacrifice] on one count {not one for each kind of bread}.
> [If a person took] an oath, [saying 'I swear] that I will not eat wheat bread, barley bread, and spelt bread,' and then he ate [them]—he is liable [to bring a sacrifice] on each and every count [one for each kind of bread].

> Mishnah Shavuot 3.2

The two passages appear virtually identical but deal with two different oaths. The order of events are the same – someone vows not to eat, then eats and becomes liable to offer a sacrifice, to make amends for breaking his vow. The wording in each passage is the same, other than that the 'plug in' concerning the bread has changed. In the first formula the 'plug in' is included as part of the violation of the oath, in the second formula it is part of the formulation of the oath. People would find it easy remember the outlines of these passages because of the fixed, repeating 'building blocks'. The only effort they had to make in memorizing the tradition was to put the 'plug ins' in the right places.

2

# The origins of the Talmud

Rabbi Ila'i said: 'By three things may a person's character be determined: By his drinking and spending habits and by his anger.' Some say: 'Also by his laughter.'[1]

## The destruction of the Temple

The struggle for religious power between the Pharisees and Sadducees continued until the year 70 CE. By this time the military situation in the land had completely deteriorated. Guerrilla groups were launching attacks on the Romans on a daily basis; the mighty Roman legions had suffered considerable setbacks.

The Empire decided it was time to flex its muscles. Roman forces besieged Jerusalem, starved the population into submission then burnt down the city and destroyed the Temple. It is hard for us, two thousand years and as many miles away, to grasp the full impact of this event.

It was far more than the mere demolition of a building. It was more even than the razing of a city and the destruction of its population, horrendous as that was. The Temple was not only the centre of the Israelite religion, it housed the legislature and the judiciary. It was the commercial centre. The destruction of the Temple threatened to herald the end, not just of the religion, but even of the last vestiges of Israelite autonomy. Like so many before them, the Israelite nation was threatened with extinction.

Desperate times tend to produce remarkable people. The rebuilding of Judaism, and the emergence of Christianity, which was taking place in the same place at exactly the same time, can be directly attributed to the vision and skill of two people; Paul for the Christians and Yohanan ben Zakkai for the Jews.

---

[1] Eruvin 65b.

Paul's story is well known. Ben Zakkai's less so. The legend[2] is that when the situation inside besieged Jerusalem became absolutely desperate, disease and famine having already decimated the population, ben Zakkai pleaded with the militants guarding the city gates to allow him to leave and negotiate a surrender. The militants would have none of it. Ben Zakkai was the leader of the peace camp, and the confrontational militants were diametrically opposed to everything he stood for.

However the leader of the militants, a man called Abba Sikra, or Red Father,[3] just happened to be ben Zakkai's nephew. He vowed to help his uncle slip past the gatekeepers and reach the Roman camp. Abba Sikra told the rabbi to climb into a coffin, play dead and get his students to carry him out of the city on the pretence that he was being taken for burial. Abba Sikra then made sure that guards let the coffin through with the appropriate amount of respect.

Once outside the city walls, ben Zakkai climbed out of the coffin and went to see the Roman commander, probably Titus (although the legend says it was his father, Vespasian). According to the legend ben Zakkai, knowing that the city would fall, performed some minor miracles which endeared him to the Roman commander and allowed him to negotiate the safe passage of the Pharisee rabbis and their students out of Jerusalem. Titus granted him a refuge in Yavneh, a small town in the south-west of the country.

The Roman authorities probably didn't think much about this. They couldn't imagine that giving a refuge to Yohanan ben Zakkai, his colleagues and students would be of any great consequence. After all, a bunch of holy men and scholars could hardly present a threat to the rampant Roman Empire. Had they thought it through though, the Romans could have saved themselves a century or more of trouble. If they'd only realized what ben Zakkai and his colleagues were about to do for the national morale, and the faith of the Jews.

The destruction of the Temple was a tragedy for the nation but for the Pharisees some good came out of it. The Sadducees no longer had their power base and their priestly allies had virtually no role at all, since the whole of their religious mission had been to conduct the services in the Temple.

In Yavneh the Pharisees were faced with a stark reality. Unless they could find a way to save the religion that now lacked its Temple and sacrificial cult,

---

[2] Gittin 56a, Echa Rabba 1.
[3] It has also been conjectured that his name meant 'Father of the Sicarii', one of the militant, anti-Roman gangs then active in Israel, who took their name from their trademark curved dagger or Sicarius.

their civilization would disappear. The proud, independent Israelite culture with its rich biblical and prophetic heritage would be eradicated, their people would become just another subjugated nation under the Roman thumb.

The tools the Pharisees had at their disposal were the written Torah, the oral traditions and their perfect faith. That was enough. Under Yohanan ben Zakkai's leadership the Pharisees were about to set in place a process that would eventually result in the composition of the Talmud and two thousand years of unbroken study.

## The vineyard at Yavneh

The academy that Yohanan ben Zakkai established at Yavneh was known as the Vineyard. It's not clear why. It's possible that the discussions took place in a field amongst grapevines, or that whatever buildings they had were erected on the site of an old vineyard. One theory, however, has it that the scholars sat in rows, planted and fruitful, just like grapevines.[4]

According to Chapters of the Fathers, after the Men of the Great Assembly received the Oral Law from the prophets they passed it to a pair of scholars, who passed it on to another pair, and so on, for five generations.[5] The names of the fifth pair were Hillel and Shammai, and although they were long dead by the time the Vineyard was established, their respective students would have been amongst those who sat in rows in the academy.

It is said of Shammai that a non-Jew approached him and offered to convert to Judaism if he could be taught the whole of the Torah while he stood on one leg. Obviously it was an impossible request and Shammai angrily drove him away. The man then approached Hillel and made the same proposal. Hillel replied, 'That which is hateful to you, do not do to your fellow. The rest is commentary. Go and learn.[6]' Shammai, who is also credited with saying 'Greet everyone cheerfully'[7] was no doubt having a bad day.

Hillel and Shammai held differing views on many issues. But the things they disagreed about are less important than the fact that they disagreed. Indeed,

---

[4] J. Berachot 4.1 7d.
[5] M. Avot 1.2ff.
[6] Shabbat 31a.
[7] M. Avot 1.5.

their disagreements were considered by the scholars in the Vineyard to be not just valid, but essential.

> For three years there was a dispute between Hillel's students and Shammai's students, the former asserting, 'The law is in agreement with our views,' and the latter claiming, 'The law is in agreement with our views.' Then a voice from heaven announced, 'These and these are the words of the Living God.'[8]

Nothing illustrates the process of Talmudic debate better than the fact that different opinions can each be 'the words of the Living God'. Even though the Talmud is concerned with laws, behaviours and beliefs, it's less interested in reaching conclusions than in presenting different ways of looking at a problem. It's not so much the final decision that counts as the process which leads to it.

The discussions in the Vineyard were not recorded in writing and anything we know about them comes from sources written long after. It's clear that the immediate priority for Yohanan ben Zakkai and his colleagues was to make sure that their knowledge of the Torah and its oral interpretation didn't get lost in all the national turmoil and upheaval. The Vineyard was the forum for transmitting their knowledge to the next generation of scholars.

But the Vineyard wasn't just a school or an academy. Sure, it contained young students who learned at the feet of older, venerated scholars. But rather than delivering lessons according to a curriculum, it seems that the method of teaching was for the students to sit in on the discussions of the older scholars, who were collaborating to collect and clarify the entire body of Jewish law; creating a belief system and legal code that no future group of dissenters, whether Sadducee or anyone else, could come along and challenge.

The discussions would start with a senior scholar stating their memory of how a particular ritual had been performed, or legal matter handled. Others might disagree, if they had different memories. Someone might quote an earlier authority; to support their own view, or to challenge another. Whatever opinions were put forward had to be in line with the text of the written Torah; if the law that Moses had written in the wilderness couldn't be interpreted in such a way as to underpin a point of view; it wasn't accepted.

---

[8] Eruvin 13b.

A key topic was how to deal with rituals that used to be performed in the Temple. Animal sacrifices had been abolished altogether; the Torah had confined the offering of them to the Temple. But many rituals had not involved sacrifices and the Pharisees believed in making the religion open to everyone. So wherever they could Yohanan ben Zakkai and his colleagues instituted new procedures that allowed ordinary people to perform those rituals that had once been in the exclusive domain of the Temple.[9]

But the most important task of all for the rabbis in the Vineyard was to inspire, enthuse and motivate their demoralized and traumatized nation; to encourage people to reconnect with a faith which seemed to have failed them so badly. In doing this they demonstrated a remarkable aptitude for creativity. Just as Moses's Torah had woven together stories, laws and grand ideas, so too the Yavneh scholars engaged in flights of imagination, illustrating their ideas with parables, folk tales and imagery.

On that day Rabbi Eliezer brought forward every imaginable argument but the other scholars did not accept them. He said: 'If the law agrees with me, let this carob-tree prove it!' Thereupon the carob-tree was torn a hundred cubits out of its place. 'No proof can be brought from a carob-tree,' they retorted. Again he said to them: 'If the law agrees with me, let the stream of water prove it!' Whereupon the stream of water flowed backwards — 'No proof can be brought from a stream of water,' they rejoined. Again he urged: 'If the law agrees with me, let the walls of the study house prove it,' whereupon the walls began to incline.

But Rabbi Joshua rebuked the walls, saying: 'When scholars are engaged in a legal dispute, what right have you to interfere?' So they did not fall, in honour of Rabbi Joshua, nor did they resume the upright, in honour of Rabbi Eliezer; and they are still leaning to this day.

Again he said to them: 'If the law agrees with me, let it be proved from Heaven!' Whereupon a Heavenly Voice cried out: 'Why do you dispute with Rabbi Eliezer, seeing that in all matters the law agrees with him!' But Rabbi Joshua arose and exclaimed: 'The Torah is not in heaven!'

What did he mean by this? — Said Rabbi Jeremiah: That once the Torah had already been given at Mount Sinai; we pay no attention to a Heavenly Voice, because it also says in the Torah, You shall follow the majority view.[10]

---

[9] The best-known examples of these are the blowing of the shofar (the sounding of musical notes using a ram's horn) at New Year, the waving of palm branches at the festival of Tabernacles and the festive meal at Passover, all of which were originally Temple rites.

[10] Bava Metzia 59b. I have based all translations from the Talmud on Epstein, 1935–1952, with occasional amendments.

## Recording the Oral Law

The following century was amongst the most tumultuous in Israelite history. A series of rebellions by the Jews led to harsh reprisals by the Romans. The fighting reached a head in 132 CE when a band of guerrillas under the leadership of Bar Koziba staged a successful revolt, put the Romans to flight and declared an independent Jewish state.

It didn't last long though. Three years later the revolution was over and the Jews were subjugated once again. A harsh period of intense religious and personal persecution orchestrated by the Roman emperor Hadrian began.

Traumatic social and political conditions make it difficult to preserve oral traditions. People move around, communication becomes difficult, things get forgotten or misrepresented. At the same time the Vineyard had expanded far beyond its original borders, it had spawned a generation of major scholars, who were now dotted all over the country, teaching when they could but mainly in hiding from the Romans. The sheer volume of material that had been taught since the opening of the Vineyard, and the difficult conditions under which it was now being disseminated meant that the oral tradition was tottering.

The rabbis began to realize that they would need to commit their teachings to writing. If they didn't, the teachings would be lost. So gradually, written codifications of the Oral Law began to emerge.

We don't know who started the process of writing down the Oral Law. One theory is that its recording began on the day that Eleazar ben Azariah was appointed as head of the Academy, in place of the hereditary leader Rabban Gamaliel II, the great-grandson of Hillel and grandson of Paul's teacher Gamaliel I.[11]

Gamaliel had inherited the title of *Nasi* from his father. Literally meaning 'prince', the *Nasi* was the leader of the rabbinic community. Hillel had been the first *Nasi*, the title was granted to him in recognition of his scholarship. The title was hereditary, which reflected the fact that the *Nasi* could trace his descent back to King David, but although he was called a prince, and had formal contacts with the Roman authorities, he didn't have a royal lifestyle in the sense we would think of it today.

Gamaliel II was a severe, but probably quite insecure leader. Like many weak men he tried to impose his will even at times when it would have been politic

---

[11] Acts of the Apostles 22.3. Despite his strong Pharisaic credentials Gamaliel I was canonized by the Roman Church.

for him to hold back. He often found himself in conflict with the other senior rabbis, notably Rabbi Joshua. On one notable occasion he publicly humiliated Joshua by ordering him to remain on his feet whilst he sat and taught. The other rabbis, who'd had enough of his autocratic behaviour took the unprecedented decision to depose him, and appointed Eleazar ben Azariah in his place.[12]

On the day that Eleazar was appointed, according the Talmudic account, the gates of the academy were thrown open and up to 700 new students, who had not matched up to Gamaliel's strict admission criteria, were admitted. Any law about which there was a doubt was apparently discussed on that day, clarified and codified in a collection known as Eduyyot, or Testimonies.

Eduyyot, which was later absorbed into the Mishnah, contains a vast number of laws, and it is probably an exaggeration to say that that they were all clarified on one day. But the deposing of Rabban Gamaliel II towards the end of the first century seems to have heralded a sea change which not only expanded the Academy but also began the process of crystallizing and recording legal decisions.

Gamaliel's office was held in high respect by the scholars. They did not want to depose him permanently. But he could not be reinstated until he apologized to Rabbi Joshua. This he agreed to do.

As he entered Joshua's hovel – no more than a simple clay brick structure with an earthen floor and timber strewn roof, he saw that the walls were black. 'It seems to me,' said Gamaliel, 'that you are a charcoal burner.' Joshua, no doubt raising his eyes to heaven replied, 'Alas for the generation of which you are the leader, seeing that you know nothing of the troubles of the scholars, their struggles to support and sustain themselves.'[13]

Even after he had apologized it wasn't easy to restore Gamaliel to his office. Many of the scholars objected, not just because they didn't want Gamaliel back but also because of the slight they thought this would cast on Eleazar ben Azariah, who had succeeded him. It fell to a younger colleague, Rabbi Akiva to propose a solution through which they would share the office.

Akiva is the best known and most highly regarded of all the rabbis. Legends and stories about him abound. Unfortunately this makes it hard to know his true life history, which is concealed somewhere beneath layers of folklore and fable.

---

[12] Berachot 27b, J. Ta'anit 4.6 (68d).
[13] Berachot 28a.

We do know that he was amongst the first to systematically compile and classify the Oral Law. We know this because in a small number of places the Mishnah itself quotes an earlier work which it either calls the 'Mishnah of Rabbi Akiva'[14] or 'The First Mishnah'.[15]

Akiva is said to have started life as a shepherd, with no education. He worked for a very wealthy man and fell in love with his daughter Rachel. Her father was resolutely opposed to the match but Rachel was willing to run away with Akiva on the condition that he immediately went off to get himself an education. Akiva jumped at her suggestion and went to the Vineyard, or one of its offshoots, for twelve years. On his return he overheard an old man asking his wife how long she would endure the life of a widow. 'If I had my way', she replied, 'he would stay for twelve more years.' Akiva promptly turned around and went back. When he finally came home, according to this tale, he was accompanied by twenty four thousand students.[16]

Although Akiva's life story is cloaked by legend and hyperbole, we get a good idea of his character and intellect from his teachings and legal rulings. As his twentieth-century biographer puts it:

> Akiva ranks in depth of intellect, breadth of sympathy and clarity of vision with the foremost personalities of the Hebrew tradition, Moses and Isaiah amongst the prophets, Maimonides, Crescas and Spinoza amongst the philosophers. He dominates the whole scene of Jewish history from the period of the Second Isaiah, about 540 BCE until the rise of the Spanish school of philosophers, about 1100 CE.[17]

Akiva never forgot his humble origins. Time and again his interpretation of the Oral Law reflects a concern for the poor and needy; for example, upholding the rights of impoverished farmers to inherit tiny parcels of land which his wealthier colleagues considered too small for the law to concern itself with.[18] When the Temple had stood and the Levites were unable to earn a living because of their official duties, they had been compensated by a system of tithes, each farmer giving a tenth of his crop. Now that the Temple had been destroyed

---

[14] M. Sanhedrin 3.4.
[15] M. Eduyyot 7.2, M. Gittin 5.6, M. Nazir 6.1.
[16] Ketubot 62b.
[17] *Akiba: Scholar, Saint and Martyr*, Louis Finkelstein, Jason Aaronson Inc., New York, 1936, p. ix.
[18] M. Bava Batra 6.4.

and small farmers were struggling to survive Akiva put in place measures which effectively abolished the system, obliging the Levites to become economically independent.[19] On another occasion he limited the exclusive rights of priests to eat the flesh of a first-born lamb that was unfit to be sacrificed, ruling that anyone, Israelite or not, may eat of it.[20]

But he did not allow his sympathy for the poor to override his belief in the integrity of the law. When his colleague Tarfon, a wealthy olive farmer, tried to introduce a humanitarian solution to a dispute between various creditors over who could seize the land of someone who had died, Akiva protested. Tarfon had wanted to give the land to the poorest claimant. 'No', argued Akiva, 'the law is not charity. The land must be given to the deceased's heirs.'[21]

In similar vein, if two people found themselves stranded in a desert with only enough water for one of them to survive, Akiva argued that they shouldn't share it, otherwise they would just watch each other die. Saving life is important, but it is not right to sacrifice two lives when one can be saved. Nor should the owner of the water sacrifice his life for his companion. Akiva quoted Leviticus 25.36, 'that thy brother shall live with you', emphasizing the word 'with' to infer that in such a case your life takes precedence over your companion's.[22]

Akiva found himself caught up in the ongoing struggle against Rome. His involvement began round about the year 95 CE when a distinguished Roman and member of the emperor's family, Flavius Clemens, converted to Judaism. This so enraged the emperor that he planned a series of punitive measures against the Jews. Akiva joined a diplomatic mission to Rome, along with Gamaliel, Joshua and Eleazar ben Azariah, to try to assuage the emperor's wrath.

As relations with Rome worsened, Akiva declared his support for the Jewish rebel, Shimon bar Koziba. When bar Koziba won his improbable and short-lived victory, Akiva proclaimed him to be the Messiah.[23] This was a rare lapse of judgement on Akiva's part, as he realized when the rebel state was ultimately defeated and a period of merciless brutality, which history would name the Hadrianic Persecutions, began. The practice of the Jewish faith was banned and

---

[19] M. Ma'aserot 3.5, M. Ma'aser Sheni 4.8.

[20] Tosefta Bekhorot 3.15.

[21] Mishnah Ketubot 92.

[22] Sifra, Behar 5.3.

[23] J. Ta'anit 4.6 (68d).

Akiva, whose whole life had been dedicated to Torah study, found himself at the head of a religious resistance movement.

When a colleague, Pappus, castigated him for teaching Torah in public, Akiva responded with a parable. He told of the fox who tried to persuade a fish that he could be saved from the fishermen's nets if he would only come and live with him on the dry land. The fish replied that if he could not be safe in his natural environment, he would certainly not be safe in an unnatural space. 'So it is with us', said Akiva, 'if we are not safe in the Torah, which is our natural condition, how can we be safe elsewhere?'[24]

Shortly afterwards Akiva was captured and imprisoned by the Romans. He was put to death in the year 135 CE, defiantly proclaiming the words of the *Shema*, the Jewish declaration of faith, whilst the Romans tore his flesh from him with iron combs.

## The Mishnah

Akiva may have been dead but his reputation and authority lived on through his students. Led by his pupil Meir, they continued his work of recording the Oral Law, compiling collections of laws and arranging them in topics, almost certainly using the same arrangement that Akiva used for his earlier Mishnah.

If Meir had followed the style of the Five Books of Moses, and simply written down the laws, albeit in greater detail, the Talmud would never have been conceived. He would have created a rule book and nothing more. But it was Meir's great genius to preserve the fluidity of the oral tradition by recording not only the official, majority rulings but also the views of those who disagreed. Today, when several judges sit together on a case it is usual for each of them to give their opinion, even if they disagree with the majority verdict. Meir's Mishnah did the same thing, except the opinions were condensed into three or four words, not paragraphs or pages.

Meir's was the work of a lifetime. It fell to one of his younger colleagues, a descendant of Hillel and Gamaliel to undertake the final stage in the creation of the Mishnah. Rabbi Judah the *Nasi*, often known just as Rabbi, collated and edited the Mishnahs of Akiva and Meir. He adopted a practice introduced by

---

[24] Berachot 61b.

Meir of using anonymous opinions to indicate his teacher's view. Meir had expressed Akiva's opinions anonymously, in Judah's Mishnah the anonymous voice belonged to Meir, not Akiva. However, in most cases Judah only gave Meir's view anonymously if it was generally accepted as the authoritative ruling. Otherwise he would state clearly that it was Meir's opinion.

The opening chapter of Rabbi Judah's Mishnah gives a good illustration of how this worked. The Torah had ordained that a passage known as the *Shema*, which declares God's unity, should be read 'when you lie down and when you rise up'. But it is also to be said 'when you sit in your house and when you walk down the road'. Unless they had clearer guidelines as to when they should say it, people would be reciting the *Shema* all day long. The Mishnah rules that the *Shema* should be said twice a day, and wants to know how this operates in practice.

> From what time can one read the Shema in the morning? From the time that one can distinguish between blue and white. Rabbi Eliezer said, between blue and green and until sunrise. Rabbi Joshua said until the third hour, for it is the practice of kings to arise at the third hour.[25]

This passage contains three opinions. The first one 'From the time that one can distinguish between blue and white' is anonymous, the others are attributed to Rabbi Eliezer and Rabbi Joshua. The anonymous opinion reflects Rabbi Meir's view, based on what he learnt from his teacher Akiva. By giving it anonymously Rabbi Judah the *Nasi* is flagging up that this is the view to follow.

When Judah finished his Mishnah, the process of recording the Oral Law was nearly at an end. The Mishnah became accepted as authentic, comprehensive and authoritative. Indeed in some circles studying Rabbi's Mishnah was so holy a task it became an acceptable substitute for the now defunct sacrifices.[26]

Although the Mishnah that has come down to us today is Rabbi Judah's work, it contains the names of several people who lived after him.[27] It even mentions his death.[28] Clearly some editing work was done to Judah's Mishnah,

---

[25] M. Berachot 1.2.
[26] Vayikra Rabbah 7.3.
[27] E.g. M. Avot 2.2, 6.2.
[28] M. Sotah 9.15, 'When Rabbi died humility and the fear of sin disappeared.'

even after he had finished. Indeed, Rabbi Hiyya, one of his pupils, is said to have had a secret scroll which contained emendations to the Mishnah.[29]

The prevailing view today is that it took some time for the Mishnah to become accepted as authoritative. It seems that once the Mishnah was complete, people in different parts of the Jewish world deliberately edited the text to fit in with a tradition they believed was more authentic.[30] This explains why there is more than one version of the Mishnah (even though the differences between the versions are very slight). It was only gradually, as the authority of the Mishnah became established, that people fiddled with the text less.

When he compiled the Mishnah, Judah had to decide what to include and what to omit. Much of what he left out was collected together in a compendium called the *Tosefta*. Thought to have been compiled by Rabbi Hiyya, Judah's student who kept the secret scroll, the *Tosefta* is structured in the same way as the Mishnah. Although the Talmud is a commentary on the Mishnah it often quotes from the *Tosefta*, as well as from other collections of material dating from the same period.[31]

The Mishnah is a stand-alone work that's often read independently of the Talmud. It's systematic, terse and direct in its language. Although, as we have seen, it offers different points of view as to what the law may be, unlike the Talmud it does not create debates or conversations. It simply records facts and moves on.

But laws, beliefs and rituals are complex things. There is plenty of opportunity to explore and interpret the principles that lie behind the bare rulings that the Mishnah states. And just as Moses' Torah became an object of study and interpretation, so did the Mishnah. In fact it wasn't until the Mishnah was finished, and was being circulated amongst the study houses in Israel and Babylon, that the story of the Talmud really began.

---

[29] Shabbat 96b.

[30] מבוא לנוסח המשנה (*Introduction to the Text of the Mishnah*) J. N. Epstein, Magnes, Press, Jerusalem, 1948.

[31] This material, known as *baraita* (pl. *baraitot*) in Talmudic terminology, is principally drawn from the Halachic Midrashim – the Mechiltas, Sifra and Sifreis as well as from sources now lost.

# 3

# Returning to Babylon

R. Mersharsheya told his sons: Better to sit on the dung heap of Matta Mahsya than in the palaces of Pumbedita.[1]

## Life in Babylon

The seeds of the Talmud were sown long before it was dreamt of, in 586 BCE. That was when the Babylonian king Nebuchadnezzar invaded ancient Israel, destroyed the Jerusalem Temple and resettled its population in his kingdom. Amongst them was the prophet Jeremiah who advised the uprooted families to 'Build houses and dwell in them, plant gardens and eat their fruit ... and seek the peace of the city'.[2]

The forced exile didn't last long. Less than fifty years later the Babylonian Empire had fallen, wiped out by Cyrus the Great, king of Persia. But although Cyrus issued a decree allowing Nebuchadnezzar's captive nations to return home, not all the exiled Jews did. Babylon, one of the world's leading cities, with international trade links, fabulous architecture and the latest technology offered a far more sophisticated lifestyle and much greater opportunity than the provincial backwater they now considered Jerusalem to be.

No longer exiles, the émigrés sank their roots deep into Babylonian soil. Any guilt they may have felt at being seduced from their divinely bestowed homeland to a foreign, heathen capital was cancelled out by their pride in living in the land where Abraham had been born. Babylon was not Egypt, Moses hadn't told them they couldn't live there.[3]

---

[1] Horayot 12a.
[2] Jeremiah 29.5–7.
[3] Deuteronomy 17.16, 28.68.

The Jews remained in Babylon for thousands of years, a handful still remain today. Empires came and went. Alexander the Great conquered it, establishing his capital in the famed city. He died there in 323 BCE, after drinking a bowlful of suspect wine in the palace that Nebuchadnezzar had built nearly three centuries earlier.

Alexander's death marked the beginning of Babylon's decline. A succession of warlords and invaders fought over it, gradually emptying the city of its population. Its once-famed ziggurats fell into desolation and ruin, its hanging gardens throttled with weeds. Eventually Babylon became as much of a cultural byway as the land from which the ancestors of its Jews had first hailed. Today it is a ruin, close to Baghdad, in Iraq.

The mists of time have concealed ancient Babylon's Jews from view. But a second wave of immigration took place from the Holy Land in 135 CE. The Roman occupiers had brought about the second destruction of the Temple sixty years earlier. Now they had savagely put down a revolt led by Shimon bar Kochba; an uprising which for three short years had kept the might of Rome at bay. When Bar Kochba's forces could hold out no longer, Roman retribution was harsh and vicious. Judea, as the Romans called Israel, was in tatters. Those who had the resources to leave did. Many of them went to Babylon. It is from this time on that Babylon's Jews became more visible on the historical stage.

In those days the ruling power in Babylon was the Parthian Empire. The Parthians, who hailed from Iran, to the East, had driven out the warlords who had squabbled over the territory after Alexander the Great's death, nearly half a millennium earlier.

## The exilarch

The Parthian Empire covered over a vast area, encompassing almost all of modern Syria, Iraq and Iran. Their approach to government was fairly hands off; they made no great demands of their subjects and delegated administrative power to semi-autonomous regions, run by local dynasties. One such dynasty was that of the exilarch, a hereditary Jewish leader who claimed descent from King David.

According to a letter written in the tenth century by a Jewish religious leader, Sherira *Gaon*, to a correspondent in the North African city of Kairouan, the first exilarch had been the biblical king, Jehoachin of Judah. He had been taken into exile in the first wave of captives whom Nebuchadnezzar had transported to Babylon, ten years before he destroyed the Temple.

Sherira's letter is the source for much of our information about the early Babylonian community.[4] Of course a letter written fifteen hundred years after the event, even one ascribed to a premier rabbinic authority, is not the same as evidence from a contemporary source. The earliest evidence we have of an exilarch comes from the fourth century CE,[5] long after Jehoachin's time. The problem is that, unlike the Jewish community in Israel during Talmudic times, the history of which is well attested in archaeology and Roman literature, the only major source of information about the Jewish Babylonian community in the same period is the Babylonian Talmud itself.[6] As Seth Schwartz points out, nearly everything we know about the historical environment of the Talmud must be wrested from the Talmud itself; we only know what the Talmud tells us and we have very little other historical context to set it against.[7] Sources such as Sherira's letter do not constitute hard evidence; as Ivan Marcus writes, medieval chroniclers were not historians, the facts they chose to recount, and the way they presented them, were intended only to support their own theological or cultural view, not to provide an objective reality.[8]

Jehoachin may not have had the title Exilarch but he was an ex-king and would have been held in high regard by those who were exiled with him. In 1939 archaeologists found cuneiform tablets listing the rations of oil and barley given to captives in Babylon.[9] Jehoachin, king of the Land of Judah is listed as one of the recipients. He almost certainly retained his personal authority and perhaps he had some degree of autonomous power over his former subjects. Whether this authority was handed down through his descendants is harder to know. The origins of the exilarchy are just as likely to lie in power struggles over the years between wealthy families who had grown rich in the silk trade.

---

[4] Lewin, 1921. Gafni, 1986 argues for the existence of some sort of chronological record that was available to Sherira but it seems clear that much of the historical narrative in the Letter is derived from Talmudic anecdotes and independent, unverifiable traditions.

[5] J. Ketubot. 12.3, 35a.

[6] Gafni, 2006.

[7] Schwartz, 2007. Yaakov Ellman makes a similar point – 'our data is restricted to the Bavli (=Babylonian Talmud) … and we are thus at the mercy of the redactors of that compilation and the rabbinic classes they represent', Ellman, 2007b, p. 190.

[8] Marcus, 1982.

[9] *Mélanges syriens offerts à monsieur René Dussaud: secrétaire perpétuel de l'Académie des inscriptions et belles-lettres*, Ernst F. Weidner, Geuthner, Paris, 1939, II.

Jehoachin was a descendant of King David, whose monarchy it was believed would one day be re-established. The exilarchs also claimed David descent. This gave them quasi-royal status. They enjoyed all the trappings of power and wealth, including an armed force that allowed them to enforce their will. The exilarch was answerable to the emperor and was responsible for the good governance and administration of the communities under his control. His powers, which varied depending on who was running the Empire at any particular time, would have included the right to appoint judges, impose capital punishment and collect taxes. He could also appoint an *agoranomos*, an overseer who took responsibility for the smooth functioning of the markets, including regulating weights and measures and controlling prices. There are accounts in the Talmud of measures to prevent overcharging or deceptive practices by traders.[10]

The distance from Israel to Babylon is a little over five hundred miles. Even in those days it was a relatively easy journey. There had always been contacts between the Jewish communities in the two countries, dating back to Temple times when the courts in Israel despatched messengers to announce the sighting of a new moon and the festival calendar for the coming months.[11] From at least the first century BCE young scholars would travel from Babylon to study in the Land of Israel; indeed according to legend it was from Babylon that Hillel, the first *Nasi*, had originally hailed. Seeking to establish a new life for himself as a scholar in Israel but too poor to enrol in the study house, the newly arrived Hillel had climbed onto the roof and listened to the lectures through the skylight, shivering in a snowstorm until the outline of his freezing body cast a shadow inside, and he was brought down to thaw out.[12]

## The founding of the academy in Nehardea

Sherira *Gaon's* letter also tells us that the exiled king Jehoachin founded the first school for religious study in Babylon, in the town of Nehardea, the largest of the Jewish settlements. According to Sherira, Jehoachin and the prophets who had been exiled with him had built the academy using clay and stone that they had brought from the Jerusalem Temple. Again we have to take this with a pinch of

---

[10] See, for example, Bava Metzia 60a–b, 61b.
[11] M. Rosh Hashanah 2.1–4.
[12] Yoma 35b.

salt; it's not likely that a throng of captives in the sixth century BCE were able to transport building materials with them. The first we hear of Nehardea is when the Mishnah mentions Rabbi Akiva travelling there to announce the onset of a leap year. This would have been around the end of the first century CE and it's the earliest record of any academy in Babylon.

Akiva was a seasoned traveller but it couldn't have been an easy trip for him. When he arrived in Nehardea he was approached by a certain Nehemia of Bet Deli who complained that he had been unable to travel in the opposite direction because the country was 'swarming with troops'.[13] Akiva had clearly considered that showing his support for the academy in Nehardea was worth the hazards of the journey.

Early in the third century CE an intense, young, lanky scholar arrived from the Land of Israel. Like Hillel he had been born in Babylon, had gone to Israel to study and had made a name for himself. Now he was returning home. His name was Abba; his friends gave him the nickname Abba Arikha, or tall Abba, but everyone knew him as Rav. Rav was a title, an honorific which acknowledged his intellectual prowess and depth of learning. It corresponded to the title Rabbi, used in Israel.[14] Just as Judah the *Nasi* was known simply as Rabbi, Rav was considered to be so distinguished that no name was necessary; all he needed was the title.

When Rav arrived in Nehardea he found a flourishing academy.[15] He worked there as an interpreter and was appointed market commissioner by the exilarch, but he soon outgrew the job. Leaving Nehardea he founded a new academy further down the Euphrates, at Sura. From that time on the Nehardean and Suran academies would compete with each other for prestige.

The head of the Nehardean academy, Shmuel, was esteemed as highly as Rav and they frequently differed on matters of law. Their disagreements sharpened the acuity of debate between the two academies. Prior to Rav's arrival the Babylonian students had considered their educational level inferior to that of their counterparts in Israel. Now the intellectual rivalry between Nehardea and Sura boosted their self esteem, and not just in matters of learning. Rav himself

---

[13] M. Yevamot 16.7.

[14] The title Rabbi could only be conferred in Israel, and only by another rabbi. It represented a continuous chain of tradition stretching back to the time when Moses ordained Joshua as his successor by placing his hands on his head. Scholars outside Israel who could not be ordained were given the title Rav.

[15] According to other documents from the ninth or tenth centuries; *Seder Tannaim V'Amoraim and Seder Olam Zuta* the first academies were not founded until after Rav's death (Katz, 2006).

pointed out to his students the difference between Babylon and the other major Jewish diaspora centres: 'Babylon is healthy; Mesene is dead; Media is sick, and Elam is dying'.[16]

Babylon's flourishing reputation probably contributed to the new wave of immigrants who arrived from Israel early in the third century. They left their homeland due to the ongoing economic and political difficulties of life under Roman occupation, hoping to make a fresh start elsewhere. A message sent around this time from Israel to the Jewish authorities in Babylon asked them to 'take care of the sons of the poor, for the Torah proceeds from them'.[17] Since the Torah was regarded as emanating from Zion, another name for Jerusalem, the sons of the poor must have been immigrants who were on their way to Babylon to carve out a new life for themselves.[18]

In the year 226 the Parthian Empire fell, brought to its knees by dynastic struggles. The coup de grâce was delivered by the Sassenid warlord Ardeshir who defeated the last Parthian king, Artabanus. Babylon now became part of the Sassenid Empire.

The rabbinic scholars in Babylon were keenly aware of the change in regime. Not only did the Sassenids introduce a far more centralized form of government than their predecessors, limiting the independence of the exilarch, but two developments in particular upset the smooth course of their lives. First, the new dynasty entered into a prolonged conflict with the Roman Empire, sparking a series of battles that lasted for more than a century. Major devastation ensued, including the destruction of the city of Nehardea and the slaughter of twelve thousand Jews in Cappadocia, in what is now central Turkey.

The other disruptive factor was the rise of the Zoroastrian religion, which the Sassanians encouraged as a means of consolidating power across their new, vast empire. Relations between the Zoroastrian Magi and the many diverse ethnic communities in the Sassanian Empire would fluctuate between peaceable and intolerable over the coming centuries. Fire, earth and water have a special sanctity in the Zoroastrian religion and their priests, or *haberim*, were zealous in proscribing their use for secular purposes. The Talmud recounts stories of fire-priests forbidding the lighting of fires or seizing candles from Jewish homes, even if these were only being used for domestic purposes. There were

---

[16] Rav Papa the Elder quoting Rav in Kiddushin 71b.
[17] Nedarim 81a.
[18] Jacobs, 1957.

even tales of corpses exhumed from their graves since dead bodies were deemed to violate the sanctity of the ground.[19]

Nevertheless, as Isaiah Gafni points out,[20] these troublesome incidents in no way compared to the wholesale persecutions taking place in Roman Palestine. With the exception of the frenzied Kirdid, a third-century Zoroastrian priest who was over-zealous in imposing his faith's strictures on the minority populations, relations between the Sassanians and their non-Zoroastrian subjects, seem to have been relatively benign. Indeed the Talmud recounts amicable contacts between leading Jewish rabbis and the Sassanian rulers, particularly between Shmuel and King Shapur I,[21] and although these accounts may be exaggerated they do suggest a general atmosphere of political and religious tolerance. Things would change with the ascent of King Yazdegerd II in the middle of the fifth century.

## Land and rivers

The Jewish settlements in Babylon were located in an area bordered by the Rivers Euphrates and Tigris, the mythical site of the Garden of Eden. Genesis identifies one of the four rivers in that utopian land as the Euphrates and an ancient Bible tradition renders another as Tigris.[22] The area forms part of the Fertile Crescent, which stretches north from the Persian Gulf, through Iraq to the southern border of Turkey, then turns to follow the Mediterranean coast across Syria, Lebanon and Israel to the Nile Delta and Valley.

The two Babylonian rivers were connected by a network of tributaries and canals. Water flowed in abundance. A statement by Rav in the Talmud suggests that the land was so well irrigated that even when the rains failed its harvests were secure.[23]

The rivers played an important part in daily life. Dotted with towns along their length, the watercourses functioned as modern highways, transporting people and goods. Inundations could be sudden and unpredictable, rivers might

---

[19] E.g. Shabbat 45a, Gittin 16b–17a, Beitzah 6a,
[20] Gafni, 2006.
[21] Sukkah 53a, Avodah Zarah 76b, Moed Katan 26a.
[22] Genesis 2.14, Targum Onkelos and Targum Pseudo Jonathan ibid.
[23] Taanit 10a.

change their course, swallowing up agricultural land,[24] there are even instances of barren fields becoming fertile through the sudden deposit of alluvial soils.[25] The Talmud discusses questions such as water disputes and the ownership of items washed up by floods.

Most people lived modest lives but owning a small amount of land, typically one or two fields, seems to have been quite common. When a couple married, the husband was obliged to make provision for his wife in the event of his death. The Talmud discusses how a widow is to collect her money in a case when her husband has made out his will in favour of his children from a previous marriage. The solution is for her to distrain upon the children's landed property, but not upon their chattels. This could only work if most people owned land; the solution would have been pointless if they didn't.

The ownership of the little land they had was not absolute. One of the two principal taxes that the Sassanian rulers levied on their subjects was the *taska*, a form of ground rent. When they paid the *taska* people effectively had the right of ownership of their land. If they did not pay they would be evicted.

Owning land doesn't seem to have been a big deal in most people's eyes. It appears to have been a completely natural state of affairs. We can see this in context if we compare the Talmud with the Roman law code, Justinian's Digest or its Sassanian equivalent, the Book of a Thousand Judgements. Only two of the Talmud's five hundred and thirty chapters deal with questions of land inheritance. The other works each devote more than a third of their content to the same subject.[26]

Most people who lived off the land were smallholders or tenant farmers, mainly growing dates, grains and rice, or rearing sheep and goats. But even though they lived in the idealized land which gave rise to the myth of the Garden of Eden we shouldn't picture a pastoral scene in which everyone tilled their own fields, with crops growing in abundance. Poverty seems to have been rife; 'Ten measures of poverty descended into the world, nine of them were taken by Babylon.'[27]

Still, despite the poverty it was possible to advance economically. Not everyone farmed a smallholding. The Talmud frequently introduces us to tanners, weavers,

---

[24] E.g. Gittin 41a.

[25] E.g. Bava Batra 124a.

[26] Ellman, 2007b.

[27] Kiddushin 49b. Louis Jacobs points out that this *baraita* in the Talmud predates the Sassanian Empire and refers to the entire population, not just the Jewish community (Jacobs, 1957).

tailors, cobblers, blood letters and even camel drivers, although the latter seem to have been less prominent than in Israel; the camel which, in the gospels, cannot pass through the eye of a needle, is an elephant in the Babylonian Talmud's proverbs.[28]

Not everyone was poor. Large estates were owned by families who had been settled in the area for generations, long before the tide of immigrants began to swell. The family of the exilarch owned tremendous estates, much of which they rented out to tenants. The trading city of Mahoza, situated on a caravan route on the Tigris, in the centre of the area of settlement, was fabled for its good living[29] and its wealth; it was rumoured that whilst in the whole city of Nehardea only twenty four women possessed a golden coronet, eighteen such owners could be found in a single alley in Mahoza.[30]

Unlike their colleagues in Israel, who often eked out a living as workmen or artisans, many of the scholars in Babylon were of independent means, typically owning larger than average land holdings. Not having to worry too much about earning a living gave them the freedom to study, but it could also lead to divisions with working people. The rabbinic elite was only a small segment of the overall population.[31] Richard Kalmin argues that the Babylonian scholars, at least in the early part of the Talmudic period, were much more detached from the general population than their counterparts in Israel, who were integrated into the general community.[32] He puts this down to differences between Persian and Roman society, but wealth would have played a part as well. Kalmin suggests that Babylonian scholars were internally focused, avoiding contact and marriage with non-rabbinic Jews, and reluctant to admit them into the scholarly environment. He likens them to monks who 'managed to be both dissociated from and part of the world, detached from society in certain contexts and capable of exercising a leadership role in others'.[33]

But at least the rabbis seem to have been aware of their aloofness. In a discussion about why so few scholars produced children who became learned

[28] Berachot 55b: A man is shown in a dream only what is suggested by his own thoughts ... Raba said: This is proved by the fact that a man is never shown in a dream a date palm of gold, or an elephant going through the eye of a needle.
  Bava Metzia 38b: 'Perhaps you are from Pumbeditha' he retorted, 'where they draw an elephant through the eye of a needle.'
[29] Taanit 26a, Shabbat 109a.
[30] Shabbat 59b.
[31] Gafni, 2006.
[32] Kalmin, 2006a.
[33] Kalmin, 2006a, p. 9.

men we find four different but equally revealing opinions. Rav Yosef said it was so that the scholarly classes could not claim to have a hereditary right to the Torah. Rav Shisha said it was so that scholars would not have an arrogant attitude towards the community. Mar Zutra said it was because they acted high-handedly against ordinary folk, whilst Rav Ashi said it was because they called people asses.[34]

Standoffish they may have been but the Babylonian rabbis didn't live in a cultural vacuum. They didn't just study religion and law. Ancient Babylon was renowned for its mathematical and astronomical knowledge and its complex systems of magic and demonology. The Talmud is replete with passages on these subjects, from calculations of the size of the earth and the thickness of the sky[35] to legends about demons[36] and medicinal cures.[37] Although mention of mythical creatures can be found in many branches of ancient Jewish literature, the Babylonian Talmud, under the influence of the local culture, takes a particular interest in them.[38]

We also find formulae for spells and incantations in the Talmud, the wording of which is often similar to the inscriptions found on 'magic bowls', a uniquely Babylonian practice in which earthenware vessels inscribed with enchantments were placed in the earth to guard against demons. The similarity of language suggests that Jews were involved in the production of these bowls, perhaps for their own use, or because the local Persian population considered the Jews as particularly skilled in getting rid of demons.[39]

---

[34] Nedarim 81a.

[35] E.g. Pesachim 94a–94b.

[36] E.g. Gittin 68a–68b.

[37] E.g. Shabbat 108b–111b.

[38] E.g. this passage in Berachot 6a: Abba Benjamin says, If the eye had the power to see them, no creature could endure the demons. Abaye says: They are more numerous than we are and they surround us like the ridge round a field. R. Huna says: Every one among us has a thousand on his left hand and ten thousand on his right hand. Raba says: The crushing in the Kallah lectures comes from them. Fatigue in the knees comes from them. The wearing out of the clothes of the scholars is due to their rubbing against them. The bruising of the feet comes from them. If one wants to discover them, let him take sifted ashes and sprinkle around his bed, and in the morning he will see something like the footprints of a cock. If one wishes to see them, let him take the after-birth of a black she-cat, the offspring of a black she-cat, the first-born of a first-born, let him roast it in fire and grind it to powder, and then let him put some into his eye, and he will see them. Let him also pour it into an iron tube and seal it with an iron signet that they should not steal it from him. Let him also close his mouth, lest he come to harm. R. Bibi b. Abaye did so, saw them and came to harm. The scholars, however, prayed for him and he recovered.

[39] Gafni, 2006.

Zoroastrian superstitions also account for a passage in the Talmud which urges the burying of cut fingernails, or at very least burning them and not simply throwing them away. This must be avoided 'lest a pregnant woman steps over them and miscarries'.[40]

But spells and magic, astronomy and mathematics were probably light relief for the Babylonian rabbis. They were known as the 'condiments of wisdom',[41] tasty appetisers but a bit of a luxury. The real hard work, the essential curriculum in the Babylonian academies, was the detailed analysis of the minutiae of the law. Everything else was simply icing on the cake.

---

[40] Moed Katan 18a, Daiches contends that the root of this custom (and also that of looking at one's nails at the close of the Sabbath) derive from an ancient Babylonian practice of 'thumb nail magic' by which the future could be divined through the reflections of spirits which appear when gazing into in the thumb nail (Daiches, 1913).

[41] Mishnah Avot 3.23.

# 4

# *The compilation of the Talmud*

Rabbi Tarfon said, The day is short and there is much work, the workman are lazy but the wages are high, and the master of the house is pressing.[1]

## The academies in Babylon

The starting point for every discussion in the Babylonian academies was the Mishnah, a structured work which is arranged systematically under six main headings, each one containing many sub categories. But we can assume that the discussions in the academies rarely remained on topic; it is highly likely that they would digress, often wildly. To appreciate this we can think of a class of school students discussing, let's say, *A Midsummer's Night's Dream* with an enlightened teacher. On the face of it the task of the class is to analyse the text in front of them, but their observations might easily become a launching pad for discussions about love, fairy lore, theatre, ancient society, magical potions, loss of personal identity and much else. The play itself would simply be the place they started.

We find a similar thing happening over and again in the Talmud. There is a passage in the Mishnah that deals with the water-drawing ceremony in the Temple, a spectacular public ceremony during the Tabernacles festival.[2] The Talmud starts its discussion of this subject logically enough with a description of the Temple where the ceremony took place, but then rapidly digresses into an excursion which surveys a basilica synagogue in Alexandria, discusses the

---

[1]  Avot 2.20.
[2]  M. Sukkah 5.1.

Messiah, considers the nature of evil, strong men and demonology, before turning to juggling, world peace and the physical depth of the earth.[3]

However, unlike our fictional classroom discussion on *A Midsummer Night's Dream*, the four densely printed pages of Talmudic text which discuss the water-drawing ceremony do not record the deliberations of a single academy session. The printed discussion didn't even take place in a single generation or in one location. It contains contributions from people who lived a century or more apart, who taught in different academies, even in different countries; the lands of Babylon and Israel. This is because the Talmud is a literary construction in which debates, opinions, proofs and rulings that took place over nearly three hundred years are woven together by later editors into a coherent whole.[4] And we can assume that the individual discussions in the academy were equally varied in their scope because, if they had been rigidly focused on a single subject, it is highly unlikely that their structure would have been broken up and recorded for posterity in such a wide-ranging and discursive manner.

The formal sessions in an academy, or *yeshiva*, took place in a large hall. The head of the academy would sit at the front, on a pile of cushions or a settle and the students would sit in rows in front of him. The number of rows wasn't fixed; in one place we read of an academy with seventeen rows[5] but the preferred number seems to have been seven, with ten people in each; mirroring the numbers and seating pattern in the ancient Sanhedrin.[6] As we have already seen, the Vineyard at Yavneh may have been called that because the scholars sat there in rows, like vines.

The term students is a little misleading because many of the participants in the *yeshiva* sessions were distinguished scholars in their own right, even if they were subordinate to the head of the academy. The most senior scholars would sit in the front row, the younger participants to the rear. As students progressed in their studies they would gradually be brought towards the front. It was a bit like the arrangement in old schoolrooms where pupils sat at the front, middle or back of the class depending on their ability.

The academy head would have a memory man alongside him. Known as a *tanna* he was a scholar who could be called on at any moment to recite a passage

---

[3] Sukkah 51b–53b.
[4] Jacobs, 2005.
[5] Hullin 137b.
[6] Bava Kamma 117a.

by heart, usually from the Mishnah but occasionally from the *Tosefta* which, as we saw earlier, Rabbi Hiyya had compiled out of material which hadn't been included in the Mishnah. The *tanna's* prodigious memory also contained a mental database of biblical commentaries dating from the same, early period. All this material, which was not in the Mishnah but had emanated from the same schools, was known as *baraita*, which means 'external'.

The passages that the *tanna* would be asked to search his memory for played a central part in the argument that the academy head was presenting and the *tanna* was the closest he could get in the ancient world to having a database of references at his fingertips.

In a large gathering the head of the *yeshiva* would also have someone, known as an *amora*, who acted as his mouthpiece, declaiming his words loudly so that everyone could hear. The terminology is confusing because the scholars of the Talmudic period are also known as *amoraim*. A similar confusion exists with the term *tanna* which refers both to rabbis of the Mishnaic period as well as to memory men of the Talmudic era.

The participants in each session would have prepared the material to be discussed in advance. Frequently the head of the academy would be challenged by one of the students and a debate would ensue in which the protagonists would make their points either by logic, by appeal to a biblical verse or by calling upon the *tanna* to recite a passage from the earlier literature that they hoped would clinch the argument for them.

These study sessions weren't always as dry and formal as they sound. A weird account in the Talmud tells the story of Rav Kahana, an experienced Babylonian scholar who had been forced to flee from the Sassanian authorities after taking it into his own hands to impose the death penalty on an informer. His teacher, Rav, advised him to go to Israel, to Rabbi Yohanan's academy in Tiberias. Rav counselled him to keep his head down and not challenge Yohanan's authority. Unfortunately Kahana found it difficult to blend into the background. The first time he attended a session he kept raising objections to assertions that Yohanan made. Yohanan, as befitting the head of the academy was sitting at the front, on seven cushions. Every time Kahana scored a point against him in the debate, a cushion was pulled from under Yohanan, until eventually he was sitting on the ground. At this point Yohanan was so enraged that he pronounced a curse upon Kahana, who dropped dead. Some days later Yohanan, full of remorse, went to Kahana's tomb. It was guarded by a snake, Yohanan had to pronounce three separate charms on the animal before he could enter. Once inside Yohanan sought Kahana's forgiveness and prayed that he would be brought back to life. His unfortunate victim only agreed to be revived on condition that Yohanan promised that the same thing would not happen again should Kahana happen to best him in a future debate.[7]

This odd story has been subjected to considerable analysis by both ancient and modern scholars. Nobody argues that we should take it literally and several academics have argued that it is in fact a polemic which weaves together Persian motifs and stories from different periods including a boast about the superiority of the Babylonian scholars over those in Israel.[8] But it needn't be as complicated as this. Babylon was a place of mystery and magic; it could just have been a story that was told and retold, because people believed it was true.

Twice a year, the academies would put on a major, public event. During the months preceding the spring and autumn harvests, when there was little else to do but wait for the crops to grow, hundreds of teachers, lay scholars and graduates of other *yeshivot* would leave their homes and travel to their nearest academy. These month-long study sessions, known as *kallah,* were carefully orchestrated; everyone knew what subject was to be studied and should have spent the weeks since the previous session memorizing the material and coming to grips with its meaning.

As the years passed the discussions held by one generation of scholars would become material to be studied by the next. In the time of Rav and Shmuel, the only material available to be studied was the Mishnah, and other works dating from the same period. Succeeding generations would have included Rav and Shmuel's analyses in their curriculum, and their discussions would in turn be pulled apart in due course by succeeding cohorts.

The style of material changed from one generation to another. David Weiss Halivni points out that the earliest teachings were not unlike the terse style of the Mishnah, laying down absolute rulings on the law. As time elapsed and the quantity of material grew, the later Babylonian *amoraim* grew more interested in why, rather than what; they wanted to know the rationale that lay behind those rulings.[9] They were rigidly logical in their analysis, they had no patience with incoherent thinking. When Rav Nahman, who lived half a century after Rav and Shmuel, heard a ruling from the Mishnah that a guarantor for a loan

---

[7] Bava Kamma 117a–b.

[8] For different interpretations of this story see, for example, Gafni, 1990; Herman, 2008; Sperber, 1994.

[9] Weiss Halivni, 1986.

cannot be forced to pay up, it made no sense to him; if that was the case, what would have been the point of guaranteeing the loan? He complained that it was 'like a law of the Persians who don't give reasons for their decisions'.[10] As Weiss Halivni puts it, the Talmud prefers law that is 'expressly reasonable, that seeks to win the hearts of those to whom the laws are addressed'.[11]

But the Talmud knows that that not everyone cares about reasons, they just want to know how to act. We find a similar conflict amongst the Greeks. In response to Plato's argument that laws had to be explained so that they wouldn't just be 'brusque injunctions'[12] Seneca had responded 'Tell me what I have to do. I do not want to learn. I want to obey'[13]. The Talmud gives its version of this dilemma in a story about the Israelites at Mount Sinai. When Moses tells them that they are to receive the Ten Commandments they say, 'We will do and we will listen'.[14] This means, says the Talmud, that they pledged their obedience even before they understood what was involved. As a reward for their trusting loyalty, six hundred thousand angels descended from heaven and gave them each two crowns, one for their promise to do and the other for their promise to listen. A few weeks later, when Moses had failed to return from the mountain top on the day they expected him, they assumed he was dead. They lost their faith in God and made themselves a Golden Calf. And when Moses did return and found that their reasoning had got the better of their loyalty, twice as many angels came down and took the crowns away.[15]

## Words and deeds

People might have thought them aloof, and they probably were detached from mainstream society, but the heads of the academies and their leading students didn't spend their whole lives in ivory towers. They were called upon to intercede in local disputes and some were appointed by the exilarchs as judges for their town.

---

[10] Bava Batra 173b. Nahman argued that the Mishnah could only mean that the guarantor cannot be forced to pay until the debtor has failed to do so.
[11] Weiss Halivni, 1986, p. 4.
[12] Plato's laws 722D–723B, cited in Weiss Halivni, 1986, p. 5.
[13] Seneca's *Writings* 94: 38, also cited in Weiss Halivni, 1986, p. 5.
[14] Exodus 24.7.
[15] Shabbat 88a.

Of course the Sassanian authorities were the ultimate arbiters of the law and there was always the possibility that the demands of the Empire might come into conflict with the Oral Law. To keep such differences to a minimum Shmuel introduced a landmark ruling known as *dina malchuta dina*, that in all areas of civil and monetary law, the law of the state is the law. This applied in every arena of life other than religious law; if Jewish civil law came into conflict with Sassanian law, Sassanian law prevailed. Minorities throughout history with their own customs and traditions have established similar principles; it is a necessary pre-condition for preserving cultural identity and a degree of autonomy.

The rabbinic courts heard cases on matters of religious and family law and adjudicated in disputes, usually concerning land, money or contracts. They had the power to levy fines, to act as legal guardians for orphans, to rule on ownership of disputed items and to dispose of expropriated property. They also had the power to ostracize or excommunicate offenders although this was an extreme sanction, rarely applied. But although biblical law permitted capital punishment in certain cases, the rabbinic courts did not have this power. Not out of deference to Sassanian jurisprudence but because according to Jewish religious law the sanction to condemn someone to death was only available to the Sanhedrin when the Temple stood.

Despite their twin roles as judges and interpreters of the Oral Law, the scholars in the academy rarely saw themselves as law makers. As we have seen, academic debate focused on the arguments underpinning the law, but the scholars weren't much bothered about its practical application.[16] Indeed this disconnect between theory and practice is stated clearly in the Jerusalem Talmud in Shmuel's name; practical laws can't be learnt from the outcome of debates in the academy.[17] If anything, the reverse was true; the practical law was established by the way the judges acted.

On one occasion Rav Assi, a Babylonian scholar who'd gone to study in Rabbi Yohanan's academy in Israel, heard a *tanna* recite. 'The law may not be derived from a theoretical conclusion unless one has been told that it is to be taken as a rule for practical decisions.' So Assi asked his teacher, 'When you tell us that

---

[16] Halivni argues that there were collections of laws, known as *hora'ah* or instruction, which were formulated by the Babylonian rabbis even though they didn't have the same force as laws in the Mishnah (Weiss Halivni, 1986).

[17] J. Peah 2.6 (17a).

something is the law, may we act on it accordingly?' 'No,' replied Yohanan, 'you cannot, unless I say that it is a law that can be acted upon.'[18]

On the other hand a ruling by a court can be used to support a theoretical argument. In a discussion about how much space there needs to be between a group of trees for their purchaser to also automatically acquire the land they stand on, one rabbi builds a case by quoting from the Mishnah. His colleague overrules him by citing a court decision. 'But the outcome is the same,' complains the first rabbi. 'Yes,' comes the answer, 'but a real life example is preferable.'[19]

This principle crops up in the Talmudic discussion about whether it is better for a person to study Torah, or to go out and perform good deeds. Learning Torah is considered a holy task, and according to one source it outranks any good deed or act of charity.[20] The scholars debate the relative merits of a life of study or a life of good deeds – in their terminology the question is framed as 'what is greater, study or action?' It turns out that study is greater ... because study leads to action.[21] In a nutshell this sums up the Talmudic dilemma about decision making. Decisions must be made, action is important. But even more important is why the decision is reached, and what other valid possibilities were rejected along the way. Alternative points of view can exist side by side. In the Talmudic world view there is only one absolute Truth, the rabbis never lost sight of the fact that their sole authority was the divine. In the face of that Truth everything else is relative to the circumstance.

It was their awareness of living in a created world which allowed the scholars of the academy to digress from discussions about the law without feeling they were being frivolous. The whole of nature is part of a coherent, divinely ordained and immaculately governed system, every aspect of which was revealed to Moses; it all fell within the scope of their investigation. And so about a quarter of the Talmud is not law in the accepted sense at all. It belongs to a category for which there is no adequate English word and which is usually referred to negatively and unimaginatively, as 'non-legal material'. Technically it is known as *aggada*, which literally means story-telling, but although the *aggada* contains stories in abundance, it is far more than just that. Much of the *aggada* is devoted to explaining biblical texts,

---

[18] Bava Batra 130b.
[19] Bava Batra 82b–83a.
[20] M. Peah 1.1.
[21] Kiddushin 40b.

either to introduce new ideas or to make a theological point, but other sections contain fables, folklore or discussions of the natural or supernatural worlds.

On the face of it the *aggadic* passages are less challenging than the legal sections, and they have attracted far less scholarly attention. But while it's true that to fully grasp the intricacies of the legal passages requires the ability to think logically, systematically and to keep several steps of an argument in one's head at the same time, the *aggadic* content needs a different sort of mind. It appeals to people whose skills lie in grappling with ideas and abstractions, who are more interested in looking at a conceptual framework than the minutiae of an argument. Comparing the merits of the two types of material is a bit like comparing pure mathematics to philosophy. Our preference for one over the other depends on our interests, and our skills.

## Compiling the Talmud

The debates carried on in the academies for generations. Sura continued to be a major centre but the city of Nehardea was destroyed in 259 CE, a casualty of the frequent skirmishes between the Roman and Sassanian Empires. By the time the town was rebuilt its academy had moved further up the Euphrates, to the north-west. It would still be called the academy of Nehardea; but it was now located in a new home, in the town of Pumbedita.

New academies opened, notably at the wealthy city of Mehoza where the most well known of its heads was Rava, who was in charge from around 320 CE onwards. Along with his contemporary Abayye, who headed the college in Pumbedita, Rava is counted amongst the greats of Talmudic scholarship.

Rava's relationship with the townspeople of Mahoza wasn't too good. On one occasion he applied the prophet Amos's description of the people of Bashan 'who oppress the poor, who crush the needy'[22] to the women of Mahoza 'who eat without working.'[23] On another he criticized a prominent doctor's family for not showing sufficient respect to the rabbis.[24]

These character insights are unusual; generally the personal lives of the rabbis are only of passing interest to the Talmud, unless they can be used to

---

[22] Amos 4.1.
[23] Shabbat 32b.
[24] Sanhedrin 99b.

glean an ethical, religious or legal point. Such as the occasion when Rav Ashi, one of the last *amoraim*, broke a glass at a marriage ceremony,[25] a custom which still prevails in Jewish weddings today.

Rava has the further distinction of posing more problems than anyone else in which the solution is so finely balanced between two possibilities that neither can be preferred over the other.[26] These problems, which conclude with the word *teyku*, meaning 'let it stand', will, according to folklore, all be solved by the prophet Elijah in the utopian future. In the meantime both solutions to the problem are equally valid. There may only be one Truth, but there can be multiple realities.[27]

Around about the year 500 CE the debates in the academies gave way to a process of rounding up all the material from the preceding centuries, which circulated as verbal traditions, collating it and eventually editing it into the Talmud. A hundred years earlier harsh economic and political conditions in Israel had brought about a premature completion of the Jerusalem Talmud, but the completion of the Babylonian Talmud doesn't seem to have been abrupt. There may even have been a long period of overlap during which the process of compilation had begun even though the final discussions were still going on.

The difference between the Jerusalem and Babylonian Talmuds is glaringly stark, and not just because the dialect and terminology is different. The Jerusalem Talmud, which received very little editing and was almost certainly not constructed as a literary unit, is very terse, almost staccato in places, listing very little more than the basic outlines of its arguments. In contrast the Babylonian version is far more fluent, presenting its reasoning in greater detail.

But the two Talmuds are by no means independent of each other. Many of the discussions that took place in the academies in one country crop up in the Talmud of the other. So do the names of many of the rabbis. There was a continual ebb and flow of scholars between the two centres, creating a two-way flow of ideas, insights and information. There are numerous examples of

---

[25] Berachot 31a. Rav Ashi broke the glass to introduce a note of solemnity into the occasion, based on the principle that since the destruction of the Temple all celebration is to be tempered somewhat with reflection.
[26] Jacobs, 1981. Of the two hundred and fifty seven *teyku* problems which are attributed to a specific teacher, Rava accounts for forty seven, far more than anyone else.
[27] See Chapter 8.

problems with which the Babylonian rabbis are grappling being resolved by a visitor from Israel who is able to provide a solution.[28]

It had never been the intention of the *amoraim* to have their discussions collected into a literary compilation. They weren't working to fulfil a grand project; they studied to clarify and explain the law, not to go down in history. Something must have happened around the year 500 CE to make the scholarly elite feel it was necessary to draw the intellectual threads of centuries together, into a single, coherent form.

The catalyst may have been turmoil within the Sassanian kingdom and upheavals in the local, social environment. An uprising led by a Persian priest, Mazdak, had led to the Sassanian king being temporarily deposed. At around the same time there was a briefly successful attempt by the exilarch, Mar Zutra to establish an autonomous state in Mahoza. None of these disruptions lasted long though; the Empire soon retook control, order was eventually restored and both the Exilarch and his grandfather Haninah, the head of the academy, were hanged on the bridge of Mahoza.[29] It was a very unstable time.

We don't know who compiled the Babylonian Talmud, nor how they went about it. The early medieval view, which is set out in Sherira *Gaon*'s letter, is that the final editors of the Talmud were Rav Ashi, who died in 428 CE, and Rabina, who lived until 499 CE, both of whom are described in the Talmud as being 'at the close of teaching'.[30] But it has long been recognized that this view is untenable, since they are both frequently mentioned in the Talmud, as indeed is Rav Ashi's son, Mar, and indeed Rav Ashi's encounter with the Angel of Death.[31] It seems pretty clear that the editing process was still going on long after their time.

---

[28] Oppenheimer, 2005, pp. 417–20 shows that the main period of activity for the *nahotei* – scholarly travellers between Israel and Babylon – was concentrated in the period between the end of the third century and the first decades of the fourth. The best known of the *nahotei* are Ulla, Rav Dimi and Rabin. Many of the rulings they brought with them are transmitted in the name of Rabbi Yohanan, the most prominent of the *amoraim* in the Land of Israel.

[29] Gafni, 2006; Ben Sasson, 1967.

[30] Bava Metzia 86a. One of the reasons why Rav Ashi was regarded as the final editor may be a statement in Bava Batra 157b which has Rav Ashi ruling one way in his 'first revision' and another way in his second. But of course this could also simply refer to his personal revision of what he had learnt.

[31] Moed Katan 28a.

## Layers upon layers

For the last few centuries readers have become used to books which were written at one time, by one person, or occasionally a team of people, They begin at the beginning and end at the end. The Talmud is not like this. It contains layers of material from different places and different times, which have been woven together skilfully, almost seamlessly, in a more or less uniform manner. We can identify these layers by their language, for example a change in the middle of a passage from Hebrew to Aramaic, by their style and particularly through the use of 'keywords' such as 'we learnt' or 'an objection was raised' which flag up content that had been imported into the discussion.

There are at least four chronological layers of material in the Talmud, not counting over eight thousand biblical verses[32] which are woven into the narrative to explain, justify or clarify a particular point.

The base layer comprises quotations from the Mishnah itself or from other rabbinic literature of the same period, which we looked at in Chapter 1. The second layer, which makes up the core of the Talmud, comes from the study sessions in the Babylonian academies and is usually attributed to one of the scholars of the time. The third layer has no names attached, it is anonymous, connects everything together and provides the framework for the discussion. The people who wrote this third layer are the original editors of the Talmud.[33] Finally there is another stratum of even later material which was probably added after the first drafts of the Talmud were concluded. This layer tends to introduce a topic or to provide the logical conclusion to an argument.

A classic example demonstrating these layers occurs in a discussion on the laws of damages.[34] The section opens, as do all Talmudic topics, with a citation from the Mishnah (first layer). This enumerates four 'principal categories' of damages. An anonymous editor (third or maybe fourth layer) then points out that if these are called the 'principal' categories then there must also be 'secondary' or derivative categories. The same voice asks whether the derivatives have the same standing in law as the principal categories. A view from a Babylonian academy (second layer) is then cited: 'Rav Pappa said "some of the derivatives are equal to their principals, whereas others are not."' Finally the

---

[32] Jacobs, 2005.
[33] David Weiss Halivni terms these the *Stammaim* or the Anonymous.
[34] Bava Kamma 2a–3b.

editors (third layer) cite a number of *tannaitic* (first layer) and *amoraic* (second layer) sources to clarify which derivatives Rav Pappa considered equivalent to their principals, and which he considered were not.[35]

The scale of the task facing the editors of the Talmud is hard to contemplate. Not only did they have vast amount of material to work with, most of it only existed orally. Yaakov Ellman makes out a convincing case that not only the first two layers, but even much of the third and fourth, were handed down by word of mouth, generation after generation.[36] This method of oral transmission is known as *gemara*. Printed editions of the Talmud use this word to separate the material that was composed in Babylon (second layer or later) from the introductory quotations from the Mishnah (first layer).

At least some of the Talmud was written down by the eighth century[37] but most of it probably circulated in an oral form for another three hundred years.[38] We don't know exactly when it was given its literary form. We don't even know if it was given a literary form before it was written down, or if that was a consequence of the transcription process. All we do know is that the process was carried out by editors who, whether deliberately or not, managed to successfully conceal their identity. Louis Jacobs points out that 'nowhere in the Talmud is there any definite statement about the process of redaction, and how it was done and by whom'.[39]

To pull all the material together the editors of the Talmud are likely to have worked in teams. Shamma Friedman suggests that typically there would have been an 'arranger' who fixed the early layers in place so as to construct the framework for the argument, and an 'explainer' who created the argument that linked the pieces together.[40] The teams would have worked together for an extended period of time, older scholars handing over to younger ones as the generations passed. The process may have gone on for centuries.

Yet, for all its complex composition the Talmud appears to the reader to be a seamless work. It's not until we analyse it closely that we can see the joins between the layers. Although written in Babylon the Talmud can quote the

---

[35] For a full discussion on this passage see Jacobs, 1973.
[36] Ellman, 1999.
[37] Fishman, 2011 and the sources cited in the note thereon. The earliest known, written fragment of Talmud text dates from the late seventh or early eighth century.
[38] Fishman, 2011.
[39] Jacobs, 2005, p. 4.
[40] Friedman, 2004.

opinions of people who lived their whole lives elsewhere.[41] yet it will have us think they were standing in the same room as native Babylonians. We don't know the names of the people who wove all this material together and the nature of their work is such that when studying the Talmud we are rarely aware of the scale or complexity of the task they undertook. But whilst the voices of rabbis who are quoted in the Talmud echo through history to the modern reader there is a second group of truly astonishing people, for there must have been many of them, who pulled the whole thing together but have altogether disappeared from view. The Talmud contains many paradoxes; but this is surely the greatest paradox of all.

---

[41] Most notably Rabbi Yohanan and Resh Lakish who are mentioned hundreds of times in the Talmud yet as far as we are aware never set foot in the country.

# 5

# The flowering of Babylon

Ben Bag Bag said: Turn in it and turn in it for everything is in it, and gaze into it, and grow old and weary in it and don't depart from it, for you have no better measure than it. Ben Hé Hé said, according to the trouble, so is the reward.[1]

Despite the immensity of the Talmud project, most sixth-century Jews knew nothing of it. Much of the Hebrew nation had long since scattered from its ancestral homeland, and whilst the greatest concentrations of population could still be found in Israel and the land they anachronistically called Babylon, their compatriots could now be found as far away as Spain and India, the Arabian Peninsula and France. Most of them did not belong to the rabbinic elite. What bound them together was a common belief system, a common language, family ties and, too often, a painful awareness of what it was to be part of a minority. They had their customs and traditions, they had their Torah and holy writings. Of the Talmud, most of them were blissfully unaware.

All that was about to change. But not because of anything they did.

## Limits of influence

In the year 622 CE the prophet Mohammed and his followers embarked on a series of military campaigns from their base at Medina in the Arabian Peninsula. Within a remarkably short period of time the political and religious map of the Middle East would look very different. No nation, faith or institution which fell under their influence would emerge unchanged. The Talmud was no exception.

---

[1] Avot 5.22.

Mohammed had an extensive knowledge of Judaism and Jewish practice. This is clear from the Qu'ran itself, as well as from later commentaries and legends. He may even have been influenced by Jewish teachers.[2] One legend has the Prophet discussing the names of the stars in Joseph's dream with the son of the exilarch Bustanai,[3] of whom we will soon hear more. At first Mohammed instructed his followers to face Jerusalem when praying, as the Jews do, and he instituted a fast on the tenth day of the first month, corresponding to the Jewish Day of Atonement. When he eventually abandoned these practices it was most likely the result of an early alliance with local Jewish tribes turning sour.

Medina, in modern Saudi Arabia, is several hundred miles south-east of the Land of Israel. Jewish tribes were amongst its earliest inhabitants; Moshe Gil explains that the first Jewish settlers in the Arabian Peninsula were refugees from the Romans whose numbers increased as they converted the surrounding Arabian tribes.[4] Unlike the nomadic Bedouins, with whom they shared the region, the Jews lived in walled towns and farmed the land, growing dates and vines. The Jewish tribes played an active role in the governance of Medina.[5] In fact their presence in the Arabian Peninsula was so influential that for a short period in the sixth century the royal household of Yemen converted to Judaism.[6]

Early relations between Mohammed's followers and the Jews in the area were good. In the Constitution of Medina, which Muslim sources describe as a pact between the Muslims and the Jews, Mohammed states that 'the Jews have their religion and the Muslims have theirs'. But the amity wouldn't last. Despite the contact they had with the Prophet, not all of the Jews of Medina warmed to the Islamic revolution. Mohammed fought and won separate battles against three different Jewish tribes, expelling two of them, massacring most of the men in the third and taking the women and children into slavery.[7]

It has been argued that the hostility of the Arabian Jewish tribes to Mohammed was due to his alliances with dissenting Jewish sects.[8] Our modern conception of religion prevents us from appreciating just how fluid the ancient

[2] Goitein, 1952.
[3] Gil, 2004.
[4] Gil, 2004.
[5] Gil, 2004.
[6] Stillman, 2012.
[7] Cohen, 1994.
[8] Goitein, 2005.

faiths were. Major religions today have a clear set of doctrines, well-established rituals, clergy who are responsible for the faith's propagation and buildings dedicated to worship. But the early days of a faith are rarely so well structured. The history of Judaism, Christianity and Islam is full of competing sects vying for influence.

The Talmud sat at the centre of Jewish life in Babylon and Israel but it was probably unknown to the remote desert communities. Even if the Jews of Arabia were aware of it, there is no reason to assume that its teachings remained unchanged as they diffused from the centre to the periphery of Jewish settlement.[9] Far from it; the Talmudic centres were so distant from Arabia, and the prevailing lifestyles so different that we can imagine a local, exotic Jewish culture which would have been virtually unrecognizable to a Jew from Babylon.

The Mishnah had cemented the religious authority of the rabbis amongst the Jewish communities in Israel and Babylon, but that wasn't the case elsewhere. The ideological victory that the Pharisees had gained over the Sadducees all those years ago hadn't universally standardized Jewish belief and practice. Nor had the birth of Christianity stopped other messianic groups from emerging within Judaism; the best known of whom were followers of the eighth–century, sectarian Abu Isa.[10]

One of the ideological battles the Talmud was yet to fight would be to bring dissenting Jewish groups, such as those in the Arabian Peninsula, within its sphere of influence. It was the spread of Islam over the next few centuries which allowed the battle to be won.


## Baghdad – city of culture

Once they had consolidated their stronghold in Arabia the Prophet's followers moved to challenge the powerful Sassanian and Byzantine Empires to the north and east. The first assault against the Sassanians was in 633 CE. Within a few years the Islamic victory was complete; four hundred years of Sassanian rule

---

[9] Lassner, 2012.

[10] Abu Isa was a Jewish schismatic. He promoted the doctrine of the one True Prophet who has revealed himself successively in every religion, and held that all religions are repetitions of each other. See Friedlaender, 1912, p. 121 and the sources quoted there.

over Mesopotamia came to an abrupt end. From his stronghold in Medina the Caliph Umar was redrawing the map of the world.

Umar's successors, the Umayyads, built upon his successes. The caliphate grew rapidly. By the middle of the eighth century Muslim rule extended from Spain in the west, across the whole of North Africa, to Iran and India. But despite their territorial gains the Umayyads could not suppress internal dissent. The Umayyad caliphate fell in 750 CE, defeated by the Abassids, descendants of Mohammed's youngest uncle, Abbas ibn Abd al-Muttalib.

In one of those fortuitous accidents of history, al-Mansur, the Abbasid caliph commissioned a new city to be built as his capital. He chose a new name for it but people continued to refer to it by the name of the settlement that had previously stood there. They called it Baghdad. Had al-Mansur not chosen Baghdad as the site of his capital it is quite possible that the history of the Babylonian Talmud would have run a completely different course. It may not even have run a course at all.

Baghdad's rise was brisk. Within a few years of its founding it was echoing the former glories of Babylon, the ruins of which lay a day's journey to the south. Baghdad became a flourishing centre of culture and knowledge, a dazzling capital of honeyed bazaars and scented gardens, gilded palaces and gaily bedecked caravans. Its citizens paraded through its market streets garbed in coloured silks and wools, its air hung heavy with the beguiling scents of exotic spices. The city's salacious romances and perfumed intrigues have been immortalized in *The One Thousand and One Nights*. But its greatest achievement surpassed all sensual experiences.

The Abbasid caliphate regarded learning as one of the highest of virtues, an attitude that was embodied in the saying 'the ink of a scholar is more holy than the blood of a martyr'. From the ninth century onwards their capital, Baghdad, became a magnet for scholars from across the Empire. Deeply conscious that language was a barrier to knowledge, that the Greeks had produced a branch of philosophical literature barely understood by Arabic speakers and that an inward-looking Islamic empire risked losing sight of the wisdom and ideas of the great world cultures that it was his ambition to surpass, the Caliph Harun al-Rashid embarked on a major intellectual project.

Al-Rashid, and after his passing, his son, al-Ma'mun, oversaw the creation of a new library, the House of Wisdom, which was charged with the massive task of translating the major literature of all languages into Arabic.

This project, which would soon embrace every known field of scholastic endeavour, laid the foundations for the great advances that the Islamic world would make in mathematics, philosophy, poetry, astronomy and medicine. Advances which would fulfil Harun al-Rashid's ambitions to make Islam the most advanced civilization the world had ever known.

The significance of the developments in Baghdad was not lost upon the scholars of the Talmudic academies, in their traditional halls of learning a little way down river. Baghdad was both the intellectual centre of the world and the capital of the expanding Islamic Empire. The hegemonic aspirations of the Babylonian *yeshivot,* the Sura and Pumbedita Academies, were just as bold, within the far smaller Jewish orbit. They already considered Babylon to be the leading spiritual authority in the Jewish world, whilst reluctantly accepting that there were still regions over which the Palestinian *yeshiva* held sway. The finalizing and editing of centuries of Talmudic study was to be the pinnacle of their intellectual achievement, the *yeshiva* would become a fitting equal to, and companion for, the House of Wisdom. They gave the heads of their academies; first Sura and later Pumbedita, the title *Gaon,* or Excellency, to reflect their new self image.[11]

The formative discussions in the Academy had already come to an end by this time and the process of compiling and editing the Talmudic discussions had quietly been going on, though we know virtually nothing about it. We do know though that the twice yearly, month-long study sessions were still taking place, just as they had done for generations.[12]

All we can say with confidence is that when we left the Talmud the final discussions were taking place in the provincial academies of Sura and Pumbedita; and by the time we are able to pick up its story again it is fully formed, albeit in a fluid, oral form, at the centre of a bustling and intellectually thriving Baghdad, poised to begin its journey from a local scholarly exercise to a classic of world literature.

The highly charged intellectual environment in Baghdad created one of the two conditions the Talmud needed if it was to break out of the academies into the wider world. The other was Baghdad's geographical location, at the centre

---

[11] As Gil remarks 'Any attempt to determine when the use of their title began is a waste of time' (Gil, 2004).

[12] The month-long sessions, known as *kallah,* are mentioned in the *Iggeret* of Pirkoi ben Baboi, reproduced in Lewin, 1930–1, p. 120. Moshe Gil (Gil, 2004) maintains that the academies continued their regular sessions of study, analysis and debate, just as they had always done, and although he is probably right there is very little confirmatory evidence for this, or indeed any other, view.

of the caliphate's unified polity and international communication network, stretching from the Atlantic coast of North Africa to the borders of India.

More than anything else it was these two factors which would bring about and facilitate the dissemination of the Babylonian Talmud to Jewish communities throughout the Islamic world, and eventually beyond.


## Shared ideas – the Talmud and Islam

As their links with the new metropolis strengthened the luminaries of Sura and Pumbedita found they had much in common with their opposite numbers in the Islamic world. They discovered they were grappling with similar issues, actively applying their scholarship, legal and religious traditions, to regulate the day-to-day lives of their co-religionists.

Each faith influenced the other. This is obvious both from the structure of their legal systems and some of the legislation itself. Their influence upon each other was more than just a simple two-way process; Gideon Libson explains it as a feedback model in which the Talmudic system first impacted Islam, which at a later stage left its imprint on Talmudic law.[13]

Both Islam and Judaism are religions which minutely regulate every aspect of the believer's life. They're each based on a God-given written document – the Torah for Judaism and the Qu'ran for Islam. These divine texts are each interpreted and expanded upon by an oral tradition – the Talmud and the Hadith respectively. Both traditions contain legal and ethical material, and the legal material in each distinguishes between religious laws and social laws. The Jewish system of law is called *halacha*, the Islamic system is called *shar'ia*. Both names mean a 'pathway' or a 'way to go'. Unlike Christianity, the laws and beliefs in Islam and Judaism are derived through a process of reasoning and scholarship; there are no councils or synods to rule on doctrine, ethics or behaviour.[14] In fact the two religions are so close in terms of their structure that the tenth-century rabbinic leader Saadia *Gaon* would unselfconsciously refer to Jewish law as *shar'ia*, to the prayer leader in a synagogue as an *imam* and the direction in which Jews faced when praying as *qibla*.[15]

---

[13] Libson, 1995.
[14] Goitein, 2005.
[15] Cohen, 1994.

Although in these twin systems the Qu'ran and Torah parallel each other as divinely revealed written texts, the Qu'ran was written down long after the Torah. So whilst we find characters, ideas and motifs from the Torah in the Qu'ran,[16] we shouldn't expect to find them the other way round.

However, the Talmud and Qu'ran do originate from a similar period and it's not hard to find concepts from the Talmud occurring in both the Qu'ran and Hadith, and vice versa.

One such case is the ritual definition of daybreak. The Qu'ran defines the moment of daybreak, when the faithful must begin to fast during Ramadan, as when the 'white thread of dawn becomes distinct to you from the black thread'.[17] Similarly, the Jewish Mishnah rules that the morning prayer is to be said when the worshipper can distinguish between blue and white.[18]

Both traditions use the same analogy to emphasize the sanctity and uniqueness of every human life. The Qu'ran states that 'We decreed upon the Children of Israel that whoever kills a soul ... it is as if he had slain mankind entirely. And whoever saves one – it is as if he had saved mankind entirely'.[19] This is a reference to the passage from the Mishnah that:

> Adam was created alone to teach you that whoever takes a human life is considered by the Bible to have destroyed an entire world. And whoever saves a human life is considered by the Bible as if he preserved an entire world.[20]

Initially Jewish ideas found their way into Islam but the process's subsequent reversal can be spotted in matters of finance and commerce. Talmudic law matured in Baghdad in a commercial, Islamic environment and Shmuel had already declared that when it came to civil law 'The law of the land is the law'. This gave the *geonim* flexibility in commercial matters to amend or even abrogate Talmudic sanction as necessary.

We can see an example of this flexibility in the laws governing money transfers. The Talmud had instituted that, as a precaution against fraud, merchants could not transfer money by bills of exchange even when these were

---

[16] E.g. Qu'ran Sura V.44.
[17] Qu'ran Sura II.187.
[18] See Chapter 1.
[19] Qu'ran Sura V.32.
[20] M. Sanhedrin 4.5.

countersigned by witnesses.[21] However a *geonic* ruling overturned this ruling on the basis that people were already doing it, and that it was in accordance with the Islamic laws that regulated merchants.

> It is true that the sages said we should not send money by bills of exchange, even if witnesses have signed them. However, since we have seen that people use them we have begun to accept them in court in order not to impede trade between people, and we give judgement according to the traders' law; neither more nor less.[22]

Mark Cohen points out that this 'shared judgement of Muslim and Jewish legal experts … could only occur in a market atmosphere that knew no confessional boundaries'.[23]

An extensive survey by Gideon Libson has shown similarities between the rulings of a tenth-century *gaon*, Shmuel ben Hofni, and Islamic legal writing of the same period. Of course, as Libson concedes, the fact that there are similarities between two legal rulings in different systems doesn't necessarily mean that one system was dependent upon the other; they may both have independently derived their rulings from a third source that they each knew.[24] But with all the other evidence of contact and cross-influences between the faiths, it's pretty likely that the Talmudic and Islamic systems of law influenced each other.

Talmudic and Islamic scholars cross-fertilized in legal matters because they lived in the same mercantile society. But the two traditions didn't just overlap when it came to the law. Story telling was an art in the folklore-rich Arabian world.

Amongst the few things that the patchwork of Jewish sects in the Arabia Peninsula had in common was a repository of folklore. The Talmud had drawn on some of it, but there was much more which it did not absorb, including literature linked to the secessionist priestly sect at Qumran, who are best known as the authors of the Dead Sea Scrolls.[25] Early Islam had drawn in Jewish converts who recounted these Dead Sea tales along with everyone else, based on their memories of legends they had heard as Jews.

---

[21] Bava Kamma 104b.

[22] Teshuvot Hageonim (Harkavy) 423; Goiten, 1967 vol. 1, p. 328.

[23] Cohen, 1994.

[24] Libson, 1995.

[25] Halperin and Newby, 1982. On the Qumran sect as a secessionist priestly sect see Elior, 2004.

As these stories began to circulate they took on an Islamic guise; the more they were repeated in the Islamic world, the more they were adapted to fit the cultural context.

This folklore, which became known as *Isra'iliyyat,* was not always looked upon kindly by Islamic leaders. It frequently came in for fierce censure. The Egyptian scholar Ahmad Shakir explains that *Isra'illiyat* literature can only be regarded as supporting mainstream Islamic traditions, it should not be relied on unless it is confirmed by the Qu'ran and Hadith.[26]

Amongst the many Jewish converts whose stories entered Islamic hagiography, two in particular stood out. K'ab al-Ahbar, a Yemenite Jew, is thought to have been one of Caliph Umar's closest advisers. Amongst the sayings attributed to him is that all human history is alluded to in the Jewish Torah; a Talmudic idea first expressed by the intriguingly named Ben Bag-Bag.[27]

Another convert, or possibly the son of one, Wahb ibn Munabbih, wrote, or contributed to, a work known as *Kisas al-Anbiya,* the Tales of the Prophets which recounts Jewish Biblical legends, recast in an Islamic guise. Kisas al-Anbiya is considered to be the source for the Islamic belief that Abraham is commanded to sacrifice Ishmael, rather than Isaac as the Hebrew Bible has it. The Qu'ran does not say which son was nearly sacrificed. Wahb's other major work, *Kitab al-Isra'illiyat,* or Book of Jewish Matters, no longer exists but some of its tales appear, in an Islamic context, in the *Thousand and One Nights.*

## Temporal power and scholarly authority

The *geonim* as heads of the academies had a far more exalted status than their counterparts during Talmudic times. We know the names of hundreds of *amoraim:* academy heads, senior scholars and students. In the later period, however, with very few exceptions we only know the names of the *geonim.* They seem to have ruled with far greater authority than the heads of the *amoraic* academies, and they kept their office within the leading families. The position of head of the academy frequently passed from father to son or from one brother to another.

---

[26] Shakir, 1956. For a detailed discussion of the relationship between Isra'iliyyat and the Jewish folklore, or *aggadic* tradition see Heller, 1934, p. 383–405.

[27] Mishnah Avot 5.22.

Unlike their compatriots in Israel, the Jews of Babylon were tolerated by the Islamic rulers. Together with other minority religions they were free to worship according to their faith, as long as they did nothing to offend Islam. Pirkoi ben Baboi, a ninth-century Talmudist recounts that the 'two academies in Babylon did not witness imprisonment, forced conversions or plunder; nor were they dominated by Greece or Rome'[28]

Nevertheless the caliph ruled supreme. His empire was vast and diverse; to hold it all together required strong military, political and diplomatic control. Even though the exilarch was appointed by the heads of the *yeshivot* and the elders of the community, his tenure was now to be ratified by the caliph.[29] And his court was to be relocated from Mahoza to Baghdad. There was to be no repetition of Mar Zutra's attempt to establish an independent Jewish state. Nor would the Commander of the Faithful permit a repetition of the Exilarch Bustanai's alliance with the Sassanian Empire when Caliph Umar's forces had first invaded. We encountered Bustanai's son discussing the names of the stars in Joseph's dream with the prophet Mohammed in Medina.

Most of Bustanai's life is the stuff of legend and it is hard to unravel the historical detail. But as versions of his legend are attested in several Muslim and Jewish sources,[30] there is probably an historical core to it. Bustanai's father, the previous exilarch, had been slain by one of the Sassanian kings; the accounts differ as to which monarch it was. One night King David, the traditional ancestor of the exilarchs, appeared in a dream to the Sassanian monarch and warned him, on pain of death, to stop slaying his descendants. Seeking to put right his offence, the king took the orphaned Bustanai under his wing and appointed him exilarch.

Bustanai's followers fought with the Sassanians against the Muslim invaders but it was no more than an alliance of convenience. Following the Muslim victory he signed a peace pact with Caliph Umar. As part of the deal Umar gave him one of the daughters of the defeated Sassanian king as a wife. Bustanai now had two wives, one Jewish and one Persian. However, the Persian wife, as a prisoner of war, was technically a slave and the sons of his Jewish wife tried to exclude her children from inheriting their father's title. The scholars of the Babylonian academies found in favour of the children of the Persian princess,

[28] Iggeret of Pirkoi ben Baboi, reproduced in Lewin, 1930–1, p. 395.
[29] Gil, 2004.
[30] A comprehensive review of the sources and various forms of the legend appears in Gil, 2004.

ruling that Bustanai had liberated her from her status as a slave. Bustanai's descendants from each branch of his family eventually became exilarchs but three hundred years later the matter was still being hotly disputed; the legitimacy of the Persian line challenged by the then leader of the Babylonian community, Hai *Gaon*.

The powers of Bustanai's successors under the caliphate, although diminished from their peak under Sassanian rule, were nevertheless considerable. Although the exilarch no longer had the right to judge criminal cases, other than in exceptional circumstances, he was still able to levy taxes upon his Jewish subjects. According to one report he would collect 20 per cent of their income together with a proportion of any produce and additional levies whenever a house was built or a wedding conducted.

The exilarch resided in state in a palace stretching from the Barley Gate to the Harranian Arch in the Western quarter of the city. Once 'crowned', in an elaborate feast, during which he would be showered with gifts, he remained in his palace. He would only leave if summoned to visit the caliph, when he would travel in a royal carriage accompanied by his entourage, their numbers swelled by onlookers who would join the throng as the exilarch travelled through the city.[31]

But for all the exilarch's grandeur he was merely the embodiment of temporal authority. He sat at the head of society but he did little for it that was not ceremonial. His memory endures solely due to the enterprise of his scholarly colleagues, those who were working to fulfil their perceived spiritual mission. It was the *geonim* who were responsible for the legal and social structures that would allow the Talmud to grow beyond Baghdad, and to exert its influence on a world that was growing ever more connected.

[31] Gil, 1995.

# 6

# From your father's house

Ben Zoma said: Who is wise? He who learns from all men. Who is mighty? He who subdues his passions, Who is rich? He who rejoices in his portion.[1]

## The Talmud's expanding influence

Both the Talmudic and Islamic scholars shared the same imperative, to extend their authority beyond their immediate neighbourhood. It was important for the Islamic scholars because the faith was relatively new, the empire was still expanding and there were many areas that were not yet fully Islamized. It mattered to the Talmudic scholars because the small Jewish nation was scattered over a vast geographical area, and the danger was that without a centre of influence the faith may weaken and dissipate.

There was also the question of the Jerusalem Talmud, which still exerted its authority in regions which the Babylonians wished to reach. Although Israel was the ancestral homeland its impoverished community was lacking in leadership and serious legal scholarship. Its main cultural activity had for some time been the production of poetry and biblical interpretation; disciplines which the scholarly *geonim* considered relatively unimportant. In the early days Babylon had accepted the authority of the scholars in the Holy Land without question; now this was no longer the case. The last time we hear of a Babylonian scholar applying to the Academy in Israel for the answer to a problem was in the late fifth century.[2]

---

[1]  Avot 4.1.

[2]  Ginzberg, 1909, Hullin 59b. The characters named in this account, who are disputing whether or not it is permissible to eat the fat of a certain species of wild goat, are amongst the last of the *amoraim* and their discussions occur right at the close of the Talmudic period. We don't have evidence of subsequent scholars sending questions from Babylon to Israel.

As scholarship in one centre blossomed and the other faded the contest between the two Talmuds for influence was to grow increasingly trenchant. The Babylonian Talmud's position at the heart of the Islamic Empire gave its advocates an advantage over its hard-pressed rivals in Israel; the majority of Jews lived under Islamic rule and it was far easier to communicate with them from Baghdad than from Jerusalem.

Additionally, and perhaps most importantly, the sectarian threat had not been dispelled. There was a growing body of dissenting voices within the Jewish world; sects which had never been part of the rabbinic camp or which had become disillusioned with it and now, tolerated by the caliphate, were becoming more vociferous. Spreading the Talmud far and wide was one of the strategies the *geonim* would try to use to bring these communities into the mainstream.

It was no coincidence that the scholars of both faiths used identical tools to promote the fruits of their labours. One was the new science of codification; which reduced complex legal discussions to systematic, logically arranged summations of the law. The other was the well-established craft of letter writing.

Even today, when printing has standardized the Talmud text, it is astonishing how few of the discussions it contains end up with a definite legal conclusion, most of which were added in by later editors. The Talmud was not then, and is still not, a rule book. Its genius lies in taking the detailed case law of the Mishnah, defining the principles and concepts that underlie it and advancing arguments that can be used to underpin a subsequent legal ruling.[3] Its lack of clarity, its tendency to avoid decisions, was not unusual for its time, the whole business of making laws evolved very slowly in all ancient societies, over a period of several centuries. In fact up to this point the connected world had only ever known one true legal code.

When the Byzantine emperor Justinian I assumed power in 527 CE he found Roman law in a terrible mess, completely disorganized and with no formal structure. He immediately appointed a commission to go through all the legal material, verbal and written, to eliminate contradictions, get rid of redundancies and put the whole thing into a systematic order. The result was the Justinian code of Roman civil law. It functioned as the law book of the Byzantine Empire

---

[3] For example, *berirah*, retrospective designation, is a concept developed by the Talmud to explain a series of specific rulings in the Mishnah. *Muktzeh*, set aside, although touched upon in the Mishnah is another (Jacobs, 1984).

and influenced all subsequent legal developments wherever Roman influence was still felt.

The Justinian code had been formulated in the Roman west in the sixth century but it wasn't until the late eighth century that a flurry of codification activity broke out amongst major religions in the east. Islam, Zoroastrianism, Monophysite Christianity, Nestorianism and Judaism all produced legal codes. Benjamin Jokisch[4] suggests that the starting point for all these activities was in and around Baghdad. He conjectures that the caliph Harun al-Rashid and his childhood teacher, subsequently to be appointed vizier, Yahya ibn Khalid, organized round-table sessions in which leading representatives of the different faiths had the opportunity to exchange ideas. Jokisch even proposes that, just as Justinian had done, al-Rashid may have set up a legal commission comprising both Islamic and Talmudic jurists, with the different religious parties each laying down a codex of their own. He suggests that Shimon Kayyara and Pirkoi ben Baboi may have been amongst the Jewish members of the commission.[5]

Shimon Kayyara has gone down in history as an instrumental figure in the process of codifying and systematizing Talmudic law. A ninth-century, comprehensive legislative code, *Halachot Gedolot*, is attributed to him. If Jokisch is right then it would have been this code that he worked on in the caliph's inter-faith legal commission. But *Halachot Gedolot* was only one of at least three codifications of Talmudic law that emerged around the same time. Another was *Halachot Pesukot*, said to have been produced by Yehudai *Gaon*. It's hard to know which came first. Modern academic opinions are divided as to which of these two codes (if either) influenced the other, whether or not they really are different versions of the same work and even whether Shimon Kayyara and Yehudai *Gaon* really were the authors! But while all this is unclear there is no doubt that the production of these two codes was a seminal development in clarifying the legal rulings of the Talmud and projecting its influence beyond Babylon.[6]

The third summary of Talmudic law was written by the head of the Pumbedita academy, Ahai *Gaon*. Known as the *She'iltot*, it was very different

---

[4] Jokisch, 2007.

[5] Jokisch, 2007.

[6] For an overview of the various scholarly opinions about the relationship of the two works see the article by Yehoshua Horowitz in the *Encyclopaedia Judaica*, 2nd edn., vol. 8, pp. 2601 s.v. *Halachot Gedolot*. For a contradictory view see the article in the same volume by Mordechai Margoliot, idem, pp. 262–3 s.v. *Halachot Pesukot*. The traditional religious view is that Halachot Gedolot was the first of all Talmudic codifications.

from the other two works, and became much more popular. Ahai had spent thirteen years living in Israel after the exilarch refused to appoint him as the head of the Pumbedita academy. It was there that he learnt new techniques for drawing ideas out of the biblical text[7] and he used them to good effect in his *She'iltot*. Unlike the authors of *Halachot Gedolot* and *Halachot Pesukot*, Ahai didn't arrange the laws according to topic. Instead he linked them to the text of the Five Books of Moses, and he did so with a homiletical eye, often leading to some quite odd results. The laws of robbery are not included, as one might think, after 'Thou shall not steal' in the Ten Commandments. Instead they are used to expand the story of Noah which the Bible introduces with the words 'And the earth was filled with violence'. For Ahai that violence was characterized by robbery.

*She'iltot* is based on the Talmud and draws its material from there, yet it was composed before the final version of the Talmud.[8] This shows us just how fluid the editing process of the Talmud was; and how long it survived in an oral form before it was finally written down.

## Questions and answers

Codification enabled people to access a concise summary of the law but codes in themselves didn't help much in building relationships between the academies and distant communities. A far more effective way for the Talmudic and Sharia scholars to establish their authority was by corresponding with their co-religionists, answering their questions and providing religious guidance. The Jews called these answers *teshuvot*; the Muslims called them *fatwas*. Academics of all faiths and none call them *responsa*.

In the second half of the ninth century, the leader of the Sura academy, Amram *Gaon*, received a question from a Jewish community in Spain; possibly Barcelona. It concerned a Talmudic injunction that one should recite a hundred blessings each day.[9] This injunction doesn't receive a lot of attention in the Talmud, the discussion in which it occurs moves on quite quickly. But it was

---

[7] *Midrashic* techniques of biblical interpretation were typical of the Palestinian school; all significant *midrashic* compilations emanated from there.
[8] Epstein, 1935.
[9] Menachot 43b.

important to the people who sent the question. They wanted to know, what are these hundred blessings? Amram's predecessor and teacher Natronai[10] had previously been asked a similar question by the people of Lucena in Cordoba but whilst he refers to Natronai's answers, Amram's response was far more detailed.

Amram's reply, addressed with the flamboyant courtesy of the age to 'Rabbi Isaac son of our rabbi and teacher Shimon, beloved, exalted and honoured by us and the entire *yeshiva*', is effectively the earliest known prayer book.[11] In it he sets out the blessings, the times they are to be recited and manner of their recital. Of course, he didn't intend it to be a prayer book; such a thing was unheard of in those days.[12] All Amram was doing was to answer a question posed by a remote community, but in such detail, and in such a prescriptive manner, that he reinforced the Babylonian Talmud as the natural, and only, source for determining Jewish law and practice.

The *geonim* didn't invent the practice of sending *teshuvot;* missives containing legal decisions were already well established by their time. The Roman emperor Augustus had long ago appointed official jurists who had the right to issue *responsa* on behalf of the Emperor. The Talmud itself contains a dispute in which Rav Kahana, whom we met when he was forced to flee Babylon for Israel, was accused of erecting a fence which encroached on his neighbour's land. This was in the days when the Academy in Israel was still considered the supreme authority. Kahana denied the charge and offered to bring a letter from 'the West' (i.e. Israel), confirming that his understanding of the law was correct.[13]

But although the practice was well established, the sending of written answers accelerated in the *geonic* period; sometimes, as in the case of Amram, the answers were in response to a question from a distant locale, at other times

---

[10] Brody, 1994.

[11] Amram's prayer book, *Seder Rav Amram*, has been extensively edited and elaborated by successive generations of scholars. We no longer have a record of his original letter to the Spanish community and we don't know how much detailed was contained in his reply. A critical edition was published by Daniel S. Goldschmidt, Mossad HaRav Kook, Jerusalem, 1971.

[12] Louis Ginzberg argued that there must have been some sort of written text that the prayer leader used, since a responsa of Amram's teacher Natronai permits a blind person to act as prayer leader, and the question would not have been asked if prayers were recited from memory. But Ginzberg may be wrong, there may have been other reasons why a congregation might have thought a blind person was ineligible (Ginzberg, 1909, p. 120–1) .

[13] Bava Batra 41b. Similar instances in the Talmud in which aggrieved parties offer to bring a letter appear in Sanhedrin 29a and Shevuot 48b.

the 'answers' were sent at the *Gaon's* initiative, to make a particular point or pre-empt a forthcoming situation from developing.

Some of the earliest *responsa* sent to local towns or communities dealt with issues that arose due to the interlocking of Talmudic and Sharia law. One early incident concerned the laws of divorce. The Talmudic custom had been that when a wife wanted a divorce, there should be a twelve-month cooling off period.[14] This restriction did not apply in Islamic law and, some Jewish women, unwilling to wait a full year, gave up on their Jewish divorce and married Muslim men. This seems to have obliged the Jewish courts to order an immediate divorce; though it's not clear whether this was due to pressure from the Islamic authorities. In any event around the year 650 CE two of the early *geonim,* Huna and Rava sent out letters authorizing divorces to be given immediately, so that women would no longer need to resort to the Islamic courts.[15]

The system of sending written answers to distant communities was less than sophisticated. Very often no record of either the question or the response was preserved in the Academy. So the Talmud scholars in Babylon frequently did not know decisions circulated by earlier generations, even though these decisions were known elsewhere. Some of the rulings of Yehudai *Gaon,* who was active around 760 CE, only became known in Babylon a hundred years later, when they arrived back in Baghdad, brought by Jewish captives from Christian countries.[16]

By Amram *Gaon's* time *responsa* were being sent to communities throughout the Islamic Empire. Most of the traffic was with settlements in Egypt, North Africa and Spain. The nineteenth-century discovery of a thousand years of religious and secular Hebrew documents stored in a synagogue attic in Fustat, Cairo, has unearthed hundreds of *responsa*, covering everything from the most technical laws about ritually unfit meat to obscure religious customs and ceremonies that were unique maybe only to a handful of villages.[17] One

---

[14] Ketubot 63b–64a.

[15] *Iggeret of Sherira Gaon,* ed. Lewin, p. 101, discussed in Mann, 1919.

[16] 'Or *Zarua* 2, #432, p. 177 cited in Mann, 1917, p. 461.

[17] The Cairo Genizah, was a ancient storeroom discovered in the late nineteenth century in the synagogue in Fustat. It contained nineteen thousand Hebrew and Arabic documents including lost fragments and manuscripts of the Talmud dating back to 870 CE. Its discovery, and the work on its contents which is still going on in universities around the world has revolutionized historians' understanding of ancient and medieval Jewish and Islamic life, has helped explain many obscure or corrupted Talmudic passages and thrown light on life and conditions in Egyptian communities. See Chapter 8.

tenth-century letter found in the Cairo *Genizah*, which made its way to the Bodleian Library in Oxford and was published in 1906, tells us that in the middle of the ninth century another of the *geonim*, Paltoi, was asked by a group in Spain to send them a copy of the Talmud, together with explanations, and this he duly did. Unfortunately we have no other evidence of this so it is hard to know exactly what is meant. It's pretty certain that the full, 1.8 million-word document that we know today had not yet crystallized into a format that could be written down. It is likely therefore that Paltoi sent them extracts, an abridgement or an explanation of what the Talmud was.[18]

The *responsa* functioned as more than just ritual guides and legal decisions. A *gaon* might sometimes decide to send one for propaganda purposes, or to drive home a polemical point.[19] None was better at this than Pirkoi ben Baboi, even though he wasn't a *gaon*. Pirkoi was born towards the end of the eighth century and was a pupil of Yehudai *Gaon*, whose *responsa* had been brought back by captives to Baghdad a century after they had been written. What makes him particularly interesting is that he used his *responsa* to fight two battles at the same time.

Pirkoi's most famous letter, known quite simply as the Letter of Pirkoi ben Baboi was ostensibly written to communities in Israel, pointing out that many of their practices were not in line with the rulings of the Babylonian Talmud. His teacher Yehudai had tried something similar and had been rebuffed, the heirs to the Jerusalem Talmud were not going to be dictated to by those of the Babylonian version. The Academy in Israel had told Yehudai that their traditions were firmly established, and that in matters of ritual, a long-established tradition overrides a theoretical law. Paltoi tried a different approach. He sent his letter not just to Israel but to the Jews in Kairouan, then an important city about a hundred miles from the modern Tunis.

Kairouan had a large and thriving Jewish community. The city enjoyed economic stability and its Jewish community was well educated, with close ties to their co-religionists in Spain, whom they helped to establish their own centres of learning. Pirkoi pointed out to the Jews in Kairouan that the traditions observed in Israel were unique to that country and had been forced upon them by persecutions. Even though the citizens of Kairouan were in close

---

[18] See Fishman, 2011, p.72 and notes.

[19] Talya Fishman suggests that towards the end of the *geonic* period, when the academies were struggling financially, sending *responsa* and legal guides to wealthy foreign communities was part of a proactive fund-raising strategy.

contact with, and travelled frequently to Israel, there had been no persecutions in Kairouan. There was no reason therefore for the Jews there to mimic practices in Israel. They couldn't use the same argument as the Jerusalem Academy to do things that were not in accord with the Babylonian Talmud.

What Pirkoi was really doing, in copying his letter to Kairouan, and probably elsewhere as well, was to raise the stakes in the battle between the two Talmuds for religious authority. He recognized the strategic value of establishing the authority of the Babylonian Talmud in Kairouan. By starting from a position which claimed Israel was wrong and Babylon was right, he was doing what polemicists have done since time immemorial; he was framing the debate in terms which made his position correct from the outset.

But this wasn't all. Pirkoi may have believed firmly that the Babylonian Talmud was the more authentic because it had never been forced to seek compromise with oppressors, but nevertheless the struggle between the two Talmuds was an internal matter. There was a far more urgent battle looming. Against a Jewish sectarian group known as the Karaites. Who, like the Sadducees some centuries earlier, did not accept the Oral Law at all. Overcoming the Karaites was Pirkoi's real aim, and he couldn't argue for the validity of the Oral Law if there were two Talmuds with conflicting practices, each claiming to represent the authentic tradition, each contradicting the other. That was the real reason Pirkoi was insistent that the Jews of Kairouan followed the dominant Babylonian Talmud. He wanted to take the Jerusalem Talmud out of the picture altogether.

## The Karaites

The two Talmuds may have struggled for dominance out of a competing sense of superiority, but they were about to be hit by a challenge that was wholly out of their control. Nobody had seen what was coming when, in the second half of the eighth century, the exilarch-in-waiting, Anan ben David was passed over for the job in favour of his brother, nor when, some years later, his grandson Daniel became embroiled in a separate dispute over the succession. The fact that another member of Anan's family, a man named Josiah, was the head of the Academy in Israel did nothing to help.

Anan was a charismatic intellectual who attracted followers towards him, polymaths with interests in law, philosophy, language and biblical interpretation. His disenchantment with the Talmudic establishment may have been why he didn't get the post of exilarch, or it may have been a consequence of his rejection. Either way, he began to explore the origins of Talmudic religion and to enter into dialogue with other dissenting Jewish sects, including Abu Isa's movement, and the Yudghanites, a Jewish sect influenced by Sufism.[20] An amalgamation of sorts began to take place and by the ninth century the coalition, although patchy at first, had developed its own distinctive identity, and taken a name that implied 'followers of the Bible', thus making it clear they were no disciples of the Talmud.[21]

The Karaites actively recruited converts and established communities across the Islamic and Byzantine Empires. The two Academies of Babylon and Israel, still eyeing each other suspiciously, had a bigger threat to deal with than anything they had previously known.

The Karaites' fundamental premise was the rejection of Talmudic Judaism, in favour of a literal interpretation of the Bible. This did not mean that they had no traditions or biblical interpretations of their own, it would be very difficult to take the Bible at face value without any need for interpretation or explanation. The Karaites had their own principles for interpreting the Bible, but they rejected out of hand the idea of an Oral Law handed down from Mount Sinai, of which the Talmud was the summation. Just as the earlier Sadducees, with whom they share many similarities, had rejected the Oral Law adhered to by the Pharisees.

Pirkoi ben Baboi believed the Karaite threat could only be contained if the struggle between the Academies was resolved. A divided Talmud played into the hands of those who opposed it; dissent could only be contained by a single, universally accepted legal authority. He used his letter to highlight seemingly minor points of law which he believed illustrated the failings of the Israel Academy. He railed against them for hesitating over whether the Sabbath regulations prohibiting the lighting of fires could be overruled to heat water for a woman in labour. All agreed that preservation of life came ahead of everything else and therefore, he argued, there was no question that a fire must be lit. But his real purpose in this argument was to point the finger at the Karaites who

---

[20] According to al-Qirqisani, Yudgahan's followers assert that he was the Messiah; he did not die, they expect him to return at any moment. Their asceticism led them to abstain from meat and strong drink and to observe many fasts.

[21] The distinctive practices of the Ananites, as opposed to other sects belonging to the pre-Karaite coalition, are detailed by al-Qirqisani (Nemoy, 1930).

took the biblical prohibition against lighting a fire on the Sabbath literally and would spend the whole day with no heat and no light. By accusing the scholars in Israel of endangering women in childbirth by not lighting fires he was by implication accusing the Karaites of an even greater recklessness; in ignoring the Oral Law's interpretation of a biblical commandment they risked the lives of anyone who needed to be warmed on the Sabbath for the sake of their health.

Pirkoi didn't just use legal arguments against the Karaites. He appealed to their interest in biblical interpretation by adapting a well-known homily on a verse at the end of the Book of Deuteronomy, one which implies that God had offered the Torah to other Middle Eastern tribes before offering it to the Israelites.[22] In the original homily all the tribes had rejected the Torah because it contained too many restrictions. In Pirkoi's adaptation, the tribes had agreed to accept the written Torah, but it was not given to them because they would not accept an Oral Law. The homily implied that the Karaites were beyond the fold; by not accepting the Oral Law they had implicitly rejected the written Torah.

Nevertheless, despite Pirkoi's best efforts, the Karaites were far and away the most successful of the anti-Talmudic groups, and the only one from that period to survive to the present day. They based their interpretation of Bible upon reason. Despite doctrinal differences they were considered by all parties, including the Talmudists, to be part of the Jewish community. It was their membership of the community, coupled with their opposition to the Talmud, that caused emotions to run so high, and made the dispute so bitter.

Much of our knowledge of the Karaites comes from the writings of their tenth-century apologist, Abu Yusuf Yaqub al-Qirqisani. His *Book of Lights and Watch Towers*[23] is a detailed description of the many Jewish sects in Babylon, and the differences between them. Al-Qirqisani's charge against the Talmud is exactly that which Pirkoi had tried to eliminate; namely that differences of opinions between Talmudic scholars undermines their doctrine of a divinely given Oral Law that by definition should be clear and unambiguous. Karaites, on the other hand, says al-Qirqisani, 'arrive at our knowledge by the mere deduction of our reason; since this is so, it cannot be denied that controversy may possibly arise'.[24]

Pirkoi ben Baboi did manage to keep the North African communities on side; they didn't place themselves under the authority of the Israel Academy, as

---

[22] Mechilta d'R.Ishmael, Haḥodesh 5 on Deuteronomy 33.2.

[23] Nemoy, 1930.

[24] Nemoy, 1930.

he had feared. But other than that his evangelism for the Babylonian Talmud wasn't particularly successful. Not just because the Karaites were growing more numerous and confident daily. He also hadn't really gained any territorial advantage in the battle between the academies; the communities of Syria, Lebanon and most of Egypt still looked to Israel for guidance. It would take a stronger, more assertive character to strengthen the Babylon Academy, and to take decisive steps towards eliminating the Karaite threat.

## Saadia's controversies

Pirkoi was an important figure at a particular moment in the story of the Babylonian Talmud, but few people remember him today. Not so Saadia, *Gaon* of Sura.

At the beginning of the tenth century the Sura academy was in decline. According to Sherira *Gaon's* letter many of the scholars had died within a three-month period around the year 886 CE; Moshe Gil suggests this may have been the result of a plague.[25] The number of scholars fell away so sharply that when the academy head died in 924 CE the exilarch had to recruit from outside the academy. He appointed a local lay scholar, a weaver by profession, as *gaon*. Four years later, when the weaver died and the academy was in danger of closing, the exilarch, David ben Zakkai appointed another outsider, this time Saadia ben Yosef, who had been making something of a name for himself in Baghdad.

Saadia had been born in Fiyum, in Egypt. He was known locally as al-Faiyumi. Like the Karaites, Saadia had been influenced by the rationalist, Islamic school of Mu'tazilite philosophy. He wrote prolifically, on philosophy, biblical interpretation and grammar. People still read his works today.

Saadia was a great scholar but a quarrelsome man. He had been involved in controversy before his appointment as *Gaon* of Sura. David the Exilarch had been warned off the appointment, for Saadia 'feared no one, deferred to no-one in the world, because of his great wisdom and his large mouth and his long tongue …' .[26]

Saadia's attitude towards the perceived dangers of Karaism was far more impassioned than his fellow Talmudists; he had no interest in communal

---

[25] Gil, 2004.
[26] Quoted in Gil, 2004, p. 224.

reconciliation, he considered the Karaites to be apostates who should be ostra-cized by the community. At the age of twenty three, whilst still in Egypt and long before he was appointed *gaon*, Saadia had fired his first shot in his war against them, publishing a fierce polemic against the followers of Anan, who at that time still retained a separate identity within the Karaite movement. Not surprisingly the Karaites regarded him as their main opponent and they counter-attacked vigorously. Salmon ben Jeroham was particularly abusive towards him: 'You have written lies ... where do you flee to hide yourself in utter ruin ... may your steps be hampered as you walk.'[27]

But Saadia wasn't just quarrelsome; he was a good strategist. His persistent attacks achieved the outcome he had wanted, a complete break between the Talmud academies and the Karaites. He didn't get everything right; he strengthened the Karaites by propelling the Ananites, who were his intellectual equals and could hold their own against him in polemic, into a dominant position in Karaism. Saadia's attacks helped the Karaite ideologues to create a unitary position out of quarrelling sects. 'Karaism honed its intellectual edge on the confrontation with Saadia ... without Saadia, Karaism might have had a very different fate & form.'[28]

Saadia's quarrelsome reputation wasn't confined to his war against the Karaites. He also had a go at the Jerusalem Talmud. Six years before his appointment as *gaon* he had instigated the fiercest of all disputes between the adherents of the two Talmuds, a dispute which to all intents and purposes finally established the hegemony of the Babylonian school. It all had to do with the fixing of the calendar, and a squabble over a couple of missing days.

The Talmudic calendar is a unique and complex combination of both the lunar and solar cycles. The months are determined by the new moons, the years are dictated by the position of the earth relative to the sun. There are twelve months in the Talmudic year, but a lunar month is less than thirty days. Twelve of them do not add up to a solar year of three hundred and sixty five days. To bring the lunar and solar cycles into line a rigorous calculation had to be implemented, in which some years had additional months inserted, and two particular months could vary between twenty nine or thirty days. Tradition has it that this calculation was introduced in the year 358 CE by the *Nasi* Hillel IV

---

[27] Schur, 1995, p. 225.
[28] Schur, 1995, pp. 247–8.

but Sacha Stern has shown that the development of this hybrid calendar was far more complicated than that.[29]

Until Saadia's time, responsibility for performing the calculation and announcing the leap years had rested with the Israel Academy. This was a relic of the custom in the days of the Temple, before the calculation was introduced, when the rabbis in Jerusalem would call for witnesses to come forward to testify they had seen the new moon. When a pair of reliable informants arrived, the rabbis would proclaim the new month.

In the year 922 CE a dispute broke out, for highly technical reasons, over whether the two flexible months should have twenty nine or thirty days. The *gaon* in Israel, ben Meir, held that the two months should have twenty nine days. The Babylonian scholars disagreed; they argued for thirty days. The details of the disagreement may have appeared trivial, they were arguing over a matter of a few minutes here or there, but the consequences were that, unless the two academies agreed, the communities over which they each held sway would celebrate their festivals on different days. Each school contended that if they followed the opinion of the other they would be eating forbidden bread on the day they had calculated to be the Passover.[30]

Saadia led the attack on the *Nasi's* calculation. He wrote to ben Meir, to his former pupils in Egypt and to 'most of the great cities' warning that if the view of the Israel Academy were to be followed this would lead to a profanation of Passover and the fast of the Day of Atonement, which would both be celebrated two days earlier than prescribed. Letters and counter-letters flew between Babylon and Israel. Ben Meir seems to have been the more short-tempered of the two protagonists, Saadia managed to keep his cool whilst protesting ben Meir's attempts to implement what he, Saadia, saw as a change to the calendrical rules.

The fury with which the dispute was conducted masked a fear which was uppermost in the minds of all Talmudic scholars. Were a schism to develop in which Israel and Babylon permanently observed different calendars, with their festivals falling on different days, the authority of the Talmud would be seriously compromised. There would in effect be two Talmudic sects. It was one thing for the Academies in Israel and Babylon to differ over minor points of law, such as heating water on the Sabbath. It was wholly another for them to

[29] Stern, 2001.

[30] For a full analysis and explanation of the technicalities behind the dispute see Stern, 2001.

create an ongoing situation in which one group regarded a certain day as holy, whilst their co-religionists profaned it, in which there was never any possibility that the entire nation would celebrate their festivals as they had been ordained. It would destroy the integrity of the Talmud, and it would hand a victory to the non-Talmudic sects; particularly the Karaites.

Despite this fear the two communities did observe separate festivals in 922 CE. We don't know how long this situation went on for, or how it was resolved, but, when all was over, it was of course Saadia who'd won the day. His 'fiery genius, profound learning and above all his superior literary skill proved more than a match for his opponent and finally brought about ben Meir's overthrow'.[31] The ancient privilege of the Israel Academy to set the calendar had been taken from them, and a decisive victory had been won in the battle for the dominance of the Babylonian.

That might have been Saadia's finest hour, but victory over the Israel Academy was by no means the only controversy he was embroiled in. Two years after his appointment he fell out with David ben Zakkai, the exilarch who had appointed him. It happened because Saadia had refused to countersign a deed which ruled in favour of one of the parties in a dispute over a large inheritance. The deed would have allowed the Exilarch to benefit from a 10 per cent levy on the money collected. A row broke out between Saadia and the exilarch. The *Gaon* of Pumbedita, who had already signed the deed, weighed in on the Exilarch's side, wealthy Baghdadis took Saadia's part. Whilst abusive letters circulated, the Exilarch's son threatened to beat Saadia's head with a shoe, a threat which misfired when the enraged students at the *yeshiva* charged at him and struck him with their footwear.

The Exilarch placed Saadia under a ban. He fled for his life, but not before he had taken his revenge by trying to appoint the Exilarch's brother in David's place.

The acrimony lasted for seven years until some of the leading families in Baghdad exerted pressure on the Exilarch to make peace with Saadia. The Exilarch gave way and consented to a reconciliation ceremony at which Saadia would appear at his house, where a feast would be held, complete with hugs and kisses.

Following the reconciliation Saadia was readmitted to his position as *Gaon* of Sura, but as part of the peace accord, was obliged to share the post with Joseph

---

[31] Malter, 1921, p. 86.

ben Jacob, who had been appointed when Saadia was expelled. Fortunately, Joseph was smart enough to know not to aggravate Saadia. Rather than actively participating in the activities of the academy he stayed at home, all the while continuing to draw his salary.[32]

Saadia was a confident and assertive man who was not afraid to stand up for his beliefs and defend his position, come what may. He may sound like a quarrelsome character, and maybe he was, but he was far more than just that.

Saadia was a pioneer in the new form of literature which would come to dominate Talmud scholarship in the medieval period. He wrote treatises on specific topics of law, in which he gives both the laws and the Talmud proofs underlying them. His topic-by-topic approach represented a significant development in codification; the earlier works of Shimon Kayyara and Yehudai *Gaon* had followed a far more fluid, less systematic arrangement. It wasn't just that he explained the law and made it accessible, he wrote in Arabic, the language which everyone now spoke, rather than Hebrew or Aramaic. This enabled his writings to reach a far wider audience.

But the Talmud was only one of his literary activities. Saadia spoke and wrote Arabic but he pioneered the study of the Hebrew language, composing some of its most enduring poetry. He wrote commentaries on much of the Hebrew Bible. But more than anything else, he was a philosopher. Drawing on the rational principles of the Mu'tazilite school in which he had been raised, he sought to establish a rational basis for articles of faith, a synthesis between reason and tradition.

Saadia was without doubt the greatest scholar of the *geonic* period. He was also one of the last *geonim*. He lived at a time when Baghdad's influence on the world was beginning to wane. The Abbasid caliphate was losing control of its empire, the dominant centres of Islamic life were becoming more diffuse. The Talmud was on the move too. Its story was shifting, to North Africa and Spain, Provence and the Rhineland. Saadia had laid the foundations for the next phase in the life of the Talmud; one in which Babylon would play a far smaller part.

---

[32] Gil, 2004, pp. 228–33.

# 7

# Coming of age

Rabbi Akiva said: Everything is foreseen yet freedom of choice is given.[1]

## The liberation of the Talmud

The Talmud may have been spawned in Babylon but its future lay far away. Rather like an adolescent, there came a time when its origins began to constrain it; it needed to get out in order to grow.

For centuries it had been declaimed, discussed and analysed in the academies. Even though every generation had something new to add, while it dwelt in its ivory towers the Talmud was content to remain an elite and complex work; a theoretical underpinning of the law rather than a legal manual. The majority of scholars were no doubt happy with that, and it mattered little to any one else. The Talmud existed, its students studied it, and that could have been the end of the story.

The fact that the story didn't end there makes the Talmud, in Nassim Nicholas Taleb's terminology, a Black Swan.[2] Nobody imagined black swans could exist, until they were discovered in Australia. Similarly, nobody would have thought, in seventh-century Baghdad, that the Talmud could morph from a fiercely debated, self-contained work of scholarship into the minutely examined, core text of a complex, all-embracing and rigidly prescriptive legal system. That it would become a manual of life which prescribed every conceivable aspect of human existence,[3] from the most sublime to the seemingly mechanical. Regulating all human activity, from intense religious devotion through the

---

[1] Avot 3.15.
[2] *The Black Swan: The Impact of the Highly Improbable*, Nassim Nicholas Taleb, Penguin, London, 2008.
[3] Fishman, 2011, Introduction; Ta Shma, 1999.

minutiae of social legislation to the correct way to wash one's body or put on one's shoes (the right one first then the left, removing them in the opposite order).[4]

It's hard for us to avoid projecting our modern perspectives back to an earlier time. Because the Talmud is acknowledged today as the final authority on Jewish religious law and practice, it is easy to assume that's what it always was. But the way observers of the Talmud see it in the twenty-first century is shaped by the way it was used and interpreted throughout history. The status of the Talmud today bears very little relation to the vision of its original editors who, like all of us, could not see into the future.

The responses that Natronai and Amram wrote to distant communities marked the beginning of the Talmud's unshackling from the Academy. But a complete uncoupling from the sanctum sanctorum would require more than that. The process which in time would lead the Talmud to influence kings and revolutionaries, to be adored and reviled, to be published in multiple editions and cast to the flames, was not an inevitable consequence of people in far-flung Jewish communities getting answers to their questions from the geonim in Baghdad. Any more than it was the result of Saadia's victory in the calendar dispute, which to all intents and purposes ended the struggle between the Babylonian Talmud and its Palestinian counterpart.

The change in the manner in which the Talmud was perceived and used, its liberation from the academies of Babylon, came about largely by accident. It echoed the events of the seventh century, when the scholars of Babylon found that living in proximity to the savants of Baghdad made it so much easier for them to refine and develop their learning. This time, in North Africa, the equally serendipitous emergence of another city of Islamic culture would help their intellectual creation to reach new horizons.

The catalyst for the Talmud's metamorphosis was the city of Kairouan, with whose scholars Pirkoi ben Baboi had corresponded. Set in the heart of the Maghreb region, which extended the width of North Africa from Morocco to Libya, Kairouan had been founded about fifty years before Baghdad by the rulers of the Umayyad dynasty. The legend is that when the first Muslim settlers arrived their leader ordered all the snakes and scorpions to leave. He had to

---

[4] Shabbat 61a.

repeat his order three times, but eventually they left. From the next forty years no snake entered the city.

The twelfth-century cartographer Al-Idrisi describes Kairouan as 'the greatest city in the Arab West, the mother of cities, the most populated, prosperous and thriving'.[5] The city has been a centre of pilgrimage since the ninth century and today its Great Mosque is considered the fourth holiest site in Islam.

Kairouan was one of a chain of trading centres established at the junctions of caravan routes by its commercially minded founders. Like their other trading hubs Kairouan was close enough to the sea to take advantage of the opportunity for maritime trade, yet sufficiently far inland to be safe from attack by vessels of the rival Byzantine Empire which controlled the Mediterranean. Goods would be offloaded in the seaport and swiftly transported the forty miles to depots in the city where they would be unpacked and stored.[6]

In its heyday Kairouan was a bustling commercial and scholarly locus as splendid as any in the Islamic Empire, far surpassing anything its Byzantine foes could offer. Muslims, Christian and Jews walked its streets, traded in its markets and, untroubled by scorpions and snakes, swapped tales beneath the fountains in its squares. Dominated by the Great Mosque of Uqba, with its massive dome, paved courtyards, towers and intricately sculpted wooden pulpit, it is little wonder that the desert Berber tribes frequently cast a jealous eye on the city. With its sophisticated water storage and distribution system, comprising immense cisterns of up to 120 metres in diameter and a network of aqueducts, Kairouan rapidly shrugged off its arid, dusty setting to become a cosmopolitan centre, whose citizens paid heavily in taxes for the privileges they enjoyed.

Just as Baghdad had done, Kairouan acted as a magnet for the curious and the creative, for the enterprising and for pleasure seekers. It drew in traders, poets, intellectuals and artists. But its full value was realized in the wake of the Islamic conquest in 711 CE of Al-Andalus, better known today as Spain.[7] The city acted as a natural and accessible connector enabling Spain to trade with the Mashriq; the area of Islamic domination to the east of the Mediterranean which we now call the Middle East.[8] And in the ninth century, after the Byzantine

---

[5]  Al-Idrisi: Nuzhat al-Mushtaq, in The Conservation and Preservation of Islamic Manuscripts: Proceedings of the Third Conference of al-Furqān Islamic Heritage Foundation: 18–19 November 1995.

[6]  Hirschberg, 1974.

[7]  The earliest evidence of Jewish settlement in Spain is the third-century tombstone of a young girl named Salomonula, found at the ancient seaport of Abdera.

[8]  Abun-Nasr, 1987.

Mediterranean ports had been captured, it also functioned as a north-south link, between the Mediterranean and the sub-Saharan region.[9] Indeed the city was so well connected that a legend asserts that a pot which had been placed in a well in Mecca surfaced in Kairouan, proving that water runs between Arabia and the Maghreb.[10]

Most importantly for the future history of the Talmud, Kairouan functioned as a communication hub for the whole of North Africa and Southern Europe. Its position at the heart of a postal and trading network explains how the Talmud was able to develop in Kairouan in a completely different way from anywhere else in the vast Islamic Empire.

## Eldad the Danite

Towards the end of the ninth century a mysterious, rather dishevelled character turned up in the bustling, baking, Jewish quarter of Kairouan. Calling himself Eldad, he claimed to be a member of the ancient Israelite tribe of Dan. Tongues began to wag. His claim was preposterous. Everybody knew that the tribe of Dan had been lost for over a thousand years. They, with the other nine tribes of the Northern Kingdom of Israel, had been taken into captivity by the Assyrian king, Sennacherib. Nobody had heard of them since. The events are documented in the biblical Book of Kings.[11] Jewish belief was that they would reappear and be reunited with their people at the end of time, but this wasn't yet the end of time, and nobody in Kairouan knew what to make of Eldad. To astound them even further, Eldad came armed with a repertoire of fantastic stories, which we wouldn't countenance today, but which were wholly believable in the streets and bazaars reminiscent of those that form the backdrop to Shaharazad's tales and in which Sinbad's adventures were recounted.

Eldad told his listeners that he had come from the other side of the River Sambatyon, a mythical African torrent which flowed so fast, hurling rocks and boulders as it went, that it was impossible to cross. The river only fell quiet as the sun set on a Friday evening, when the Sabbath began. Then it became as

---

[9] Abun-Nasr, 1987.

[10] *Pilgrimage: From the Ganges to Graceland: An Encyclopedia, Volume 1*, Linda Kay Davidson, David Martin Gitlitz, ABC-CLIO, Santa Barbara, 2002.

[11] II Kings 17.

peaceable as a desert oasis. But everyone knew that it was forbidden to cross a river on the Sabbath, and, since the torrent resumed the moment the Sabbath had departed, it was clear that no human could ever pass from one of its shores to the other. Yet Eldad maintained that his tribe dwelt on the far shores of the Sambatyon, and that he had traversed the river on his way to Kairouan.

Eldad told the people of Kairouan how he had been delivered from a shipwreck only to be captured by cannibals. His companion had been eaten but he had escaped. He told them of the fabulous people he had met, of tribes who make war each year with seven kingdoms and seven languages, of nations whose members regularly lived to see their great-great grandchildren, of peaceable lands where a young child could lead a flock of sheep for days in the wilderness without coming to any harm. The Kairouanites had no difficulty believing his stories. But alarm bells began to sound when he described the methods his people used to ritually slaughter their animals for meat. They didn't conform to the time-honoured practices of the Kairouan Jews, practices which were stipulated by the Talmud. Was he a fraud after all?

The Kairouan Talmudists wrote to Zemach, the *Gaon* of Sura, informing him of Eldad's arrival and his strange ritual practices. Their concern was for the veracity of the Talmudic account; was it possible that the Talmud was wrong, or that there were alternative methods of preparing meat that the Talmud scholars had overlooked? Zemach was not fazed. He replied that he had already heard of Eldad and that, whilst he was to be believed, nothing he recounted could undermine the validity of the Talmud. It was not surprising, he told them, that certain differences existed between the laws which Eldad knew and those contained in the Babylonian Talmud, for although the latter was indeed the correct and only interpretation of the Oral Law, Eldad's tribe had been cut off for so long that they were bound to have got some things wrong.[12]

Eldad the Danite disappeared as mysteriously as he had arrived. But his legends remained; they resurfaced in the fables of Prester John which circulated in twelfth-century Europe, and told of a Christian king who ruled over a nation not dissimilar to that from which Eldad claimed to hail.

---

[12] Neubauer, 1889. Many groups around the world claim descent from one of the ten lost tribes. A modern solution to the Eldad problem (if his stories were indeed true) would be that the lost tribes left the Holy Land long before the Mishnah was compiled. Unlike the Sadducees and Karaites who rejected the Oral Law, the ten tribes just didn't know of it.

## The prominence of Kairouan

Kairouan's contribution to the Talmud's story was brief, but seminal. Its place at the centre of the Empire's communications network facilitated a continual flow of correspondence between Baghdad and Kairouan. The *geonim* were able to correspond with communities across the Islamic Empire, which by now included those in Palestine, Egypt, Sicily, Morocco, Italy, and Spain. Baghdad didn't even need to be in the loop, Kairouan's postal links allowed remote centres to communicate directly with each other and created a flourishing industry for the city's scribes, who copied Babylonian manuscripts and redistributed them to the Jewish centres.[13]

Just as had happened with Baghdad, Kairouan became a home for intellectuals. A library to rival Baghdad's House of Wisdom was established there. The ancient catalogue of books stored in the Kairouan mosque is the oldest in the Islamic world.[14] Public education for both men and women was commonplace. A study of tombstone inscriptions shows that Kairouan was home to a far higher proportion of people carrying out intellectual professions than was the case in Egypt's great cultural heartland.[15] Had Kairouan not played such a critical role in the cultural life of the caliphate, the chances are that the Talmud would have had little or no impact there.

A popular legend in the Middle Ages recounts how four scholars, on a mission to raise funds for the Sura academy, set sail from Bari in Italy. Their boat was captured by pirates and the scholars put up for ransom. Jews in four separate Mediterranean cities raised funds to redeem them. One captive, Elhanan, was released in Alexandria where he became the leader of the Egyptian community. Another, Moses ben Hanoch, found his way to Cordoba where he rose to similar prominence. The third, Hushiel, became the outstanding scholar of Kairouan.[16] We don't hear what happened to the fourth captive.

---

[13] Gil, 2004.

[14] The Ancient Sijill of Qayrawan, Adam Gacek, MELA Notes, No. 46 (Winter, 1989).

[15] *The Living and the Dead in Islam: Studies in Arabic Epitaphs*, Volume 3; Werner Diem, Marco Schöller; Otto Harrassowitz, Wiesbaden, 2004.

[16] The best-known version of this legend is in the anti-Karaite work Sefer HaKabbalah or *Book of Tradition* by Abraham ibn Daud who lived in twelfth-century Spain (Neubauer, 1888). He may have circulated the legend to demonstrate that, with the arrival of Moses ben Hanoch in Spain, the community's independence from Babylon was complete.

Most contemporary experts believe that the legend is untrue, or at very least historically inaccurate.[17] Accurate or not, its value is that it offers reasons, apocryphal or real depending on your point of view, for the emergence of the principal centres of Talmud learning in the Islamic world. It explains why, despite the widespread dispersion of the Jews throughout Europe and Asia, the Talmud only put down early roots in Italy, where the scholars embarked, and in the three centres where they ended up. It may have been heard of elsewhere, but in no other place were schools established for its study nor were meaningful questions asked about it. It seems that in general the Talmud represented little more than an academic activity that may have been fascinating to its students but which had little or no impact on ordinary lives. Much as many people feel about certain university courses today.

That was the way the Talmudic scholars in Baghdad had seen it too. Although it is quite clear from the writings of Pirkoi ben Baboi and Saadia, amongst others, that Babylon wished to be seen as the spiritual centre of the Jewish faith, we don't find its scholars or teachers evangelizing to bring the Talmud to popular attention. The Talmud, in Babylon at least, was of the academy and for the academy; Talmudic scholars would happily base their rulings on it when responding to enquiries, but they weren't particularly bothered about laying it out in front of the masses as an object of direct study. That's what the Bible was for.

Kairouan changed all that. In her penetrating study, *Becoming the People of the Talmud*, Talya Fishman explores how attitudes to the Talmud changed once people encountered it as a fixed, written text, rather than in Babylon where it still existed largely as an oral tradition. She shows how this change in attitude began in Kairouan, where the scholars set out to make the Talmud available to people who were not rabbis,[18] and to use their extensive communication network to spread the word.

[17] Moshe Gil argues in favour of the legend (Gil, 2004). He suggests that even if the legend was embellished in its earliest known source, Abraham Ibn Daud's *Book of Tradition*, it has a historical core. He holds that the episode is likely to have taken place in the reign of Abd-al-Rahman III, the Umayyad ruler of Spain around the year 960 CE.

[18] Fishman, 2011.

## Explaining the Talmud

The turning point for the Talmud came towards the end of the tenth century. It was led by Hushiel whose arrival in Kairouan had been recounted in the legend of the four captives. Modelling themselves on Babylon, Hushiel and his colleague Jacob ibn Shahin each set up an academy in Kairouan. These were the first significant schools of Talmud study outside Babylon, and marked the end of the old country's dominance. From this point forward the Talmud would be studied across the world according to the viewpoints of its local teachers, no longer anxiously awaiting decisions sent from afar. Baghdad was still venerated as the home of the Talmud, but its decline had begun, and would become more pronounced during the following generation.

We know very little about Hushiel and even less about Jacob.[19] But we are far more familiar with the works of their sons, Hananel and Nissim. Hananel, according to the twelfth-century Spanish philosopher Ibn Daud, had nine daughters. He was supported by wealthy merchants in the city, to such a degree that when he died he left ten thousand golden dinars.[20] Nissim had no children, and no wealth either.

Despite their different circumstances Hananel and Nissim were both revolutionaries. They may not have known it; in their eyes all they did was to continue to teach in their fathers' schools and write commentaries on the Talmud.[21] But nobody had done anything like it before, and they paved the way for hundreds

---

[19] Solomon Shechter published a letter found in the Cairo Genizah which Hushiel wrote to Shemarya, possibly the son of Elhanan, another of the 'four captives'. *The Jewish Quarterly Review*, 11(4) (July, 1899), pp. 643–50.

[20] Ibn Daud, Sefer HaKabbalah (Neubauer, 1888).

[21] The two men had very different styles. Hananel's approach was to give his reader an overview of the topic being discussed. Although the Talmud switches languages freely from Hebrew to Aramaic, and back again, Hananel wrote only in Hebrew. He provided the etymological roots of difficult words, referring to Greek, Arabic and Persian as necessary and was not afraid to quote the Jerusalem Talmud, which had been far better received in Kairouan than it ever was in Baghdad, giving rise to Pirkoi ben Baboi's concerns. Indeed, his use of the Jerusalem Talmud is so extensive that Hananel has often been cited as the person who began the process of bringing that work back into the mainstream, after it had been sidelined by the spread of the Babylonian version.

Hananel's commentary needs to be read alongside the Talmud text. Nissim's in contrast can be followed without even having a copy of the original (Ta Shma, 1999, Chapter 4); (Steinsaltz, 2009). Whereas Hananel only dwells on those parts of the Talmudic discussion which he feels are relevant, Nissim's style is to paraphrase the whole debate, referring the reader back to the sources which underlie the Talmudic discussion and providing a simplified summary of the topic.

of commentators, scrutineers and analysts who followed in their wake. What made them so radical was that, rather than continuing the process of debate for its own sake, which had been such a prominent feature of the Babylonian academies, they set out to explain the Talmud to people who were trying to understand it. They were educators in Talmud rather than contributors to it. Large parts of their commentaries are still printed in standard editions of the Talmud today.

The sharp contrast between both commentaries and the Talmud itself is that the commentators try to reach a conclusion. Keen to provide practical guidance and therefore not content with the way the Talmud often leaves discussions open, both men give their views on what the legal rulings should be. They may not have known it but they were pioneers in a process of legal decision making that would find its way from Kairouan into the schools of Spain.

As Kairouan ascended Baghdad declined. One event did not cause the other but there was a connection between the two. We take our leave of Babylon with the appointment of Hai, its last great personality, as head of the Pumbedita Academy. Hai succeeded his father Sherira, whose letter to Kairouan provided so much information on the development of the Oral Law and the academies in Babylon.

Hai was renowned as both a legal authority and an educator. His academy drew students from across the world, including Spain and Germany, the two centres which were about to serve as the launching pad for the Talmud in the medieval world. He corresponded with people across the world, answering questions from communities that Kairouan's communication network couldn't reach. But Hai was the last of his kind; with his death in 1038 Babylon's reign as the pre-eminent centre of Talmudic learning finally drew to a close.

Kairouan's influence on the Talmud may have been seminal but the city never attained Baghdad's prominence. It was always a hub, rarely a place to which other communities turned for guidance or instruction. When Bedouin tribes besieged and destroyed the city in 1057 its time had run its course; in the space of less than a generation the Talmud's world changed yet again and both Baghdad and Kairouan ceased to play any part in its ongoing story.

## The Golden Age of Spain

The Talmud alighted in Spain round about the same time as it landed in Kairouan. This is implied in the legend of the four captives and history bears it out because, as we saw in the previous chapter, in the second half of the ninth century someone in Barcelona heard or saw a reference in it to a hundred daily blessings that were to be said daily. He wrote to the *Gaon* Amram in Babylon asking for further details. Yet despite this early interest, and notwithstanding Amram's detailed reply, the Talmud didn't really catch on as a subject of serious investigation until well into the dying days of Babylon, when the schools set up in Kairouan by Hushiel and Jacob ibn Shahin were already flourishing.

Life in Al-Andalus, as Spain was known in those days, held far more opportunities than anywhere else the Jews had lived. Arabic and Jewish culture flourished alongside each other. The two languages were similar in structure and vocabulary. Their grammarians learned from each other. Their poets competed to elevate their craft to ever more exalted levels of refinement, weaving sublime verbal tapestries from gossamer lexical threads, rarely shy of introducing unheard of grammatical forms or words never before spoken.

The first Spanish Jew to break through the cultural barrier and make it in Andalusian society was Hisdai ibn Shaprut. Born round about 915 CE he trained as a doctor and practised in the court of the caliph in Cordoba. He caught the caliph's eye in 940 CE as a member of the team which translated into Arabic a Greek pharmaceutical treatise, which the caliph had been given by a visiting Byzantine dignitary. As was the way in those days the caliph promoted him to an administrative position alongside his medical duties. Hisdai was a shrewd political operator, he shot up through the ranks, was sent on various diplomatic errands and ended up as one of the caliph's most senior ministers.

Hisdai scored many political and diplomatic successes in his career. But one encounter stands out above them all, even if we don't fully know the details. The affair is so enmeshed in legend and speculation that even today we cannot uncover the full historical truth, though many have tried.[22]

---

[22] Dunlop, 1954; Golb & Pritsak, 1982; Brook, 2006. For more controversial views of the consequences of the Khazar conversion see Koestler, 1976; Sand, 2009. The conversion itself is the subject HaKuzari, of a highly stylized polemic written by the Spanish philosopher, poet and physician Yehuda HaLevi in the early twelfth century.

## The odd story of the Khazars

According to one of the many varying accounts, in 948 CE Hisdai sent a messenger to Constantinople, where he met a fellow Jew. The man told him that he belonged to the entourage of King Joseph of Khazaria.[23] He told him that the Khazars were an independent nation who dwelt in the region between the Black and Caspian Seas. They owed no allegiance to either the Islamic or Byzantine Empires, in fact their king and all his subjects were Jews. The messenger, whose name was Yitzhak bar Nathan, was astounded. He was a well-travelled man, the emissary of one of the highest placed ministers in Spanish society, yet he'd never heard of Khazaria and he had no inkling that an independent Jewish kingdom existed anywhere in the world.

Bar Nathan took word back to his employer who, it seems, had already heard rumours of this nation but had not known how to contact them. A correspondence ensued between Hisdai and King Joseph. We know this much from documents discovered in the Cairo *Genizah* in 1896.[24] The correspondence describes two events which cemented Khazaria's status as a Jewish nation. It first refers to a Jewish warrior who won a great victory for the Khazars. The warrior was proclaimed leader of the army and later become the founder of Khazar's dynasty of Jewish kings.

The bellicose origins of Khazar's Jewish dynasty are reinforced by a ninth-century account written by Christian of Stavelot in a monastery in Lorraine. Stavelot writes of Alexander the Great's frustration at his inability to defeat the 'peoples of Gog and Magog – those who are now called the Khazars'. Alexander prayed for them to be shut up in their mountain. His prayers were answered but, leaving nothing to chance, Alexander placed copper gates in front of the mountain to make sure its inhabitants could no longer trouble him.[25] Stavelot, however, complains that by the time he is writing the Khazars were even

---

[23] Brook, 2006.

[24] Golb & Pritsak, 1982.

[25] The Alexander legend is very ancient and widespread. The Qu'ran (Surat al-Kahf 83–98) contains an account of Dhul Qarnayn (= 'two horns'; Alexander is depicted with two horns on some coins) who also confined the people of Gog and Magog between two mountains, and shut them in with iron gates overlaid with copper. A Jewish source, *Vayikra Rabbah* 27.1, dating from the fourth or fifth century recounts how Alexander visited a King Katzia 'behind the mountains of darkness'.

stronger than when Alexander confined them, that they were circumcised and practiced all the laws of Judaism.[26]

The Jewish warrior king may have been fearless in war but, from the second event described in the letter to Hisdai, it seems that he was less adept at spiritual inspiration. He managed to propagate Jewish practice throughout the land but many of his countrymen didn't take it to heart. Eventually one of his descendants, Bulan, came under pressure from his Byzantine and Arab neighbours, who advised him it wasn't wise for the Khazars to continue to adhere to the religion of such a downtrodden people.

Bulan, not one to be pressurized, resolved to make his own decisions. He called in Jewish, Muslim and Christian sages, and commanded each of them to explain to him why theirs was the religion to which his people should adhere.

The letter doesn't name the sages that he summoned, but other sources make a stab at it, even if somewhat unreliably. The Byzantine emperor, so we are told, sent the theologians Cyril and Methodius. A Talmudist, Yitzhak Sangari, of whom we know very little, represented the Jews and Farabi ibn Kora spoke for the Muslims.

The three sages debated each other for several days but the king was unable to decide between them. Finally he asked Farabi ibn Kora, the Islamic *qadi*, which religion he would select if he was obliged to choose between the Christians and the Jews. The *qadi* said he would opt for the Jews. The king then asked the Christians which they would choose, if they had to decide between Islam and Judaism. They too replied that they would choose Judaism. That clinched it for the king; he declared that Judaism would continue to be the wisest choice for his kingdom.

Although the account of the conversion debate is apocryphal, there is little dispute that the Khazar nation did convert to Judaism, some time between the eighth and tenth centuries. According to King Joseph's reply, one of Bulan's descendants, King Obadiah, 'established the Jewish religion properly and correctly', bringing in Jewish scholars to teach the Bible, Mishnah and Talmud.

---

[26] Brook, 2006.

## The Talmud in Spain

Hisdai didn't just use his political skills to further the caliph's interests. He also had his own agenda. He exploited tensions between the Umayyad caliphate in Spain and their Abbasid rivals in Babylon to create a similar division within the Jewish world. If Muslim Spain could be independent of the declining Babylonian caliphate, so could its Jewish inhabitants be autonomous from the Baghdad *geonim*. Hisdai brought scholars into Cordoba and provided the funds for their upkeep. He acquired high-quality manuscripts from Kairouan and appointed Moses ben Hanoch, one of the 'Four Captives', to head up a Talmudic Academy.

The Academy prospered under Moses's charge and Hisdai's patronage. Cordoba became a pre-eminent centre of Talmud study with students arriving from all over the world to study. When Moses died there were two candidates for his job, Hanoch his son, and Joseph ibn Abitur, a well-respected scholar whose interest in making education available to all had led him, at the caliph's request, to complete the first translation of the Mishnah into Arabic. Hanoch had been raised by his father; the legend of the four captives recounts how Moses's young wife had thrown herself into the sea to escape abuse at the hands of the pirates. Moses arrived in Spain alone, with his infant son.

Hisdai lent his weight to Hanoch's candidacy and he was duly appointed. However, after Hisdai's death Joseph's supporters tried to re-open the question of the succession. The caliph weighed in and re-confirmed Hanoch in the post. At this point Joseph left the country. But when the caliph died some of his wealthy supporters bribed the new ruler to depose Hanoch and appoint Joseph. The new caliph obliged, but Joseph refused to return; arguing that he would not be a party to such shameful treatment of his rival. Hanoch kept the job, but his reputation had collapsed, he was considered to be a less-than-deserving benefactor of powerful patronage and never enjoyed public support in the way his father had.

Cordoba was destroyed in a series of Berber invasions around 1009–13. Amongst those who fled the city was Shmuel, one of Moses's star pupils. Shmuel, who had also studied Arabic and the Qu'ran settled a hundred miles to the south, in Malaga, where he opened a spice shop. According to the account written in the twelfth century by Abraham ibn Daud (who had also given us the legend of the four captives), one of Shmuel's customers was a servant in the court of the king's secretary. Shmuel helped her to write letters on behalf of her master. The secretary was so impressed with the calligraphy and the lucidity of language in the letters that he had Shmuel brought before him and appointed him as a clerk.

Shmuel became so indispensable to the secretary that on his death bed he confessed to the king that all the good advice he had given him over the years had in fact come from Shmuel. The king immediately appointed Shmuel to his staff, and from that point on his rise was meteoric. When a dispute broke out between the king's two sons, resulting in one of them engineering the death of the other, Shmuel had already come down on the right side. The victorious son, Badis, appointed him vizier of Granada; a post he held for maybe thirty years. The Jews called him *HaNaggid*, Shmuel the Prince.

Shmuel never forgot his education. He may have been vizier of Granada but he was a Talmudist at heart. Ibn Daud lists him, alongside Hananel and Nissim of Kairouan, as one of the three great rabbinic scholars of his time.[27] As Hisdai had done, he used his wealth to promote scholarship, Ibn Daud recording that:

> he acquired many holy texts, and copies of the Mishnah and Talmud ... and he would support anyone who wanted to make religious scholarship his craft. He had scribes who would write copies of the Mishnah and Talmud, which he would give to students who could not afford to buy them ... and he provided olive oil to the synagogues in Jerusalem. ... he died at a good old age.[28]

Shmuel wrote a legal compendium of law, only a fraction of which has survived. He clearly had an extensive library, because his work incorporates a wide range of sources, including both the Babylonian and Jerusalem Talmuds, much of the early literature from the time of the Mishnah and many of the responsa of the geonim. Although his work has not gone down in history as pivotal, its importance lies in the fact that he summarized current thinking and provided an accurate summary of laws as they then stood. Shmuel's legal scholarship was an advance on the earlier legal compilations which had simply based their decisions on the discussions in the Talmud. It was a first step in the trend towards the collation and formalization of the law which would eventually become the hallmark of the Spanish school.[29]

---

[27] Neubauer, 1888.

[28] Neubauer, 1888, p. 72–3.

[29] Shmuel Hanaggid's *Hilcheta Gavrata* was published with an extensive introduction by Mordechai Margaliot as Hilchot Hanaggid (Margaliot, 1962).

About thirty years after Shmuel's death an old man arrived in Lucena, a town half-way between Cordoba and Malaga where Shmuel had his spice shop. His name was Isaac Al-Fasi – his surname indicating that he hailed from Fez, in Morocco. Alfasi had fled Morocco, according to Ibn Daud, because of unknown slanders against him.[30] He lived in Spain for fifteen years, until the age of ninety, but he had already acquired his reputation before leaving Morocco.

Alfasi, who as a young man had studied in Kairouan under both Hananel and Nissim, shared their affinity for clarifying the law and explaining the Talmud text to students who found it hard to follow. His work was effectively a summary of the Talmud; he copied verbatim those parts of it which he felt were already clear enough, he explained bits which he felt needed to be explained, he wove together material from different parts of the Talmud which were better understood in one place and he simply omitted anything he did not feel was relevant. His omissions were not restricted to material which had no bearing on the law; he also left out any content which related to now-defunct practices, such as Temple sacrifices.

Alfasi's work is printed in all good editions of the Talmud. It forms part of the curriculum for all serious Talmudic study today. He was hailed by later generations as one of the most important of all Talmudic codifiers and his is one of the four 'monolithic codes of Jewish Law produced during the Middle Ages ... [which] were all produced in a Sephardic or Spanish milieu.'[31]

But for all its importance Alfasi's code was not the greatest of the four. That distinction goes to the compendium written by Moses ben Maimon, better known by his patronym Maimonides, or his Hebrew acrostic Rambam.

---

Standard printed editions of the Talmud contain a short work called Shmuel HaNaggid's Introduction to the Talmud. Although this concise work is distinguished by its clarity of language and the simplicity with which it gets its message across it has been mistakenly attributed to him. Shraga Abramson (Abramson, 1987) demonstrated that it is in fact an abridged translation of a work by the Babylonian *Gaon* Shmuel ben Hofni.

The translator begins by listing twenty one literary features of the Talmud text. These include the Mishnah text, explanations of the Mishnah, questions, solutions and refutations. The upshot is that the reader is able to navigate through what is generally assumed to be a very dense text with considerable ease. He then turns to the rules by which decisions are made in the Talmud so that when the reader encounters two authorities disagreeing on a point it is possible to determine which view is the accepted one.

[30] Neubauer, 1888.

[31] Karnafogel, 2006.

# 8

# The age of the giants

Abba Saul said: When pursuing a deer, I entered the thigh-bone of a corpse, and pursued it for three parasangs but reached neither the deer nor the end of the bone.[1]

## Maimonides

Maimonides is a giant on the Talmudic stage. His influence in the fields of Jewish thought, philosophy and law is second to none. His philosophical treatise *Guide for the Perplexed* was the first significant attempt to systematically explain the rationale behind the Jewish faith to those who, as the name implies, found it difficult to hold onto religious belief in the face of coeval, speculative thinking. Even though there is little place in modern thought for his Aristotelian approach and twelfth-century world view, the *Guide* remains pre-eminent amongst all Jewish philosophical writings. His impact on the Talmudic world was no less important.

Maimonides was born in Cordoba in 1135. When he was thirteen the city, which had been the site of power struggles for over a century, fell once again, this time to the puritanical Almohads whose attitude towards *dhimmis*, non-Muslim minorities, was far from tolerant. Faced with the option of converting to Islam or leaving the city, the boy's father, Maimon, a respected judge in the Jewish courts, chose the latter.

The next we hear of Maimonides is as a young man of twenty five in the city of Fez. Fez was also an Almohad city but the attitude of its ruler towards *dhimmis* seems to have softened somewhat as he edged towards old age. It was during the period between leaving Cordoba and arriving in Fez that the young

---

[1] Niddah 24b.

Maimonides began work on his first magnum opus, an Arabic commentary on the Mishnah, bearing the name *Sirāj*. We don't know where he was when he wrote the commentary. He must have travelled extensively, perhaps even living a peripatetic life, since at the end of his commentary he apologizes for any inaccuracies which may have come about due to his mind being 'troubled by exile and wandering', and due to his journeying by road and by boat.[2]

In the commentary Maimonides explains the legal principles behind the topics in the Mishnah and offers a summary of the law. Occasionally his explanation of a section of the Mishnah[3] differs from the interpretation placed upon it by the Talmud.[4]

Maimonides' *Commentary on the Mishnah* is probably best known for his formulation of what have become known as the Thirteen Principles of Faith; the nearest thing that classical Judaism has to an 'official' dogma, and the subject of considerable controversy and scholarly discussion.[5]

The sojourn in Fez was brief; within five years the leading Jewish scholar in the city, under whom Maimonides studied, was martyred by the Almohads, having refused to convert to Islam. Maimonides and his family didn't hang around. They spent a short amount of time in the Holy Land then travelled on to Egypt, settling first in Alexandria and then in Fostat, now part of old Cairo.

Maimonides's brother David supported the family through his trade in gemstones. When he drowned in the ocean on a business trip, they were left penniless. In those days rabbinic scholars tended not to take a salary for their work and Maimonides was now obliged to seek out a livelihood for himself. He trained as a physician and, although it took some time, he was eventually appointed as doctor to the sultan's court. In a letter he tells a friend not to visit him as he is too fatigued from the heavy duties that his royal appointment placed upon him, the demands made upon his time by his general medical practice and the responsibility he carried as senior scholar and head of the community.[6]

---

[2] Maimonides' *Commentary to Mishnah*, Uktzin, 3.12.

[3] Every subsection of the work called the Mishnah is also, confusingly, known as a *Mishnah*.

[4] Louis Jacobs suggests Maimonides believed that the Mishnah, like the Bible, can be interpreted on its own terms (Jacobs, 1995).

[5] The Thirteen Principles of The Faith are discussed extensively in Louis Jacobs *Principles of the Jewish Faith* (New York, 1964); Menahem Kellner *Must A Jew Believe Anything?* (London, 1999); Marc B. Shapiro *The Limits of Orthodox Theology* (London, 2004).

[6] Marcus & Saperstein, 1999.

His fatigue, however, did not prevent him from writing. Maimonides's major contribution to the Talmud is his legal code, *Mishneh Torah*[7] which he completed at the age of forty five in Cairo. Unlike his commentary on the Mishnah, the *Mishneh Torah* was detailed and prescriptive. Of his three main works *Mishneh Torah* is the only one written in Hebrew, indicating no doubt that Maimonides intended it for a far wider Jewish audience than just those in the Arabic speaking world.

The work is a code in the strictest possible sense. Systematically divided into fourteen books, Maimonides makes no attempt to reproduce the discussions or arguments contained in the Talmud. Nor does he cite his sources. He simply states his understanding of the law which emerges from those discussions. Unlike other legal codes he includes laws relating to defunct Temple practices; an indication that he considered the work applicable for all time, even when the Temple would be rebuilt.

Monumental as it is, the *Mishneh Torah* was not universally acclaimed. Some of Maimonides's critics believed he intended its study to replace that of the Talmud.[8] The work came under severe censure from a contemporary, Abraham ben David of Posquières, who argued that Maimonides had reduced the flexible openness of Talmudic law to a series of prescriptive statements with no room for manoeuvre.[9] He took issue with Maimonides on many of the legal statements in the work but reserved particularly fierce criticism for his assertion that anyone who believed God had a body was a heretic.

> How can he call such a person a heretic when so many who are greater and better than him thought this way because of what they read in the Bible and even more so in homilies which confuse the mind?[10]

Rabad's objection was not to promote the view that God had a body, but rather because, as Daniel Silver puts it, Judaism had 'never read the simple minded or the literalist out of the fold'.[11]

---

[7] *Mishneh Torah* can mean Second to the Torah, or Repetition of the Torah. The fifth of Moses's books is also known in Hebrew as *Mishneh Torah*. Translated into Greek it is Deuteronomy.

[8] Fishman, 2011.

[9] Jacobs, 1995 s.v. Maimonides.

[10] Rabad to Mishneh Torah, Hilchot Teshuvah 3.7.

[11] Silver, 1965.

Most editions of the *Mishneh Torah* contain Abraham ben David's criticisms, as well as other commentaries which seek to explain the reasons behind Maimonides's rulings.

Although generally acclaimed as the greatest Jewish thinker for two millennia, controversy was never far from Maimonides. Apart from the attacks by Abraham ben David, his philosophical and theological views came under repeated attacks leading, as we shall see, to public condemnation and even burnings of his works in the later centuries.

## The Rhineland

Kairouan may have been in ruins but due to its husbandry the Talmud was now known across a vast area. It was taught from Fez, on the western extreme of the Maghreb through Cairo to Baghdad in the east. In Europe it reached Spain, Provence, France and Italy, extending northwards through Germany, to the Rhineland cities of Mainz, Speyer and Worms. It was here the Talmud had its first serious encounter with an unfamiliar culture – and it was here, over the course of the next few centuries, that it was scrutinized as never before, both by its friends and by its enemies.

Throughout its history the Talmud had developed in an Islamic environment. Islam and Judaism were not so dissimilar in their world view. They shared the same cultural norms, particularly around family, trade and social organization. They had a linguistic affinity; Hebrew, Arabic and Aramaic are all part of the same family. Islam's acceptance of Moses as a prophet, coupled with the institution known as *dhimmi*, through which minorities were protected, had allowed the Talmud to develop freely alongside, and even in partnership with the Islamic legal tradition.

Christian lands were relatively unfamiliar territory for the Babylonian Talmud. With the exception of southern Italy, from where the Four Captives are supposed to have set sail, those few Christian centres which had encountered the Talmud were largely confined to the eastern Mediterranean and only knew the Palestinian work.

A few small Jewish communities had dwelt along the River Rhine in Germany since the earliest dispersions. They hadn't always had an easy life. A Church Council edict in Paris in 846 CE ordered all Jewish children to be removed from their homes and placed in monasteries.[12]

---

[12]  Malkiel, 2008.

Much later, in 992 CE, Sehok ben Esther a Jewish convert to Christianity, tried to destroy the Jews of Le Mans. He went to the local lord to tell him that the Jews were piercing his image with a goad in order to kill him. He suggested he search the local synagogue. The lord did as he was bid and found a wax effigy which Sehok had planted there, with its feet amputated and piercings on its body. Sehok urged the lord to take his revenge and a wave of violence broke out against the Jews. We don't have the full story since the one manuscript which contains the account breaks off before the end, but based on similar events we can imagine that the outcome may have included wholesale slaughter, forced conversion and expulsions from the city.[13]

Fifteen years later the king of France ordered all Jews to convert or die; those who could flee did, a group of women drowned themselves and the elderly were slaughtered.[14]

But it was by no means all doom and gloom. Compared with events soon to come, the tenth century in northern Europe was a period of relative calm. The Jews comprised a tiny fraction of the overall population, most Christians had never met one and as Jonathan Elukin points out, there must have been a general tolerance of Jews by ordinary people, because no early medieval government would have been able to maintain control if there had been constant strife.[15] In 1074 Henry IV even exempted the Jews of Worms from paying the poll tax in recognition of their loyalty.[16]

It was against this uncertain background that the legend of the Jewish Pope emerged. Undoubtedly fictional, it is just one of a number of popular medieval tales set in tenth-century Mainz. It offers a revealing insight into the insecurities and aspirations of people in a city which was becoming a major centre for the Talmud.

The legend, which circulated in various forms during the Middle Ages, tells the unlikely story of Elchanan, son of the poet Shimon of Mainz. Elchanan and Shimon were real characters, some of Shimon's poetry has survived and in one he refers to his son Elchanan.

One version of the story is that Elchanan was kidnapped as a child, placed in a monastery, told that his parents were dead and raised as a Christian. The

---

[13] Malkiel, 2003.
[14] Malkiel, 2008.
[15] Elukin, 2007.
[16] Pearl, 1988.

boy prospered and rose rapidly through the ranks of the Catholic Church, eventually being appointed Pope. Known as Andreas, the Pope grew increasingly insecure about his origins until he eventually demanded that his aides tell him the true story of his birth. The whole story came out, the Pope was reunited with his father and returned to Mainz to live as a loyal Jew.[17]

The story is the result of a powerful imagination, but no less powerful than the intellectual currents then flowing in Mainz. A shared atmosphere of intellectual curiosity prevailed in both the Talmudic communities and monasteries, as did comparable methods of education and study.[18] It had been sparked by the ninth-century Carolingian Renaissance, which saw art, culture and religion flourish across Europe. And although the Carolingian era had long subsided by the time interest in the Talmud surfaced along the River Rhine, its legacy lingered on. Talya Fishman notes that the Cathedral schools that produced the Holy Roman Empire's diplomats were situated in the very cities where Talmud study was strongest.[19]

## The ban on polygamy

The Talmud had probably first been introduced into the Rhineland by local merchants and traders, who would regularly travel great distances to obtain the goods and raw materials they needed. Whenever possible they would lodge in foreign lands with their co-religionists, with whom they shared a common language. Friendships would form amongst the regular travellers, just as they do today, and they would exchange news and ideas.

In this way the merchants heard about the new phenomenon of religious scholarship that had spread from Baghdad and Kairouan, of how the Talmud was institutionalizing their traditional religious practice. They heard about the legal authorities who were basing their decisions upon its debates; as part of the ongoing process of formalizing Jewish law. One can imagine there was a certain amount of disquiet and even cynicism about the new breed of rabbis

---

[17] For a history and thematic analysis of the legend see Bamberger, 2009, in Hebrew. Other studies include: Joseph Sherman, *The Jewish Pope: Myth, Diaspora and Yiddish Literature* (Oxford, Legenda, 2003); Hymie Klugman, 'Elchanan, The Jewish Pope', Midstream 34.1 (1988), pp. 26–7; David L. Lerner, 'The Enduring Legend of the Jewish Pope', *Judaism 40* (1991), pp. 148–70.

[18] Jestice, 2007.

[19] Fishman, 2011.

and scholars who seemed to be imposing new restrictions and changing the old ways.

The merchants didn't just bring home news and information. They carried documents and manuscripts. Some of the letters written by the Babylonian *gaon*, Hai, reached Mainz, as did books from Kairouan.[20] But the travellers were few in number, the geographical and political divide between North Africa and the Rhineland was huge and the flow of information and manuscripts was intermittent. Almost as soon as the Talmud was established as an object of study in the Rhineland its rabbis ploughed their own course, responding to local events and reaching their own decisions independently of anything happening in the Islamic world.

The pioneer of Talmud study in the Rhineland was Gershom ben Yehuda, known as the Light of the Exile. He was one of those figures who are so influential that history credits them with all sorts of things that were actually carried out by others. The earliest European commentary on the Talmud is attributed to him, even though it was probably written by several of his students, or even by some of theirs.

Gershom was the first European scholar to try to reconcile the Talmud's world view to the reality of living in a Christian society. He'd lived through good times and bad; intellectual and cultural dialogue when conditions were favourable and harsh realities when they weren't. In 1012 the entire community of Mainz, including Gershom, were expelled from the city by the Emperor Henry II. At the same time one of his sons was forcibly converted to Christianity; he died before he could be reconciled with his family.

We don't know if Gershom was really responsible for all the innovations attributed to him, nor do we know much about his style of leadership, nor his educational skills. But all that is less important than the impact he had on future generations, of which we do know much. Gershom inspired Europe's first wave of creative engagement with the Talmud, and in so doing smoothed the way for centuries of Talmudic life in the Western world.

Many of Gershom's innovations (we'll call them his, even if they weren't) were to do with new social conditions. One of the dangers that young people were exposed to was of being kidnapped and forcibly converted to Christianity, as had happened with Gershom's son. But there was little sympathy for those

---

[20] Grossman, 2011.

who had been forcibly converted; there were many instances of people choosing to submit to death rather than convert, those who preferred the path of life were often reviled. In a landmark pronouncement Gershom ruled that it was forbidden to rebuke or condemn people who had been forcibly converted to Christianity. Whether that changed people's attitudes, or just the way they behaved in public, is hard to say.

In an age when postal services really were medieval, letters were still a novelty for most people. Although it sounds strange to us, those charged with carrying or receiving letters on behalf of others didn't always think twice about opening and reading them. People lived far less private lives than today. Even though the Talmud itself had advised on ways in which privacy can be maintained[21] natural curiosity overruled any qualms most people had about confidentiality. Many letters would have contained intimate personal messages, confidential negotiations between traders or commercial secrets. In what was both a defence of privacy and one of the earliest regulations against industrial espionage, Gershom prohibited the reading of other people's letters.

The best known of the innovations attributed to Gershom, and also the most puzzling to understand, was his prohibition against marrying more than one wife, and the severe punishment of excommunication that was to be pronounced against anyone committing the offence. It's a puzzling enactment because laws are generally not made unless there is a need for them and all the evidence is that Jewish families in Mainz, as was generally the case throughout Christian Europe in the Middle Ages, were small, nuclear and monogamous.[22] It is true that in Talmudic legislation men were permitted to marry more than one wife, but it happened so rarely that even in the Talmud itself we don't find any significant mention of it taking place.[23]

Several opinions have been put forward to explain this enactment. One view is that it was directed at polygamous immigrants from Muslim countries. Another was that once they became aware of the Talmud, men who had previously been unaware of its sanction for polygamy might be tempted to follow it. Avraham Grossman suggests that it may have been directed against travelling

---

[21] Bava Batra 2b discusses whether building windows which overlook a neighbour's property constitutes a form of damages.

[22] Grossman, 1988; Stow, 1987.

[23] BT Yoma 18b records both Rav and Rav Nahman, who when travelling would call out 'Who will be mine for a day?'

merchants who stayed away from home for so long that they may have been tempted to take second wives in the lands they travelled to, perhaps even abandoning their first wife altogether.[24] The truth is that we don't know why this regulation was instituted, and like all his other innovations we don't even know whether it was Gershom who instituted it. But it remains the piece of legislation for which he is (perhaps erroneously) best known.

## The vintner of Troyes

Thirty years after Gershom's death a young wine grower from the French city of Troyes travelled to Mainz to study at the feet of Gershom's former pupils. His name was Shlomo ben Yitzhak, but he is universally known by the acrostic formed from his name, as Rashi (the 'R' stands for Rabbi). He took notes of the lectures he attended in the Mainz *yeshiva*. On returning home he composed a work that has ever since remained the first, and often the only, commentary to which every reader of the Talmud turns. Like Maimonides in Spain, Rashi dominates the story of the Talmud, the pair of them stand head and shoulders above every other. There is little doubt that without Rashi's commentary many passages of the Talmud would be indecipherable.[25]

Unlike his predecessors in Kairouan, Rashi provided a running commentary, distinguished by its brevity and simplicity. Although the reader can often follow the literal meaning of the Talmud text, the various steps in a Talmudic argument are not always clear. By judiciously inserting a few words here and there, Rashi deftly links together the staccato flow of the text, fills in gaps and clarifies difficult or ambiguous meanings.

Rashi's concern is to explain the Talmudic discussion, rather than provide a legal ruling. His occasional use of ancient French to explain the meaning of a difficult word makes him a valuable reference source for medieval linguists.[26] If there is any single figure to whom, despite its many setbacks, the survival, continual study and popularity of the Talmud can be attributed, it is Rashi. He

---

[24] Grossman, 2004.

[25] The fourteenth-century Talmudist Isaac ben Sheshet Perfet exclaims that without Rashi's commentary obscure parts of the Talmud would be 'like the words of a closed book'. Quoted in Urbach, 1968, p. 19.

[26] Brenner, et al., 2003.

democratized the Talmud;[27] armed with a copy of his commentary anyone with a command of the Hebrew language and an analytical leaning is able to read and understand it. As Haym Solovetchik points out, 'No one ever attempted again to write another commentary to the Talmud and all other commentaries were swiftly consigned to oblivion'.[28] But far from Rashi's commentary closing the story of the Talmud, the fact that he made it so much easier to understand opened the door to its future.

Rashi is distinguished for the education he gave his daughters. The status of women in France at the time was generally more elevated than elsewhere,[29] nevertheless Rashi seems to have lavished the same educational care upon his three daughters as he would have done on his sons, if he'd had any. His daughter Miriam is cited in a later work as the example to follow in overcoming a technical problem concerning the absorption by cooking vessels of the flavour of incompatible foods.[30]

Rashi lived just long enough to witness the devastating rampage of the army of the First Crusade. Heading for Jerusalem, to seize the city from its Muslim rulers, and working themselves up into a religious frenzy as they prepared for their expedition, the least disciplined of the crusader throng took it into their heads to slaughter the Jews of Europe along the way.

The assault began in the spring of 1096 in the Rhineland. In Speyer, Worms and Mainz the crusaders announced their presence with a murderous assault. Following the initial slaughter, those who survived were offered the choice of conversion or death. Most chose the latter option, many slaughtering their own children before committing suicide themselves, rather than condemning them to be tortured and raped by the blood-crazed army. Jewish property too was cast to the flames; this was the first occasion in which the Talmud would be burnt in Europe.

The drunken crusaders ripped their way through Europe, destroying and killing as they went. When they finally reached Jerusalem the small Jewish community was completely wiped out; for the first time in its history the city was empty of Jews.

The trauma of the crusade eventually subsided. It would return, but for now some sort of normality returned. Advances were being made in Christian

---

[27] Solovetchik, 2006.

[28] Solovetchik, 2006, p. 37.

[29] Fishman, 2011.

[30] Teshuvot Maimoniot, Hilchot Ma'achlot Asurot, 5.

scholarship and those who were preoccupied with persuading the Jews of the error of their ways were beginning to realize that their lack of success so far was because neither side understood the other. Each faith interpreted the Bible differently, neither side could relate to the arguments of the other.

If Christians wanted to win their arguments against the Jews they realized they would have to understand Jewish interpretations of the Bible. They also began to appreciate that by reading the Jewish Bible in its original language, instead of Latin, they were likely to learn more about the underpinnings of their own faith. They began to enquire more deeply into what the Jews were studying. They began to talk to the Jews. The Jews, for their part, were happy enough to talk back.

## Abelard and Héloise

One of the first to mention the new phenomenon of Jewish–Christian dialogue was Peter Abelard. Abelard, a Frenchman like Rashi, born forty years later, was a controversial, powerfully logical theologian. His rational approach to theology brought him into bitter, book-burning conflict with the supernaturalist Bernard of Clairvaux.

Abelard has gone down in history as the co-star of the medieval tale Abelard and Héloise, immortalized in Alexander Pope's eighteenth-century poem and recounted in plays, novels, film and music ever since. It's a true story; Héloise was Abelard's student; they fell in love and had a child. Héloise's father sought revenge, he had Abelard seized and castrated. Abelard entered a monastery, Héloise a nunnery, from where they conducted a correspondence that was both passionate and scholarly. Reunited in death they are said to be buried together, in the Père-Lachaise cemetery in Paris.

Amongst his many works, Abelard composed the *Dialogue between a Philosopher, a Christian and a Jew*. Abelard tells his readers of a dream he had, in which he is called upon to arbitrate between the three men of God (even philosophers in those days were believers). The structure of the work is reminiscent of the debate that the king of the Khazars had commanded. Although there is no evidence in the *Dialogue* that Abelard knew the Talmud, he does know a lot about Jewish practices.[31] He could only have got this knowledge through conversations with Jews.

---

[31] Cf. Marenbon & Orlandi, 2001.

In one of his letters to Héloise, Abelard tells her of discussions he has had with a Jew about the significance of a silver coin mentioned in the Book of Kings.[32] Around the same time Hugh of St Victor, a member of the twelfth–century, intellectual Scholastic school and his pupil Andrew began to study Rashi's Bible commentaries. They also studied the Bible commentaries of Rashi's grandson Rashbam. He was a key figure in what would become known as the logic-chopping, dialectical Talmudic school of the *tosafists*. It would seem, from the style in which the *tosafists* wrote, that it wasn't just Christian scholars studying Jewish texts. The *tosafists* were learning new methods of analysis from their Christian counterparts.

## Splitting hairs

The traditional Talmud page consists of three columns. The text of the Talmud sits in the centre, the commentary of Rashi is on the inside and the outside column contains a further commentary known as the *Tosafot*.

Unlike Rashi, *Tosafot* is not a person and the commentary was not written at one time. Rather, *Tosafot* is a compilation of comments from scholars who flourished from the generation following Rashi to the fourteenth century. The people who contributed to the *Tosafot* are called *tosafists*. The first *tosafists* were Rashi's pupils and amongst the most important are two of his grandsons, Shmuel, generally referred to as *Rashbam*, whose Bible commentaries Hugo and Andrew studied, and his youngest brother Jacob, known as Rabbenu Tam.

The *Tosafot* are glosses or novellae on the Talmud text. The method of the *tosafists* marked a wholly new development in Talmud study. Rather than explaining the text of the Talmud, more or less word for word as Rashi had done, they focused only on topics to which they had something to add.[33] What they have to say about the topics that interest them can be quite lengthy and they frequently resolve the issue they are dealing with by cross-referencing to other passages in the Talmud. They treat the Talmud as a unitary work which, provided the text is correct (and they sometimes are forced to concede that it isn't), should be internally consistent. If they find a contradiction or difficulty

---

[32] *Opera Petri Abaelardi* ed. V. Cousin, 2v (Paris: A Durand, 1849, 1859), Problemata, 1.237–94.
[33] Jacobs, 1995.

between two Talmudic passages that cannot be easily resolved they tend to resort to hair-splitting, casuistic analysis.

This method was not universally acclaimed. The sixteenth-century mystical Talmudist, Judah Loew of Prague, best known for his legendary creation of a *golem*, a humanoid made out of clay which inspired Mary Shelley's *Frankenstein*, is particularly censorious of the place of the *Tosafot* in Talmudic study. He notes that *Tosafot* only became well known because the first printers of the Talmud placed it in a prominent position on the page. Had it not been for that accident of printing, the study of *Tosafot* would not have become popular. Loew argues that had other works, which concentrated on interpreting the legal outcomes of the Talmudic discussions, been printed in its place, young people would find Talmud study far more interesting and engaging.[34]

The *tosafist* method was very different from that of the more conservative view of the Spanish school. The Spanish excelled in clarifying and codifying the law. They did not concern themselves with analysis of the text. It is this, more than anything else, that led to a divergence between the two schools.

The *Tosafot* were composed by students in the study houses who would record what their teachers said, often challenging their remarks, before summarizing the discussion. As can happen when an inattentive student takes notes, they sometimes got things wrong. Ephraim Urbach in his comprehensive study of the *tosafist*s notes some of the reactions of the teachers when they discovered that their words were incorrectly recorded for posterity. Rabennu Tam is recorded as vehemently disputing a comment that had been attributed to him, protesting that the student who recorded it was confused.[35] Rabbenu Tam was himself accused by a later scholar of transmitting errors; 'heaven forfend that such an astute mind as his could hold such an opinion, one in which even children do not err'.[36]

In the same way that Christian scholars were beginning to take note of Jewish Bible scholarship, the *tosafist*s were carried along by the intellectual currents pervading Christian Europe in the eleventh century. Ephraim Urbach noted that the *tosafist*s' style bears many similarities to the glosses that began to be added around this time to the Justinian code.[37] Their method of comparing,

---

[34] *Maharal, Netivot Olam 1*, p. 25, ed. H. Heinig, London, 1961.

[35] Tosafot Avoda Zara 57b s.v. L'afukei.

[36] Urbach, 1968.

[37] Urbach, 1968.

contrasting and challenging Talmudic passages and of reconciling the economic and social realities of their time with Talmudic law reflected the new style of innovative thinking that was taking root in the Church schools. This view reconciled the honour due to earlier generations with the greater knowledge of their own time; later scholars did not consider themselves as great as their predecessors but believed they could see further because, in the words of a proverb adopted from Christian scholastics, they were dwarves standing on the shoulders of giants.[38]

These developments were of course no accident. Just as had happened in the early days of the Islamic Empire, a two-way process of influence and counter-influence was taking place. Christian Bible exegetes were gaining biblical insights from dialogue with Jews. Jewish Talmudic scholars were learning analytical methods from their Christian counterparts. The Talmud would soon no longer exist within its own closed world. It would need to find its way in a new, and often more challenging, environment.

---

[38] Karnafogel, 2000.

# PART II

## The Talmud in the World

# 9

# Banned, censored and burned – the thirteenth century

*Nahum of Gamzu used to say: Even this is for the best.*[1]

It seems to me, Jew, that I dare not declare that you are human lest perchance I lie, because I recognize that reason, that which distinguishes human beings from beasts, is extinct in you or in any case buried. Truly, why are you not called brute animals? Why not beasts? Why not beasts of burden? The ass hears but does not understand; the Jew hears but does not understand.[2]

With these words the twelfth-century abbot of Cluny, Peter the Venerable, vented his frustration with the Jews. They had once again failed to listen to his arguments showing the Talmud to be false and proving the divinity of Jesus.

Peter was the head of a powerful, international monastic movement who devoted much of his life to the study of other faiths. Peter pioneered the study of both Islam and Judaism, but his interest was far from academic. In those days many religious thinkers were polemicists; anxious to prove the truth of their faith and the falseness of any other belief. By all accounts Peter was a saintly and politically influential man, who had the ear of kings and popes. He had defended Peter Abelard against the accusations of Bernard of Clairvaux and after Abelard's death had acceded to Héloise's request to grant him absolution from his sins. He was also a polemicist par excellence.

Peter first encountered Islam during a visit to Spain, sparking an interest which led him to commission the translation of Islamic texts into Latin. He then devoted much of his time to writing refutations of the Muslim faith. Eventually

---

[1] Ta'anit 21a.
[2] Langmuir, 1990, p. 207.

he turned his attention to Judaism, becoming one of the first to discuss the Talmud; a work which he held in contempt and ridicule.[3]

Peter's work came at a time when Christian scholars were realizing that their attempts, over the last thousand years, to prove the Jews wrong from the Bible were not working because the Jews had their own tradition of biblical interpretation, a tradition which was contained in the Talmud. The Christians were beginning to realize the significance of the Talmud to the Jews, and to understand that if they wanted to prove the Jews wrong they would need to do it by refuting the Talmud, not by bringing arguments from the Bible. The Jews would not accept Christian interpretations of the Old Testament. They had their own. Which were stored in the Talmud.

Peter's life-long attempts to show both Muslims and Jews the errors of their ways mark the beginning of an onslaught on both religions over the next hundred years or so. Chief amongst the aggressors were the Dominican Friars.

The American historian Salo Baron challenged the 'lachrymose' view of Jewish history. He took exception to the popular view, reinforced by nineteenth-century historians, that the Jews had been the most persecuted group in history. He argued that, for example, during the Middle Ages, life for Christian peasants was far worse. To be sure, there were horrific events; crusader assaults, pogroms and the carnage that followed in the wake of blood libels, recurring accusations that Jews had ritually slaughtered Christian children and used their blood to bake Passover bread. But to understand the history of the Jews in any particular period one had to look at what they were doing with their lives. They were not constantly under attack and when they were not, they were living creative lives, learning, working, reading, teaching, raising families and promoting the way of life they believed in.

The history of the Talmud, which has paralleled the history of the Jews, supports Salo Baron's view. By and large it has been a successful history. Followers of the Talmud have explored the deepest intellectual oceans, traversed broad plains of knowledge and ideas, created and sustained communities and attained a clear and uncompromising sense of personal identity and self-knowledge. But that's not to say there weren't lachrymose periods, tearful events in the life of the Talmud and its devotees. The thirteenth century in Christian Europe was one such time.

---

[3] Chazan, 2005.

## The disputation in Paris

Institutional prejudice against the Jews took a giant step forward when Pope Innocent III was elected in 1198. Paying lip service to the earlier papal bull, *Sicut Judaeis*, which had granted limited protection to the Jews in papal lands, Innocent introduced measures to distinguish Jews from Christians, including a requirement for them to wear distinctive clothing. He drew clear lines between orthodox and heretical Christian beliefs and urged bishops to enforce correct religious adherence in their localities. His successor, Gregory IX pushed these reforms further, handing power to mendicant orders to assert his authority.[4] Jeremy Cohen notes that the 'condemnation and persecution of rabbinic literature by the late medieval Church marked an important milestone in the history of Christian-Jewish relations'.[5]

In 1236 Nicholas Donin, a Dominican friar who had been born a Jew but converted to Christianity, appeared before Pope Gregory IX. He brought with him a list of thirty five charges that he had compiled against the Talmud. Amongst Donin's accusations were the charges that the Jews believed the Talmud came from God, that Christians who studied it were to be punished by death and that God is capable of sinning. Notwithstanding the institutional climate driven by the papacy, it has been suggested that Donin's specific motive for this was to seek revenge against his former teacher, Yehiel of Paris. Yehiel had apparently excommunicated Donin for his heretical views – the same views no doubt which had led to his conversion to Christianity.

It took the Pope nearly three years to respond to Donin's charges. When he did, he sent Donin off with a letter to be delivered to the Bishop of Paris. The Bishop was ordered to issue instructions to the kings of France, England, Portugal and the Spanish, that all copies of the Talmud and other Jewish books in their lands were to be confiscated. The Pope demanded that the confiscation was to take place on the first Sabbath in Lent, that all confiscated books be examined and any which contained material contradictory to the Christian faith were to be burnt.

The kings weren't too impressed with the Pope's edict. England, Spain and Portugal ignored it. The only king to react was Louis IX of France, and his response was far from the Pope's original demand. Instead, Louis offered the

---

[4] Lower, 2004.
[5] Cohen, 1999, p. 317.

Jews an opportunity to publicly defend the Talmud. He ordered that a public debate take place, in which Donin would confront the leading rabbis of France with his charges.

It was not the first debate, or disputation, to take place between Christians and Jews and nor would it be the last. But this debate was very different from anything that had gone before. Previously, either the Christians had sought to prove to the Jews that the Hebrew Bible had foretold the coming of Jesus, or the Jews had initiated the debate, attempting to prove the reverse. The debates centred on the interpretation of passages in the Hebrew Bible; the Christians quoting verses from the Jewish prophets that they believed supported their view, the Jews using their tradition of interpretation, which the Christians had recently discovered was bound up in the Talmud, to try to prove them wrong.

Even Salo Baron would accept that in thirteenth-century France Jews had a hard time of it. They were restricted in the trades they could perform, were subjected to blood libels, had been attacked and slaughtered by crusaders and were generally treated as inferior and unwelcome. What is interesting about the previous debates is that despite the power and authority vested in the Church, the Jews had the upper hand; Christianity was trying to justify its existence and not, as might have been expected, the other way round. In matters of religious belief, since Christianity depended on the Hebrew Bible the Jews represented the status quo; it fell to Christianity to prove it was right, not to Judaism to prove its daughter faith wrong.[6]

But the debate between Donin and Yehiel was different. This time Judaism was on the back foot, forced to defend itself. Not only that, but the heart of the debate was no longer how to interpret biblical texts which were claimed by both religions. Instead it was the validity and integrity of the Talmud which was at stake, even though it was a rabbinic text which until recently had been of no interest to Christianity at all.

The debate took place in the royal court in Paris on 25 and 26 June 1240, in the presence of the leading French clergy and Queen Blanche, the king's mother. Nicholas Donin appeared as prosecutor of the Talmud; Yehiel and his colleague,

---

[6] Eisenberg, 2008. Eisenberg sees the disputation between Donin and Yehiel not as an inquisitorial event, as earlier historians assert, in which the Church sought to expose and eradicate heresy. Rather, he shows that the disputation was part of a wider Church campaign against new ideas being promoted in the universities and 'textual communities', who were revising accepted canonical texts in new ways. Texts were a threat to established orthodoxies. The Jews with their interpretative tradition were, from the Church's perspective, just such a textual community.

Rabbi Moses of Courcy were its defenders. It was a tense and dramatic occasion, everyone was aware that the stakes riding on it were high. For Yehiel, it was an intimidating environment:

> When he came before the queen and the princes in the king's court, the Rabbi was alone there with the throng, the queen, the clergy, the rules and all the knights, great and small; of the Israelites there was not one.[7]

Our knowledge of the debate comes from the accounts written by the protagonists, Rabbi Yehiel and Nicholas Donin. Donin's account was in Latin and Yehiel's in Hebrew. Of course, they each wrote their accounts after the debate had taken place, they each had an axe to grind and the two documents therefore are neither word–for–word transcriptions, nor do they necessarily agree with each other.

Donin's account of the disputation is held in the French Bibliothèque Nationale. It is appended to the *Extractiones de Talmut*, a work composed by Jewish converts to Christianity, which purports to list all the incriminating passages in the Talmud.[8] The philosopher St Thomas Aquinas probably had a copy of the *Extractiones* in front of him when he composed his polemic against disbelief, the *Summa Contra Gentiles* in which he misunderstands the Talmud in a similar manner to Donin.[9] It might be thought that the scholarly and rational Aquinas, who used the writings of Maimonides to help him expound biblical laws, would help improve Christian understanding of the Talmud. In fact the opposite seems to have happened; his attention to Scripture led him to a literal understanding of biblical Judaism which failed to recognize the role and purpose of the Talmud in the reality of a post-biblical world.[10]

It has been argued that Yehiel was less interested in reporting the cut and thrust of the debate than writing an account which would function as a guide for future disputants. His report doesn't just set out the arguments he used, which he felt others should follow. It also helps others who might find

---

[7] Ms. Moscow – Guenzberg 1390 (Mosc.) 85a quoted in Eisenberg, 2008, p. 43. It is not clear where Moses of Courcy was.

[8] Eisenberg, 2008.

[9] 'By this is refuted the error of the Jews, who say in the Talmud that at times God sins and is cleansed from sin', *Summa Contra Gentiles* 1.95.8 (Hanover House, New York, 1955).

[10] Cohen, 1999.

themselves in a similar position to prepare, by describing the atmosphere in the court in detail, and the manner in which the audience behaved.[11]

Yehiel tried to explain that the Talmud was an essential, divinely given companion to the Bible, that without it the Bible could not be understood. He tried to rebut Donin's specific charges one by one. Many of the charges that Donin had laid were based upon the parts of the Talmud known as *aggada*, which do not deal with law or religious practice but instead introduce fables, folktales, stories, magic and cosmology. Yehiel argued that these passages are intended 'to draw the heart of a person … if he wants he can believe them, if he doesn't want to, he need not believe'.[12]

Donin mocked the Talmudic statement about the disagreements between Hillel and Shammai: 'these and these are the words of the living God'. How can God change his mind, he asked? Yehiel's answer was that the statement refers to legal decisions that are reached by majority vote. If a majority in one community decide differently from a majority elsewhere, both decisions are valid.

Yehiel refuted the charges that the Talmud is disparaging to Christians, arguing that Donin misunderstood. The passages that Donin claimed referred to Christians actually referred to pagans and idolaters. This is obviously so since the Christian faith had hardly reached Babylon when the Talmud was under composition and its authors were neither particularly knowledgeable about it nor fearful of it.

## The Talmud aflame

Donin's charges against the Talmud were artificial and Yehiel's attempt at defence tortuous, but of course this was never going to be a fair contest. It was no surprise that Yehiel didn't win the debate and what really mattered was not the outcome, but what happened next. The consequences of Yehiel's defeat were far-reaching. Two years after the debate, in 1242, a papal commission condemned the Talmud and urged Louis IX to issue an edict for all copies of the Talmud to be burnt. Louis was not slow to react. He despatched inspectors across the realm, charging them to ransack the Jewish neighbourhoods in both

---

[11] Eisenberg, 2008.

[12] Ms. Moscow – Guenzberg 1390 (Mosc.) 86b quoted in Eisenberg, 2008, p. 46.

cities and villages. The inspectors, most of whom could not read Hebrew, were unable to tell which volumes were copies of the Talmud and which were not. They confiscated everything they found.

Books were the lifeblood of Jewish life; the people may have been as poor as any in the Middle Ages but they had pride in their learning. Their books were often all they had. Study was an end in itself and the highest aspiration of any Jewish parent was that their son would become a rabbinic scholar, an authority in Talmud. They wouldn't have given up their holy books without a fight, many of those fights would have ended in bloodshed and tragedy.

The impact went far beyond those from whom the books were wrenched. Twenty four wagonloads of books were brought to the pyre in a square in Paris. This was long before printing reached Europe. Every book had been written by hand. Thousands of manuscripts, each of which would have taken weeks or months to write, were burned. Many works of which only a few copies existed were lost to the world for ever. Shmuel ben Shlomo, who may have helped Yehiel prepare for the disputation, complains that:

> My spirit is departed, my strength exhausted and there is no light in my eyes due to the wrath of the enemy. He forcefully overpowered us, he took the soul and delight of our eyes, we have no book in our hands to comprehend or to understand.[13]

No complete manuscript of the Talmud exists from before this time.

Amongst the onlookers at the conflagration was Meir ben Baruch, a young student from the Rhineland, who had gone to Paris to study with Yehiel. Distraught at the events he followed the example of so many other traumatized scholars of his time. He expressed his grief in a lamentation:

> Oh you who have been consumed with fire,
> Pray for the peace of those who mourn you,
> Who long to dwell in your court of your habitation,
> Who choke in the dust of the earth,
> Who grieve and are confounded by the immolation of your parchments.[14]

---

[13] Urbach, 1968, p. 377–8.
[14] *Shaali Serufa* forms part of the liturgy for the fast day of the 9th of Av, which commemorates the destruction of the Temple and other national tragedies.

## The censor's pen

Back in Rome, Gregory was already dead, and his successor Celestine only survived in the papal office for fifteen days. A new Pope, Innocent IV, was now on the throne. He seemed content to carry on Gregory's anti-Talmud policy.

In 1244 he wrote to King Louis in Paris, encouraging him in his work and urging him to continue burning all copies of the Talmud, wherever they were found. But his policy would shortly change. Three years later after he had written to Louis, a delegation of French rabbis appeared before Pope Innocent, pleading that without the Talmud they could not understand the Bible and reminding him that the Church had long afforded the Jews the guarantee that they could practise their religion, as long as it did not harm or undermine the Christian faith.

Innocent listened. He modified his stance, now ordering that all Jewish books be inspected, by monks well versed in Hebrew. As long as any material 'harmful' to Christianity was removed, the books could continue in use. This was the beginning of the policy of Talmudic censorship, a policy which continued for many centuries. Censorship was the means of separating out material of which the Church did not approve, whilst allowing Jews access to their rabbinic law.[15] Most printed copies of the Talmud today still reflect the work of the censor's pen.

The advent of censorship did not remove the physical threat to the Talmud. It continued to come under attack in France. Louis IX's son Philip, who was a weaker character than his father, came under continuing pressure from the Church to legislate against the Jews. In 1283 he issued an edict which, alongside forbidding them to live in villages, chant loudly or build cemeteries, forbade the possession of the Talmud. Any copies in their possession were to be burnt.

The next king of France, Philip the Fair, expelled the Jews in 1306, probably for financial reasons.[16] He allowed them back nine years later at which time the burning of copies of the Talmud and other Jewish books in France resumed. The conflagrations continued until 1319, when the Dominican inquisitor Bernard Gui built a pyre in Toulouse.[17] By this time the Talmud had virtually disappeared from France.

---

[15] Chazan, 2005.

[16] Schwarzfuchs, 1967.

[17] For a full account of Bernard Gui's attitude towards and campaign against the Talmud see Cohen, 1982.

But it would return.

In September 2008 Pope Benedict XVI met Jewish leaders in Paris. The weight of history, both recent and medieval, hung heavily on both communities. In his address to the Jews the Pope quoted from the Talmud. It was no accident. Relations between the Church and the Talmud have come a long way since the thirteenth century.

## Maimonides under attack

The Talmud was not the first rabbinic book to be burnt. There had been an incident just a few years earlier, the consequence of a fierce dispute within Jewish intellectual circles. In this case however the burning had the cathartic effect of cooling tempers and restoring a sense of perspective to the disputants.

Over fifty years had elapsed since Maimonides had first published his philosophical treatise *Guide for the Perplexed*. The book had caused quite a stir. Maimonides's attempts to reconcile the secular Aristotelian philosophy of the day with traditional Jewish belief had divided the intellectual world. The battle was between faith and reason. Traditionalists took exception to his view that there was no conflict between the Bible and philosophy, they held the position that a faith found on revelation could not, and should not, be subjected to rational examination; God's word was all that was needed. The rationalists, on the other hand, could not conceive of a world in which God's revelation could conflict with his creation.

The battle had started in the second century BCE, when the Hebrew faith first encountered Greek rationalism. A parable in the Talmud tells of four scholars in the time of the Mishnah who engaged in mystical contemplation. They entered the 'orchard', a metaphor to describe the highest levels of spiritual elevation. It was not a comfortable experience for them. Ben Azzai died, Ben Zoma went mad, Elisha ben Abuya became a heretic and only Rabbi Akiva emerged unscathed.[18] The Talmud goes on to tell us that 'Greek songs never ceased from Elisha ben Abuya's mouth' and 'when he stood up in the study house many heretical books' fell from inside his cloak.[19] Elisha's heresy was his study

---

[18] B. Hagigah 14b.
[19] B. Hagigah 15b.

of Greek philosophy. The disparaging tales that the Talmud's authors recount about him leave us in no doubt about their views on the matter.

The battle between faith and reason was ancient and in the thirteenth century it was by no means confined to the Jewish world. Christianity and Islam were experiencing the same tensions. It was the mood of the times. Although the Jews in Muslim lands had shared the long Islamic tradition of philosophical enquiry, many of them considered Maimonides's ideological rationalism a step too far. All the more so for those in Christian Europe who'd had far less exposure to speculative thought.

Maimonides's philosophical work *Guide for the Perplexed* was not written until he was in his fifties and was only made popularly available in Hebrew towards the end of his life. The storm over it did not erupt until after his death. But, as we saw previously, there had already been disquiet over his legal compendium, *Mishneh Torah,* and the embers of the earlier controversy were still hot. When his critics read the *Guide,* the storm erupted again. This time it was even more bitter.

And yet, as Joseph Dan has written, although the battle was between faith and reason, the letters and pamphlets which have survived from that time do not discuss whether Maimonides was right or wrong. They concentrate on only one thing; was there a contradiction between Maimonides and the Talmud? If there was no contradiction, if Maimonides could be shown to be in accord with tradition, then the veracity of his arguments would be proved. The rationalists, as Dan points out, succumbed to the values of their opponents, who accused Maimonides of being in conflict with the Talmud.[20]

The argument was vitriolic and raged across Europe. It came to an end unexpectedly, in 1232, when the Dominicans, who were busy investigating the Church's own Albigensian heresy,[21] suddenly turned their attention to the Jews and cast Maimonides's works to the flames in 1232. Maimonides's supporters hurled blame at their opponents for dragging the friars into the row, but whether the Dominicans burnt his works of their own initiative, or whether they were put up to it by the same type of fanatic who, some years later, desecrated his tomb in Tiberias, remains a mystery.

---

[20] Dan, 1999.

[21] The Albigensian dispute between the Pope and the Cathars in Languedoc is the only recorded example of a crusade conducted by the Church against fellow Christians.

## Disputation in Barcelona

The events that had taken place in Paris resonated throughout Europe. They particularly had an effect in Spain where the Christian reconquest of the country was proceeding apace. The Golden Age had drawn to a close, the Muslim rulers were being driven southwards as the Christian kingdoms in the north expanded their reach. When, in 1236, King Ferdinand III of Castile captured Cordova, the destiny of Spain's Jewish communities would now be shaped by events in Christian France and Germany, instead of those in the Muslim world.

The Dominicans, the Order to which Nicholas Donin had belonged, pursued an active missionary agenda in Spain, just as they did in France. Charged with operating the Inquisition by Pope Gregory and faithful to their responsibilities, they were fanatical defenders of Orthodox Church dogma. Although they focused their attentions equally on Muslims, Jews and heretics, the Jews were the easiest group for the Dominicans to prey on. Unlike the Christian heretics, Jews made no attempt to conceal themselves or to disguise their religious beliefs.[22] Fewer and less organized than the Muslims, they posed little danger; they had no retreating co-religionists in the south who may turn and launch a counter-attack. The Jews, visible, unprotected and vulnerable, were an easy target.

To make things worse, several Jewish converts amongst the Dominican friars were actively agitating against the Talmud, as if they believed that by discrediting it they could hasten the abolition of the Jewish faith. Nicholas Donin had been a convert and now in Barcelona another convert, Pablo Christiani, began to foment against the Talmud.

Even though centuries of Muslim rule had left Spanish society more tolerant towards minorities than France, the Jews were nevertheless disenfranchised. They had long been obliged to attend forced sermons at the king's command, to hear friars preach the gospels to them. In this atmosphere of strident invective, Christiani did not need to manufacture charges against the Talmud as Donin had done. He could simply take advantage of the polemical mood to persuade the Jews of the error of their ways and of the truth of Christianity. He prevailed upon the king to order a compulsory debate.

King James I of Aragon was more than willing to accede to Christiani's request. He relished the idea of a debate, particularly if it could be open and

---

[22] Chazan, 1977.

cordial. He ordered that it take place in the royal palace in Barcelona and summoned the leading rabbi in Spain, Moses ben Nachman. As is traditional for prominent rabbinic scholars, he was known by the acrostic formed by his title and initials. Ramban was to argue in favour of the Talmud.[23]

Yehiel in Paris had been a well-known and respected rabbi, but Ramban was in a different league. A physician by profession, he was one of those people who seem able to do anything and to excel at whatever they do. He'd been the head of a rabbinic school in Gerona before being appointed chief rabbi of Catalonia, and, despite his religious and medical duties, he found the time to author over fifty works, principally on Talmud, philosophy and mysticism. He also wrote poetry. His works, particularly his commentaries on the Torah and the Talmud, are still read today.

Ramban was in his late sixties when he received the king's summons. According to the account that he wrote of the debate, he only agreed to participate if he was allowed to speak freely and if the king himself agreed to take no active part. He didn't want to get into an argument with the monarch. He repeated the request to speak freely to Friar Ramon, the head of the Dominical Order. Friar Ramon agreed, just as the king had already done.

The disputation took place over four days in July 1263. As in Paris, it was attended by the leading clergy and noblemen. Pablo Christiani was the main advocate for the Dominicans, supported by four colleagues. Ramban was the sole spokesperson for the Talmud although unlike the debate in Paris, other Jews were present.

Christiani opened by declaring it was his intention to prove from the Talmud that the Messiah had already come, that he was both human and divine and that he had died to atone for human sin. He quoted Talmudic homilies in support of his view.

Ramban argued that not only had Christiani misconstrued the passages he was quoting, but that in any event Jews were not obliged to take the folklore and stories in the Talmud literally. This is the same argument that Yehiel had used in Paris. He explained that there were three levels of Jewish literature; Bible, Talmud and *aggada*. The Bible was to be believed with perfect faith. The legal part of the Talmud, which explains the commandments in the Torah, is also to

---

[23] Like Maimonides,and several others, he was also known by his patronymic, as Nachmanides.

be relied upon but *aggada* should be treated like sermons; 'if one believes it, all well and good, if not, one will not be harmed spiritually'.[24]

The debate proved inconclusive. Pablo Christiani was not able to persuade Ramban and the other Jews present that the Messiah had already come, and Ramban was not able to refute Christiani to a point where he could demand he cease his proselytizing activity. The king seems to have been won over by Ramban at least to some degree. At the end of the debate he presented him with three hundred *dineros* and said he had never heard someone who was wrong argue his case so well.[25]

However the king also decreed that he would come to the synagogue the following Sabbath with Pablo Christiani and Friar Ramon, where they would preach the gospels to the Jews. Ramban remained behind in Barcelona for the occasion, to try to reassure the frightened congregation. He listened patiently whilst Christiani and Friar Ramon each preached to them, but leapt to his feet to protest when the Friar intimated that he had been won over by Christiani during the disputation.

Despite the goodwill that the king showed Ramban, he came under further pressure from the Dominicans to impose strictures upon the Jews and their Talmud. A month later he issued a series of royal edicts in which he ordered the Jews to attend Christiani's missionary sermons whenever required. They were also required to show Christiani their books, which he would use to convince them of the truth of his case.

Two years later the Bishop of Gerona got hold of a copy of Ramban's account of the debate. It clearly did not accord with his own understanding of what had been said because he charged him with blasphemy. Ramban appealed to the king, arguing that he had promised him freedom of speech. The king supported him, demanding that the trial be adjourned until he had the opportunity of judging it himself.

The trial never took place and the Dominicans now appealed to Pope Clement IV. He in turn ordered the Archbishop of Tarragona to seize all the

---

[24]  Chavel, 1983. There has been much discussion in modern scholarly circles as to whether Ramban really believed that it was not obligatory to believe the many *aggadic* (non-legal) passages in the Talmud. Most modern Jews, aware that many *aggadic* passages contradict each other and that much of Talmudic science and medicine reflects merely the knowledge of the time, regard *aggada* as instructive, insightful or illustrative but not necessarily true. Ramban, however, belonged to a period when many people did believe in the literal truth of *aggada* and in his other writings there is little indication that he doubts its veracity.

[25]  Chavel, 1983.

copies of the Talmud and other Jewish books in his kingdom and submit them
to Pablo Christiania and his fellow friars for examination and censorship. The
Pope instructed the censors to return to the Jews all books which accorded with
the Bible and all which clearly did not contain blasphemies.[26]

By now it was obvious to Ramban that living conditions could only deteri-
orate. Although he was well into his seventies he took the decision to leave
Spain and make the perilous sea journey to Israel. He landed in Acre in 1267
where he completed the work for which he is most famous, his commentary
on the Torah. His last communal role was as the Rabbi of Acre. Ironically, his
predecessor in the post had been Yechiel of Paris, who had also upped sticks
and made the journey to Israel a few years earlier, following the trauma of his
disputation.

These were the most famous disputations of the thirteenth century, but they
were by no means the only ones. The accounts that both Yehiel and Ramban
wrote of their experiences served as a sort of manual for other, less experienced
rabbis when they were summoned to a debate.

One of the members of the committee of censors that was established in
the wake of the Barcelona disputation was an erudite friar, Raymondi Martini.
Martini had been singled out for a special education as a young man and had
already written at least two polemics against Islam. In 1278 he produced his
most famous work, the *Pugio Fidei adversos Mauros et Judaeos,* or Dagger of
Faith against the Moors and Jews.

Way back in the early fifth century St Augustine had declared that the Jews
were permitted to dwell amongst Christians due to the special status that God
had given them. Unlike Christian heretics, their presence in Christian Europe
had been ordained by God. Their exile and suffering was a consequence of their
refusal to accept the truth of Christianity and as such was a testament to its
veracity.

Successive Popes had paid lip service to the doctrine, even though as we have
seen, it was breached far more frequently than was affirmed. But despite the
breaches, in theory Augustinian protections still held good. Now, in a radical
departure from Augustine doctrine, Martini came up with a doctrinal defence
of Dominican aggression. He sought to justify their mission against the Jews
theologically. There was, he argued, a difference between the Jews who lived

---

[26] Cohen, 1999.

before Jesus, and those after. The ancient Jews, he claimed, agreed with the Christians. But the modern Jews had wilfully rejected Christianity, and should be treated as heretics.[27]

Martini used his comprehensive knowledge of Jewish sources to assert that the Talmud actually refuted the practices of contemporary Jews. Certainly his knowledge of Talmudic and other rabbinic texts was extensive and his argumentation complex and learned. He may well have intended the *Pugio* as a guide to help Christian disputants in much the same way as Yehiel and Ramban had recorded their debates as a practical manual for those Jews who found themselves forced into disputation.[28] The *Pugio* became the essential companion for any aspiring Christian disputant for at least the next four centuries. It was widely copied and recopied in manuscript form and was finally printed in 1651. It remains the most comprehensive and well-known polemic against the Talmud ever written.

Meanwhile the young student Meir ben Baruch, who had witnessed the Paris burnings and written an elegy lamenting the occasion, had acquired a reputation as the leading Talmudic scholar of his generation. Now an old man in his late sixties, Meir had authored many works on religious law, had served as the head of the supreme religious court in Germany and was the principal of the leading rabbinical academy in Europe. Over one thousand responses of his legal responses still survive today.

Back in the Rhineland, in Meir's home city of Rothenburg, conditions had greatly deteriorated. The Jews found themselves under continuing attack and his students, who included many who would become leading lights of the next generation, feared for their lives. They prevailed on Meir to leave Germany for a safer clime. The *Pugio* had already been copied and recopied many times when the young student set off with his family on the lengthy journey across land and sea to settle in Israel.

Meir and his fellow travellers had got as far as Lombardy when he was arrested and sent back to Germany. On his arrival he was delivered into the hands of the Habsburg emperor, Rudolph I. Rudolph, who needed to augment his treasury, decided that Meir was too good a catch to let go easily and imprisoned him, hoping to receive a hefty ransom. His followers raised twenty three thousand marks but Meir refused to allow it to be paid, fearing that if he

---

[27] Rooden, 2001.
[28] Wiersma, 2009.

was released this would only embolden the Emperor to kidnap and hold others to ransom. Meir's followers prevailed upon the Emperor to allow him access to his books, and he wrote several works whilst in prison. Meir was never released. He died seven years later.

## The spread of *kabbalah*

For the best part of a millennium the Talmud had been the pre-eminent, non-biblical corpus in the Jewish world. True, the Mishnah was older and the Talmud's authority was based on the fact that it interpreted the Mishnah, but the two works were so close that the older had effectively been absorbed into the newer, they were even written as one. But a new work was appearing on the scene, one which, whilst paying lip service to the supremacy of Talmud would come in time, in certain places and amongst certain people, to rival and even occasionally to surpass it.

The practice of Jewish mysticism was as old as the faith itself. The book of Ezekiel opens with the prophet's mystical vision of God's throne, known as the heavenly chariot, and the Talmud itself refers to two distinct types of mystics, those who contemplate the 'works of the chariot' and those who busy themselves with the 'works of creation'.[29] The tale above, about the four scholars who entered the orchard is one of several mystical narratives in the Talmud.

Mystical texts too had been known for centuries. The oldest, the Book of Creation, dates back to the fifth century and seems to have been in regular use;[30] Sa'adia *Gaon* composed a commentary to it in 931 CE.[31] Mystical texts were often structured similarly to the homiletical collections that were composed in the Talmudic period in Israel and recounted the supernatural exploits of Talmudic sages, even though in most, if not all cases, the name of a sage was only adduced to give the narrative credibility.

But although there was almost certainly a long-standing undercurrent of mysticism in Jewish circles we hear little of it until the twelfth century, when mystical schools emerged in both Spain and Germany.

---

[29] B. Hagigah 13a.

[30] Dan, 1999. Although only once mentioned by name (and even that may be a reference to a different work), devotees of the *Sefer Yetzirah* (Book of Creation) do however find other allusions to it in the Talmud. Cf. Kaplan, 1997.

[31] Kaplan, 1997.

All the prominent early mystics were students of the Talmud. Ramban, who had conducted the dispute in Barcelona, wrote commentaries on parts of the Talmud and on the Torah. His Torah commentary offers both rational and mystical interpretations. The Pietists in Germany produced works which used Talmudic traditions as a starting point but then set off on mystical tangents.[32] But many mystics were ambivalent about the study of Talmud, they felt it focused too much on rigid legal analysis and downplayed the importance of spiritual and ethical matters. The Talmudists had abandoned the quest for God in favour of the precise formulation of the law.[33]

In these circles a new category of ethical law emerged, the 'law of heaven'. It didn't override the law of the Talmud, a crime was still a crime. But the Talmud's mechanical application of the law was subordinated to an absolute morality; a crime which necessitated a greater struggle against the 'evil inclination', such as when a pious but starving man steals food, is to be judged less harshly than a theft instigated by wicked intent.[34] Similarly, Talmudic law forbids people spitting at each other but there is only a penalty for damages if the spit lands on the other person. Heavenly law focuses exclusively on the intent, spitting is an offence, wherever it may land.[35]

During the thirteenth century mystical pamphlets began to circulate in Castile, in Spain. By the end of the century they had been compiled into a collection known as the *Zohar*, which means 'radiance'.

As befits any mystical tome the origins of the *Zohar* are lost in the mists of time. Traditionally it is ascribed to Shimon ben Yohai, a second-century pupil of Rabbi Akiva. Until recently the academic view was that it had been composed by the thirteenth-century Spanish mystic Moses de Leon. However, the language and complexity of the work suggests that it is a compendium of texts that may well have been edited together by Moses de Leon and his colleagues, but much of which was of a significantly earlier provenance.[36] Over the coming centuries the *Zohar* would prove to be a challenging companion to the Talmud. Some considered it to be the more important of the two. Asher Lemlein, a sixteenth-century kabbalist mocked those who thought the study of mundane laws was

---

[32] Dan, 1999.

[33] Fishman, 2011.

[34] Alexander-Frizer, 1991. Alexander-Frizer discusses what she sees as a similar relation between intention and deed, between 'this-worldly and other-worldly recompense', in the writings of Peter Abelard.

[35] *Sefer Hasidim* ed. Margolis, Section 44.

[36] Rapaport-Albert & Kwasman, 2006.

more important than knowledge of the Creator. He likened the Talmudists to a king's workers and the Kabbalists to those who sat alongside the monarch in his council.[37]

---

[37] Carlebach, 2006.

# 10

# Printers and polemics

R. Hanina said: Everything comes from heaven. Except for cold draughts.[1]

## Forced, and not so forced, conversions

By the fourteenth century the southward march of Christian armies into Islamic territory in Spain, was all but over. Granada was the only area to remain in Muslim hands. The victory of the Cross over the Crescent led to an outpouring of religious triumphalism.[2] Actions to convert the Jews to Christianity increased dramatically, They were seen as not just the enemies of God and Christendom, they'd been exposed as heretics; forsaking the Bible and placing themselves under the jurisdiction of the Talmud.[3]

The conversion drive was not without success. At first a trickle of converts made their way towards Christianity, some out of genuine belief, others from expediency. The trend accelerated as the century wore on until, in 1391, an outbreak of riots and pogroms directed against the Jews led to a bursting of the flood gates. Suddenly the *conversos,* as they were called, were numbered not in their tens, hundreds or thousands, but in their myriads. About half of the Jewish population is thought to have converted.[4]

But the conversion policy backfired. Mainstream Spanish society was wholly unprepared for an event of such magnitude. Instead of just Jews and Christians (the Muslims had long been forced out), the population now comprised three

---

[1] Bava Metzia 107b.

[2] Friedman, 1987.

[3] Peters, 1995.

[4] Peters, 1995.

distinct groups. Old Christians, Jews and *conversos* or New Christians. It didn't bode well for the *conversos.*

The Old Christians resented the sudden influx of people who, almost overnight, had moved from the fringes of society to its heart and now demanded the same rights and privileges as those who had always been loyal to the Cross. What did it matter, argued the Old Christians, if these people had changed their religion? They still had Jewish blood in their veins. And wasn't it the case, they added, that most of them still kept up their Jewish practices, as if they had never converted?

The *conversos'* dilemma was that it's one thing to submit to pressure to convert to avoid persecution and oppression. It is quite another to give up the habits, practices and beliefs of a lifetime. Many *conversos* started to live a dual life. They were Christians in public. But in secret, in a clandestine, underground existence they were still Jews. Stories began to circulate of *converso* women sweeping their houses on a Friday, when surely Saturday was the time for Sabbath preparations. When these women had finished sweeping they were seen placing pots of food in the embers of their fires, to keep it warm for the following day. And when sun set on a Friday evening, they lit candles. Some were said even to be holding secret prayer services in their homes.[5]

If these practices, which were nothing more than traditional Jewish Sabbath preparations, had been ordained by the Bible, there'd have been no problem. They may not have been what native born Christians did, but nor would they have intimated a rejection of Christianity. But they weren't Bible practices. The Bible commands the Sabbath. But it's the Talmud that ordains the practices the *conversos* were following. The difference probably didn't even occur to them, they were only doing what they had always done. But they weren't doing what the Church had expected of them. They'd accepted Christianity. But they hadn't rejected the Talmud.

One man rejected it though. As a child he'd been known as Solomon ha-Levy. He was raised in a learned home, he was well educated and had grown into a skilled Talmudist, even engaging in erudite correspondence with the leading scholar in Spain, Rabbi Isaac ben Sheshet. He qualified as a rabbi and ministered to the Castilian town of Burgos. Until he converted to Christianity. He changed his name to Pablo de Santa Maria. He became a bishop. And like

---

[5]  Starr-LeBeau, 2003.

Nicholas Donin, Pablo Christiani and so many other converts before him, he
became an ideological opponent of the Talmud.

Pablo de Santa Maria was not the only distinguished *converso* Talmudist
to become a Christian scholar. Another was Jeronimo de Santa Fé. He wrote
*Hebraeomastyx,* an anti-Jewish treatise in which he attacked the Talmud, taking
his arguments directly from Ramon Martini's *Pugeo Fidei.* He caught the eye
of the Church dignitaries in Avignon, in Provence. The Catholic Church had
recently split, there was now a pope in Rome, and another, Benedict XIII, in
Avignon. Benedict, who was known as the anti-pope, had jurisdiction over
Spain. He engaged Jeronimo de Santa Fé to conduct yet another disputation,
this time in Tortosa.

There had been many disputations by this time but Tortosa hosted the
longest of them all. It lasted for over a year, with one short break. Its purpose, as
always, was to persuade the Jews of their errors of their ways and oblige them to
convert. No new arguments were raised or compelling insights evoked. But the
Jews were on the back foot, their leadership weak and their spirits shattered. By
the time it finished many of the Jewish delegates, who were so exhausted by the
year-long ordeal, and so impoverished by the time spent away from their trades,
had converted out of desperation.[6]

More than a century had now passed since the first *conversos* were baptised
but the resentment of the Old Christians hadn't abated. When nine days
of rioting broke out in 1467, the king brought in legislatation against the
newcomers. He decreed that no *converso* could hold an official position in
Toledo or Ciudad Real.[7]

The Old Christians blamed the Jews for the *conversos'* inability to integrate.
They argued that there was too much contact, the *conversos* were too close to the
Jews, and they remained under their influence. In order to bring the *conversos*
into line, to teach them to be true to their new faith, all traces of heresy would
have to be rooted out. King Ferdinand, who was himself partly descended from
Jewish stock[8] consulted the bishops. The bishops' solution took even the Old
Christians by surprise. Nobody expects the Spanish Inquisition.

The Inquisition was established in 1480 with a mandate to purge all heresy
from those *conversos,* who, despite their pledges to Christianity, were really

---

[6] Roth, 1995.

[7] Friedman, 1987.

[8] Roth, 1995.

crypto-Jews. There had been previous papal inquisitions in Spain, but this was the first to be set up under a royal mandate. Led by the notorious Thomas de Torquemada, it sought to root out and prosecute anyone who had been spotted observing Talmudic law. A handbook written to guide the inquisitors advised them that the Bible decreed eternal damnation for heretics. There was every justification therefore for guilty *conversos* to be put to death.[9]

But punishing guilty *conversos* wouldn't solve the underlying problem. To ensure that no taint of Jewish influence could contaminate those who were not yet guilty, in 1492 Ferdinand and his queen, Isabella, expelled all the Jews from Spain. Fifteen hundred years of unbroken Jewish settlement came to an end.

1492 was one of those rare years in which everything changes all at once.[10] Granada, the last remaining Muslim kingdom in Spain, fell to Christian conquerors. Christopher Columbus landed in America. By the end of the year there were Spaniards in America, but there were no longer any Muslims or Jews in Spain. Andres de Bernaldez, a Spanish priest who watched the Jews pack up and leave, reported that there was 'no sight more pitiable ... there was not a Christian who did not feel their pain'.[11]

As the departing Jews packed their bags, they took their copies of the Talmud with them. Not all were densely written manuscripts, carefully inscribed. A few of the exiles, the wealthiest and those renowned for their scholarship, carried with them the products of the very latest technology. Some even took the new technology itself. As the Talmud cast its final, backward glance at Spain, it did so from a printed folio. The age of the scribe and their manuscripts was coming to an end. Printing had arrived. And a new chapter in the history of the Talmud was about to begin.

**Printing the Talmud**

The earliest known Spanish imprints of the Talmud were produced in Guadalajara, a little way to the north-east of Madrid. The ancient town had been founded in the eighth century on the site of an old Roman settlement. By

---

[9] Baer, 1961.

[10] Felipe Fernández-Armesto records the game-changing events that took place that year, across the world. *1492, The Year Our World Began*, (Bloomsbury, London, 2009).

[11] Cited in *1492, The Year Our World Began*, Felipe Fernández-Armesto (Bloomsbury, London, 2009), p. 87.

the fifteenth century it was the seat of the Mendoza family, patrons of the arts and literature. Like so many earlier homes of the Talmud it was a cultured city. The refined atmosphere was just the setting to stimulate an interest in printing and the construction of the earliest presses.

The few surviving printed volumes of the Talmud from Spain, and contemporaneous editions from Portugal, contain Rashi's commentary in the outer margin and the main text in the centre. They don't always correspond exactly to texts printed today.

The reason is that, for the whole of its early life, the Talmud was mainly transmitted by word of mouth. There were manuscripts but not everyone possessed them, and the Talmud is such a large document that virtually nobody had a complete copy. Students were taught to memorize their studies, rote learning was the order of the day.

Oral texts are fluid and organic; not everyone has a perfect memory. When manuscripts began to be produced, successive scribes and readers inserted comments or even emended texts, an activity which was considered quite acceptable.[12] It wasn't until it was printed that the text became fixed.

Printing brought many benefits. But it set in stone an opus which had started life as an organic tradition. If we think of the transmission of an oral text as a continuous process, like a shifting landscape of desert sands, then a printed copy is a snapshot, taken at a moment in time; a random but defining, apparently authentic, configuration of the sands, or in our case the text, at the moment the shutter was pressed.[13] The reason why modern editions of the Talmud differ from the early Spanish volumes is simply that they were based on different manuscripts, with different printers making different decisions about how the text should read.

The early imprints were only of individual volumes, thirty seven of which make up a full set. In 1483, round about the same time as the Spanish volumes were being produced, Joshua Solomon of Soncino in northern Italy established his Hebrew printing press. Amongst the works he and his nephew Gershom

---

[12] Fishman, 2011.

[13] Talya Fishman has treated the whole subject of the Talmud's transition from an oral to a written text in great depth, although her work has not been universally accepted. It is too big a subject to deal with in anything other than a book, I have tried simply to give a flavour of what happens when an oral tradition is crystallized in printing.

produced were several volumes of the Talmud, complete with Rashi and *Tosafot* commentaries.

Gershom Soncino became known as one of the leading printers of his generation; in the course of his lifetime he produced over a hundred Hebrew titles and a similar number of Latin, Greek and Italian works. But although the Soncino family would go down in history as pioneers, their work on the Talmud was shortly to be eclipsed by an even more ambitious project taking place in Venice, a little over a hundred miles to the east.

Printing the Talmud standardized the text and brought it within the reach of a much wider audience. Adding commentaries to the printed page, something that was unknown in manuscripts, revolutionized the method of study.[14] But a full forty years was to elapse from when the Soncinos produced their first volume until the first complete printed copy of the whole Talmud was produced. And that full copy may well never have seen the light of day at all, had it not been for the revolution that was taking place in the Church, the challenge of the Reformation and the emergence of the early Christian Hebraists.


## The laid table

Amongst the families who had been driven out of Spain was that of Ephraim Caro. The family had hailed from Toledo and, following the expulsion, settled in Turkey where Ephraim taught the Talmud to his son Yosef. Yosef was a sensitive young man who kept a diary in which he recorded conversations he had with a heavenly mentor. He described this mentor, known as a *maggid* in mystical terminology, as a personification of the Mishnah. One of his companions, Solomon Alkabetz, records that he heard the *maggid* speaking from Joseph's mouth.[15]

Yosef Caro's mystical proclivities led him to settle in Safed, the city in northern Israel which was home to the new, burgeoning kabbalist movement. Caro became one of Safed's leading lights, with a profound knowledge of the

---

[14] Carlebach, 2006.

[15] Caro recorded his discussions over a period of fifty years with his mentor, or *maggid*, in *Maggid Mesharim*. The book was first published in Amsterdam in 1704, though probably in a truncated form. A detailed study of the work was published by R. J. Zwi Werblowsky, *Joseph Karo, Lawyer and Mystic* (Oxford University Press, Oxford, 1962).

Talmud. He could see that, in the three hundred years since Maimonides had written his legal code, the *Mishneh Torah*, the legal landscape in the widely scattered Jewish world had become almost anarchic. Caro complained about the many books of law and practice that were circulating, it was as if everyone was writing books and nobody knowing which opinion to follow.[16]

Caro's solution to this was to write a book. But it was not a book like any other. He took as his starting point a work known as the *Arba'ah Turim*, or Four Rows, named after the four sets of stones on the ancient High Priests' breastplate. The *Arba'ah Turim*, commonly abbreviated as the *Tur*, had been written by Jacob, the son of Asher ben Yehiel, a pupil of Meir of Rothenburg who had been held captive by Rudolph the Hapsburg emperor.

Jacob had written the *Tur* in the early fourteenth century. He had based it in part on Maimonides's *Mishneh Torah* but, unlike Maimonides, he cited the Talmudic sources of the law, omitted everything that was no longer relevant, such as the ancient order of service in the Jerusalem Temple, and introduced rulings by the French and German scholars who, by and large, lived and worked after Maimonides.

The *Tur* had served its purpose but Caro saw the need to expand it, bring it up to date and produce an authoritative guide to the law that would be applicable everywhere and serve to assist rabbis and judges in their decision making. He produced a commentary on the *Tur* which he called the *Bet Yosef*. It was the most comprehensive guide to Jewish law that had ever been produced, both in its breadth of content and the manner in which it explained things. Louis Jacobs described it as the 'keenest work of legal analysis in the history of Jewish law'.[17]

The *Bet Yosef* was so momentous that, once he finished it, Caro felt compelled to produce a digest. He decided to write a work for 'young students' to help them clearly know the law. Unlike the *Bet Yosef*, it would not contain complex analysis. This book would be laid out, like a table is for a meal, with everything to hand and clearly in its place. He called it *Shulchan Aruch* or the Laid Table.

Shortly after the *Shulchan Aruch* was written, Moses Isserles of Krakow in Poland criticized its Sephardic outlook (the Sephardim were the Jews who had originated in Spain, who often had different customs from the northern Europeans, or Ashkenazim). Isserles interpolated his comments into Caro's work, whenever he felt the Ashkenazi practice needed to be recorded.

---

[16] Introduction to *Bet Yosef*, various editions.
[17] Jacobs, 1995 s.v. Karo.

Caro's *Shulchan Aruch*, printed with Isserles's glosses, is still the unchallenged compendium of Jewish law. Although a changing world has led to a plenitude of new works dealing with technical, social, scientific and economic matters of which Caro and Isserles would have had no conception, the *Shulchan Aruch* still lies beneath them all as the law code par excellence, the definitive summary of how things should be done.[18] The scholars in the old academies of Babylon, with their multifaceted view of the world and their reluctance to provide definitive rulings, would have been astonished.

## Christian Hebraists

Protestantism began to take hold in Europe in 1517, in the wake of Martin Luther's challenges to Catholic doctrine. One of its chief pillars was the principle of *sola scriptura;* the belief that the Bible is all that is needed to interpret the word of God. *Sola scriptura* contends that Scripture is complete; it holds absolute authority over the believer.[19] This position is of course far removed from the rabbinic principle that the Bible can only be understood through a tradition of interpretation, which is found in the Oral Law. *Sola scriptura* is closer to the literalist, Karaite position. At first sight, therefore, the Talmud had even less in common with Protestantism than it had with Catholicism; there didn't seem to be any reason why Protestant thinkers would react to it any differently than the Catholics had done for so long.

But the leading Protestant theologians saw things differently. They believed that if Protestantism was to really get to grips with the true meaning of Scripture, the Old as well as the New Testament, it would need a much deeper understanding of biblical texts. From the days of the earliest Church Fathers the Old Testament had been taught, studied and read in Latin. But Latin was not its original language. It was a translation. And, as everyone who has studied texts in any language knows, translations are slippery things. When there's more than one way to translate a word, such as the French word *aimer,* which in English

---

[18] That's not to say there is no diversity in Jewish law and practice, there is a range of opinions on almost every topic. But those differences tend to stem from the way a ruling of the *Shulchan Aruch* applies to the case in hand, or because of a perceived latitude or ambiguity in its text. It is rare for orthodox scholars to overrule or ignore a ruling of the Shulchan Aruch.

[19] *Sola Scriptura: The Protestant Position on the Bible,* Joel R. Beeke et al., (Soli Deo Gloria Publications, Lake Mary, FL, 2009).

can mean to love or to like, the translator has to make a decision. That decision reflects the translator's personal opinion, it can radically change the meaning of a passage. Particularly if the translator lived in the fourth century, when the Bible was translated into Latin; a period in history when translation techniques were not all that sophisticated.

Understanding the true meaning of the original Hebrew text was a priority for Protestants if they were to make progress in advancing the principles of *sola scriptura*. They would have to learn Hebrew.

We can't tell whether the doctrine of *sola scriptura* led to Christian study of Hebrew, or whether it was the other way round. There is some evidence that a few imaginative scholars, humanists who admired and promoted the study of classical art, literature and language, had already started to learn Hebrew out of intellectual curiosity. In so doing, they discovered that their comprehension of the Old Testament improved and this may have led in turn to the development of the idea of *sola scriptura*.

One of these pioneering scholars was Conrad Pellican. Born in Alsace in 1478, around the time the first copies of the Talmud were being printed, he entered the Franciscan order at the age of fifteen. He is the first Christian scholar that we hear of who studied the Talmud systematically. He had a Jewish teacher, his intention being, according to Stephen Burnett, to contend with Judaism more successfully.[20] But whatever the reasons for his initial interest in Hebrew and Talmud, he was obviously drawn to the subject. He composed a Hebrew Grammar in 1501, just two years after starting to study the language.

Pellican's encounter with the Talmud was benign. Not so for his older contemporary Johannes Reuchlin, perhaps the best known of all Christian Hebraists.

## Pfefferkorn v. Reuchlin

Reuchlin was a well-respected humanist scholar who had studied in universities across Europe before moving to Basel where he taught Greek and obtained a doctorate in Imperial Law. Successfully navigating his way past a career setback, when he backed an unsuccessful move to unseat the heir apparent to the Duchy

---

[20] Burnett, 2005.

of Wurtemburg, he was appointed as a judge to the Supreme Court in Speyer and as legal counsel to the Swabian League, a newly formed political alliance in southern Germany. At the age of fifty seven he retired to concentrate on his studies.[21]

Reuchlin was a self-taught Hebrew scholar. He became interested in *kabbalah* and sought to use it to prove the doctrines of Christianity.[22] In 1494 he wrote a book in which he tried to reconcile Jewish mysticism with Christian doctrine and Greek philosophy. Like Pellican he also wrote a Hebrew grammar which became the standard in its field. Five years after he retired he wrote his classic mystical study, *On The Art of Kabbalah*.

While the Christian Reuchlin was developing his knowledge of Jewish literature and language, Josef Pfefferkorn, a Jew from Moravia or, according to some, Nuremberg, was going the other way. Around 1504 he converted to Christianity and five years later, following in the tradition of Nicholas Donin, Pablo Christiani and Pablo de Santa Maria, he declared war on the Talmud. He approached the Emperor Maximillian with a plan to destroy and confiscate all Jewish books, arguing that they posed an obstacle to the conversion of the Jews. The Emperor agreed and set Pfefferkorn to work. Unfortunately the Archbishop of Mainz took umbrage, he considered this an intrusion onto his territory, and demanded that a proper legal process be set in place. The Emperor backed down and set up a commission to investigate Pfefferkorn's proposals. He appointed Reuchlin as a member.

All the commissioners, with the sole exception of Reuchlin, endorsed Pfefferkorn's idea. Reuchlin, who shared many of the anti-Jewish sentiments of his age, argued that the Talmud should be preserved and studied by all Christians, because it contained valuable information on medicine and plants, good legal verdicts and many theological arguments 'against the wrong faith'.[23] He quoted the Jewish convert, Bishop Pablo de Santa Maria of Burgos who had cited the Talmud over fifty times in the book he had written defending Christianity.

Things didn't go well for Pfefferkorn. After much wrangling the Emperor decided not to proceed with the confiscation project. Pfefferkorn then turned his ire on Reuchlin, who had described his writings as ignorant rantings and

---

[21] Rummel, 2002.
[22] *The Wisdom of the Zohar*, Isaiah Tishby, I, 33 (Littman, Oxford, 1989).
[23] Burnett, 2005.

hatemongering. The two men swapped abuse. When he attacked Pfefferkorn's lack of education and poor knowledge of Hebrew, Reuchlin's fellow commissioners, who shared the same shortcomings, took exception. Reuchlin found himself first hauled before the inquisitional tribunal in Cologne and then to the episcopal court in Speyer. He was charged with promoting Judaism.

The affair became a cause célèbre. Reuchlin's fellow humanists saw the attack on him as an attack on them all. Reuchlin complained that once they were done with him, the scholastic theologians, who preferred the disciplines of logic and the Aristotelians to the humanist focus on art and language, would 'gag all poets, one after another'.[24]

The court in Speyer acquitted Reuchlin of all charges but the inquisitor appealed to Rome. The affair dragged on for years until finally, in 1520, the inquisitor's appeal was allowed, Reuchlin was convicted and ordered to pay the costs of the case. He died two years later, his scholarly reputation intact but his finances in tatters.

It wasn't quite the end of the story. In 1518, Gershom Soncino, who had pioneered the printing of the Talmud, published *De Arcana Catholicae Veritatis*, a virulent text by Petrus Galatino that lambasted the Jews and their Talmud. Although it seems odd for a Jew to publish such a work, Soncino knew exactly what he was doing.

The book's tortuous subtitle, in Wilhelm Schmidt-Biggemann's translation from the Latin, was *A Work Most Useful for the Christian Republic on the Secrets of the Catholic Truth, against the Hard-Hearted Wickedness of Our Contemporary Jews, Newly Excerpted from the Talmud and Other Hebrew Books, and in Four Languages Elegantly Composed.*[25] The author, Galatino, believed that the Second Coming was about to happen. The Talmud may have been the work of hard-hearted, wicked Jews but this didn't stop him from using it to support his argument. The first of the twelve books in his opus was called *On the Talmud, and Its Content*.

As far as Soncino was concerned, Galatino's book vindicated Reuchlin. If, as Galatino claimed, the Talmud contained the secrets of the Second Coming, confiscating and burning it was not only futile, it was counterproductive. If the Church could learn from it, why destroy it?

Soncino took a risk with his own community in publishing the work, even though the intricacies of theological struggles within the Church would have

---

[24] Rummel, 2002, p. ix.
[25] Schmidt-Biggemann, 2006.

been lost on most of them. But Soncino recognized the importance of Reuchlin, and the whole humanist endeavour, to the survival of the Talmud in sixteenth-century papal Europe.

Reuchlin's doggedness, at great personal cost, had saved the Talmud from the flames. But that wasn't all. He may have been defeated at the appeal in Rome but he had an admirer in Pope Leo X who had read Reuchlin's works on *kabbalah*.[26] When Daniel Bomberg, a printer working in Venice, approached the Vatican asking for a licence to print a full copy of the Talmud, the Pope agreed. It is worth contemplating what the Pope's answer might have been, had he not been an admirer of Reuchlin, and had Reuchlin not fought so hard against the Talmud's enemies.

[26] Burnett, 2012.

# 11

# A royal Talmud, a Protestant rabbi

Rav Yehuda quoted Rav: There are three things for which one should pray: a good king, a good year, and a good dream.[1]

## The Venetian printers

Andres de Bernaldez who had watched the Jews leave Spain, recounts how they screamed and wailed when they first saw the sea, hoping for some miracle.[2] It didn't come. The Spanish Jews boarded any boat that would have them and dispersed across southern Europe, settling wherever they could. Their wanderings were long, and wearisome. Those amongst them who had mastered the art of printing took their craft with them. They established presses in Fez, in Constantinople and in Thessalonika.[3] But they only printed occasional volumes of the Talmud. A full, printed edition was still some way off.

Many of the refugees from Spain landed in Italy. Those who settled in Rome became known as the Pope's Jews[4] and lived under a certain degree of protection. They fared better than their comrades in Florence where the vituperative preacher Savonarola was agitating to have the Jews expelled. A small number also arrived in Venice, hoping to find a haven amongst its long-established community of Jews.

Not long after they arrived, in 1509, Venice was heavily defeated in battle against the League of Cambrai, an alliance of European forces. Its straitened

---

[1] Berachot 55a.
[2] *1492, The Year Our World Began*, Felipe Fernández -Armesto (Bloomsbury, London, 2009).
[3] Heller, 2006.
[4] Wisch, 2003.

rulers were casting around to restore the ambitious, mercantile, maritime republic's reputation, and its wealth.

The Venetians saw an opportunity to raise taxes from the Jews. Although they'd lived in Venice for at least two hundred years the Jews had never been granted permanent resident status.[5] Until now. As if to reinforce the fact that they could remain in the city and pay their taxes they were shunted, in 1516, onto a small island containing a foundry, or *ghèto*. Venice became the site of the world's first ghetto. The Spanish exiles, squeezed into the ghetto alongside their co-religionists, found themselves enjoying a greater period of stability than they had imagined possible during the long years of their wandering.

Long before its military defeat Venice had established itself as a major centre of printing. It didn't invent the art, the Chinese did that and the Germans are considered to be the first to recreate it in Europe. But Venice in the late fifteenth century is where printing became an industry. The republic produced books in larger quantities, and distributed them over a wider area, than any other European city.[6]

To publish a book in Venice the printer had to obtain copyright. A complex system had been introduced in the late fifteenth century in which printers were to seek certification as to the value of the work, and a 'privilege' to print it.[7] Printers could also obtain patents for their inventions and in 1515 Daniel Bomberg, a Christian originally from Antwerp, did just that, for his new Hebrew typeface.[8]

Bomberg didn't pioneer Hebrew printing in Venice. That distinction went to Aldo Manuzio who mainly printed Greek classics but had experimented with Hebrew type in a 1498 imprint.[9] But Bomberg was the first specialist Hebrew printer in the city, and his workshop became the pivot upon which the Talmud's future history would turn.

In 1515 Daniel Bomberg was approached by an Augustinian monk, Fra Felice de Prato. Like so many others, Felice was a convert from Judaism. Unlike many other converts he was no enemy of the Talmud. Felice asked Bomberg to print some Hebrew books for him, one of which was the Talmud. The two

[5] Ravid, 1987.
[6] Bernstein, 2001.
[7] Brown, 1891.
[8] Brown, 1891.
[9] Bernstein, 2001.

men applied to the Pope for a copyright, and backed up their application with another to the Council of Venice. They took the opportunity to request an exclusive licence.

The Council was sympathetic to Bomberg's request but the hundred ducat fee he offered for the licence was too low. His second bid of one hundred and fifty ducats was also turned down. Even three hundred were not enough. Finally, at the fourth time of asking and after a year of negotiation the Council agreed to grant him an exclusive licence to print the Talmud, for five hundred ducats.[10]

Bomberg's workshop was a model of co-existence. Jews, Christians and converts worked together. Bomberg's first edition of the Talmud, which was completed by 1523, became the template for all future editions; even today most copies of the Talmud use his pagination and layout. Over the next few years he produced two more editions. Then he printed an edition of the almost-forgotten Jerusalem Talmud.

Gershom Soncino, whose printing of the Talmud predated Bomberg's by maybe forty years complained that Bomberg had copied his text. He probably had, both editions contain the same errors. But Bomberg was no plagiarist. Printing has the effect of giving texts an authoritative status, he would have been criticized if his work had differed from other printed texts already in the public domain. Bomberg may have copied Soncino when he could, but Soncino had only printed fourteen of the thirty seven volumes whereas Bomberg printed them all. Most of his work was new, and far more comprehensive. Instead of just including Rashi and *Tosafot* as Soncino had done; Bomberg's volumes contained appendices including Maimonides's commentary on the Mishnah and that of Asher ben Yehiel.[11]

Other than that which he copied from Soncino, all Bomberg's work was edited and typeset from manuscripts. They needed careful checking and cross referencing. Bomberg's editors faced a mammoth task which they astonishingly completed in only three years. When they finished, one, Cornelius Adelkind, wrote a paean of praise to Bomberg who had

> gathered and assembled the entire Talmud and these commentaries, which had been scattered in every land both distant and near and joined to them many other books.

---

[10] Brown, 1891.
[11] Heller, 2006.

And he accomplished more than his predecessors. He expended his fortune and his wealth and sent couriers, riding swift steeds, to call the finest craftsmen that could be found in all these regions to do this awesome work … .[12]

Bomberg achieved more than anybody else in making the Talmud widely accessible. News of his publication spread rapidly through Europe. The German printer Michael Buchfuhrer headed to Venice to purchase copies for distribution in Prague.[13]

But the story didn't have a happy ending. Marco Antonio Giustiniani, a well-heeled, aristocratic printer, set up a Hebrew press in competition to Bomberg. Where Bomberg's trademark had been quality, Giustiniani's was economy. He plagiarized many of Bomberg's titles, printed them badly on substandard paper and sold them cheaply. Bomberg's press closed in 1548, quite possibly due to unfair competition from Giustiniani.

But nor did Giustiniani prosper. A dispute broke out when he plagiarized another printer's commentary on Maimonides's law code, *Mishneh Torah*. Rabbi Moses Isserles, the leading rabbinic authority in Poland, decreed that it was forbidden for Jews to buy Giustiniani's books. Giustiniani appealed to the Pope. Leo X was long gone, this Pope was Julius III who shared none of Leo's humanist predisposition.

The Pope set up a commission of six cardinals to investigate the printers' dispute. Both Giustiniani and his opponents engaged Jewish converts to Christianity to represent them. The case disintegrated into an assault on the Talmud. The head of the commission, who would one day become Pope Paul IV, demanded that the Talmud be burnt.

The homes of the Jews in Rome were searched and all copies of the Talmud seized. Pyres were lit in the Campo dei Fiori in Rome on the Jewish New Year in 1553 and in St Mark's Square in Venice on Saturday 21 October of that year. The Talmud was once again consigned to the flames.[14] Any Christian caught in possession of a copy had their property seized, a quarter of its value going

---

[12]  From the colophon to tractate Soferim quoted in Heller, 2006, p. 75.

[13]  Heller, 2006.

[14]  Heller, 2013. It is probable, as Marvin Heller notes, that Meir Benayahu (Benayahu, 1971) is right in saying that the commission was investigating more than just the printing of the Mishneh Torah. The Pope's decree to burn the Talmud does not mention the Mishneh Torah and more than three years elapsed between the original complaint to the Pope and the burning. The true situation was probably far more complicated than historians have been able to unravel so far.

in reward to those who had denounced them.[15] The Hebrew printing shops in Venice closed. Only in the Duchy of Milan was the decree resisted, until 1559, when what turned out to be the last of the wave of Talmud book burnings was held in Cremona.[16]

## Forbidden books

Immolating the Talmud was just the beginning of the future Pope Paul IV's campaign to regulate theological thought. When he became Pope, one of his first acts was to order the publication of a register of forbidden books, the *Index Librorum Prohibitorum*. With the Protestant Reformation well under way in western Europe the Catholic Church's concerns about heresy were far greater than just worrying about what the Jews were reading. Over five hundred authors, both Protestants and humanists, were on the list, including Rabelais and Erasmus.[17] But the Talmud was on the list too. Bomberg's work had led to it becoming too widely available, even some of the great noble houses of Italy had copies, as the Roman Inquisition discovered when it began its policy of raiding stately homes. The Talmud had insinuated its way into the Medici Library in Florence; it even turned up in the Vatican itself.[18]

The policy of banning heretical works came in for severe criticism, even in the strictest Catholic circles. The Jesuits warned that outlawing books would be counterproductive and hinder, rather than assist, missionary activity. The Christian Hebraist, Andreas Maes protested against the proscription and immolation of the Talmud based on nothing more than the doubtful testimony of converts. Gradually the mood changed even within the Church, from an outright ban on suspect books to one of censorship instead.[19]

Five years after the list of forbidden books was published, the Council of Trent, which was responsible for the regulation of Catholic doctrine, decreed that the Talmud would be tolerated provided all 'slanderous attacks' on

---

[15] Godman, 2000.
[16] Raz-Krakotzkin, 2007.
[17] Raz-Krakotzkin, 2004.
[18] Burnett, 2012.
[19] Raz-Krakotzkin, 2007.

Christianity were censored out. It was both a reprieve from the flames for the Talmud, and tacit permission for printing to recommence in Venice.

The censorship of the Talmud was to be carried out by Jews, overseen by Inquisitors appointed by the Church. The Jewish censors had to walk a fine line. Book owners and printers who were obliged to present their volumes for censorship wanted to get them back quickly, with a minimum of fuss. The authorities wanted the books censored thoroughly. Rather than having the censors scour every possible book to see if it needed censoring, one Jewish censor, Abraham ben David Provençal worked with the inquisitors to produce an *Index Expurgatorius; a* checklist of which books were required to be censored.[20]

It wasn't just books which were subject to the censor's control, so too were the printing presses. It was in the interest of the printers that their works were censored judiciously. If the books were over-censored people wouldn't think them worth buying. Under-censored and their customers would worry that the Inquisition might come along at any moment and seize them.[21]

It was commercial impediments like this which ruined Ambrosius Froben, a printer in Basel. Some years earlier, in a rare display of unity, Swiss Protestants and Catholics had banded together when they'd heard of the opening of a Jewish printing press in Tiengen. They overruled the bishop who had given the printers a licence to print and demanded that the press be closed immediately. They'd heard that the Talmud was to be printed there.[22]

Ambrosius Froben didn't want the same thing happening to him. When he was approached by Simon von Günzberg of Frankfurt, who wanted him to print copies of the Talmud for resale, he tried to make sure he wouldn't run foul either of the censors or of zealous, local burghers. The contract he signed with Günzberg named Marco Marino, the papal inquisitor of Venice, as the principal censor. He also engaged his own in-house censor to supervise the day-to-day works. The result was a heavily expurgated edition, which satisfied the German authorities but not the customers. The Basel edition of the Talmud flopped. Froben had worried too much about the authorities, and not enough about his customers.

Over and again the Italian Jews tried to produce an expurgated version of the Talmud which would meet the Council's criteria. But, whatever its enemies

---

[20] Sonne, 1943.
[21] Sonne, 1943.
[22] Burnett, 1998.

believed, the Talmud doesn't dwell much on Christianity. It had developed in a Muslim environment, Christianity for the most part was outside its frame of reference. There are scattered references to Jesus in the Talmud, but many of them tend to refer to him in passing, whilst dealing with another subject. As Peter Schäfer has shown, the handful of references tend to be little more than polemical counter-narratives that parody Gospel stories.[23] They are more likely to have been directed at the competing Christian sects in Sassanian Babylon than serious attempts to undermine Christian belief.[24]

With very little material in it that dealt with Christian theology, there wasn't much for the Jews to identify and expunge. But this didn't satisfy the censors who needed to show their superiors wholesale obliteration of the text. They were forced into a corner, censoring items that didn't need censoring, just to prove they were doing their work properly.

To try to regulate the situation and pre-empt the demands of the censor, a council of rabbis meeting in Ferrara in 1554 instituted a regime of self-censorship.[25] They decreed that any newly published Hebrew book would have to carry the approbation of three rabbis.[26] But even this measure failed to satisfy the Talmud's critics and in 1596 a new edition of the forbidden books list renewed the blanket ban on the Talmud. The era of printing the Talmud in Italy had come to an end.

## Henry VIII's Great Matter

In 1529 Richard Croke, an envoy of England's King Henry VIII arrived in Venice. He had been sent to consult the Talmud. Henry was in the middle of his 'Great Matter', his struggle to get permission from the Pope to divorce Catherine of Aragon, youngest daughter of Isabella and Ferdinand, who had expelled the Jews and their Talmud from Spain.

---

[23] Shäfer, 2007.
[24] Shäfer, 2007.
[25] Popper, 1969. See also Stephen G. Burnett, Hebrew Censorship in Hanau: A Mirror of Jewish-Christian Coexistence in Seventeenth-Century Germany, in *The Expulsion of the Jews: 1492 and After*, R. B. Waddington and A. H. Williamson (eds) (Garland, New York, 1994).
[26] More recently, however, Daniel Ungar has argued that the rabbis' decree was a stratagem for protecting the copyright of the author and publisher. Daniel Ungar, Copyright Enforcement by Praise and Curse: The Colourful Development of Jewish Intellectual Property *Intellectual Property Quarterly* 1, 2011, pp. 86–107.

Initially Henry thought his chances of having the marriage dissolved were good. It was only a few years since his sister, Queen Margaret of Scotland had been granted permission to divorce, as had King Louis XII of France. But as David Katz points out, Henry had left it too late. Rome had just been sacked by the Holy Roman Emperor, Charles V; the Pope was virtually a prisoner with no authority to take independent decisions, and Charles was a nephew of Catherine of Aragon, who was fighting against the divorce with all her might.[27]

One of the stratagems that Henry used to justify a divorce was to argue that his marriage to Catherine had been invalid from the outset. She had previously been married to Henry's brother Arthur, but he had died young. The book of Leviticus in the Old Testament prohibits marriage to the widow of a brother. Henry had only been able to wed Catherine after obtaining a dispensation from the previous Pope, on the grounds that her previous marriage to Arthur had not been consummated. Now the future Bishop of London, John Stokesley, was advising him that the dispensation should not have been granted since the Pope had no power to overturn a divine law. Stokesley said the marriage between Catherine and Henry should never have taken place and it needed to be annulled.[28]

The trouble was that although Leviticus forbade a man from marrying his brother's widow Deuteronomy demanded that, if there had been no children from her first marriage, the widow had to marry her dead husband's brother. According to Deuteronomy, Henry had been obliged to marry Catherine. Unless he could find a way out.

John Stokesley argued that the requirement to marry a dead brother's widow, known as levirate marriage, only applied to the Jews.[29] He suggested that Henry find Jewish scholars who would bring evidence from the Talmud to support this view, and to show that in fact the Jews had abandoned this law.[30] Stokesley wanted to argue the Deuteronomy injunction out of existence. Henry imported a copy of Bomberg's printed Talmud into England for his advisers to consult and Richard Croke was despatched to Italy to find Talmudists who would help him.

In Venice, Croke engaged Francesco Giorgi to help him. Giorgi was a leading Christian Kabbalist with good contacts in the ghetto. Giorgi introduced Croke

---

[27] Katz, 1994.
[28] Chibi, 1994.
[29] Chibi, 1997.
[30] Katz, 1994.

to Elijah Halfon, a rabbi and Kabbalist, who confirmed that levirate marriage, like most of Jewish law, only applied to Jews. However, the Vatican also engaged a Talmudist, Jacob Mantino, an exile from Spain, who took the other side and confirmed the Pope's view.

The situation wasn't helped by a separate quarrel between Halfon and Mantino, over a messianic pretender named Solomon Molcho. Molcho was a *converso* from Portugal who believed he was the Messiah, and who had attracted a sizeable following. Mantino was an avowed opponent of Molcho, whilst Halfon was a supporter. Their conflicting opinions on the question of Henry's divorce were influenced by their personal antagonism over Solomon Molcho.

Realizing that Halfon's testimony would not sway the Pope, Richard Croke turned to Marco Raphael, a Jewish convert to Christianity whose principal claim to fame was that he had invented an invisible ink. Raphael enthusiastically supported Henry's position and Croke brought him to England to testify in front of Henry. However Raphael's evidence turned out to not be of much use since he could not confirm that Henry was free from the stricture to marry his brother's widow. Henry turned his not inconsiderable ire on Raphael and we hear no more of him.

But at the end of the day Henry's whole exercise of relying on the Talmud to legitimize his divorce turned out to be fruitless. As things turned out his lover, Anne Boleyn, became pregnant. Henry broke from the Catholic Church, divorced Catherine on his own authority and married Anne.

## The Hebrew Republic

The seventeenth century saw the development of modern political thought. Ideas that we take for granted today, such as individual rights and freedoms, the nation state and religious tolerance all began to emerge during this period. One of the drivers for these new ideas was the revival of the Hebrew language by the Christian Hebraists and their investigation of the biblical text.

Some Christian thinkers began to see the Bible's account of how the ancient Israelite nation was governed as a blueprint for the administration of their own nations. They believed that the Old Testament presented the ideal political constitution, one designed by God for the Children of Israel.[31]

---

[31] Nelson, 2010.

Some, notably Jean Bodin in France, saw the Israelite monarchy under King David and his descendants as the paradigm; for them the Hebrew Bible advocated the rule of kings.[32] They backed up their claims with a passage from Deuteronomy:

> When you come to the land the Lord your God gives you and have taken possession of it and settled there, and you say, 'Let us set a king over us like all the nations around us', you may appoint a king whom the Lord your God chooses.[33]

It is an ambivalent passage which permits, but by no means demands, that the Israelites appoint a king over themselves. Not all Hebraists read it in the same way. They didn't all believe that the Hebrew Bible advocated monarchy. Some looked elsewhere in the Bible for evidence of the ideal government. They found plenty of options; aristocracy, theocracy, even democracy. As Kalman Neuman puts it, Political Hebraists did not share a political vision, but they did create a common language of discourse. In time this discourse would influence the great political thinkers of the seventeenth century, including Hobbes and Spinoza.[34]

Although they delved deeply into the biblical text most Hebraists had neither the knowledge of Jewish law nor sufficient command of Hebrew to investigate the Talmud, nor even the many commentaries that had by now spun off from it. But some began to feel that the Hebrew Bible alone could not lead them to a full understanding of what they regarded as the idealized, divinely sanctioned form of national government. And so, from amongst the Hebraists arose a small group with the skills and erudition to look beyond the Bible itself. They had a few tools to help them do this, including an Aramaic lexicon that Johannes Buxtorf, perhaps the most erudite of all Hebraists, was engaged in producing in Basel.[35]

They based their investigations on the prophet Samuel's warning to the Israelites when they decided to ask God for a king 'to judge us, like all the nations'.[36] Samuel adjures them:

---

[32] Bartolucci, 2007.

[33] Deuteronomy 17.14–15.

[34] Neuman, 2005.

[35] Not all who cited the Talmud and other rabbinic sources were skilled Hebraists. Many, such as Carlo Sigonio, a pioneer in the field of Hebrew Republicanism, freely admitted that they had no command of Hebrew. Sigonio and many others relied on translations of rabbinic works which by now were becoming freely available.

[36] 1 Samuel 8.5.

This will be rule of the king who will reign over you: He will take your sons for himself and place them in his chariots and as his horsemen, and they will run in front of his chariots. Some he will appoint to be commanders of thousands and commanders of fifties, and to plough his ground and reap his harvest, and to make his weapons of war and equipment for his chariots. He will take your daughters to be perfumers and cooks and bakers. He will take the best of your fields and vineyards and olive groves and give them to his servants. He will tithe your seeds and your vineyards and give it to his officials and servants. He will take your menservants and maidservants and the best of your young men and your donkeys and he will put them to his work. He will tithe your flocks, and you will be his slaves.[37]

This passage seemed to prove that the Israelites had been wrong in asking for a king. Monarchy was not the way to go. Republicanism seemed to be a much better option.

Wilhelm Shickard, Professor of Hebrew at the University of Tubingen, marshalled the Talmudic and rabbinic sources on the passages from Deuteronomy and Samuel in his legal treatise, *The Hebrew King's Law*. His sources were used in a bitter dispute between Claude de Saumaise, or Salmasius, and John Milton, author of *Paradise Lost*. Salmasius had written an impassioned defence of the monarchy after the execution of England's Charles I. Milton, a staunch republican who equated monarchy with idolatry[38] had written a fierce riposte. Neither man, it appears, could read the Talmud[39] but Shickard had set out the sources clearly enough for Milton to accuse Salmasius of plagiarizing Shickard[40] and misrepresenting him.[41] The Hebrew Republic, based on Talmudic sources marks the beginning of modern republican, political theory.

---

[37] 1 Samuel 8.11–17.

[38] Nelson, 2010.

[39] On the question of Milton's ability to read Talmud see *Milton and the Rabbis: Hebraism, Hellenism and Christianity*, Jeffrey S. Shoulson, Columbia University Press, New York, 2001; *Torah and Law* in Paradise Lost, Jason P. Rosenblatt (Princeton University Press, Princeton, 1994), Mattern, 2009 and the sources cited in Nelson, 2010, p. 160n. 66.

[40] Mattern, 2009.

[41] Nelson, 2010.

## New Israel

The Dutch Republic had recently freed itself from Spanish rule. The newly independent nation bought into a founding myth that proclaimed them, like the biblical Israelites, as having been redeemed from slavery. They even called themselves the New Israel. It seems like a harmless name but it was responsible for a deep split in Netherlands Protestantism during the early part of the seventeenth century.

For the orthodox Calvinists, the victory of New Israel over Catholic Spain had been a vindication of their true faith. They believed they were now obliged to enforce that faith by regulating religious belief. Their opponents argued that by defeating Spain, New Israel had scored a victory over tyranny. As such, it was their duty to establish a free, tolerant society in which people could follow their conscience in religious matters.[42]

Hugo Grotius, one of the pioneers of modern international law and a former child prodigy who had gone to university at the age of eleven, cited the example of the Hebrew republic to support the tolerant view. In a nutshell, he argued that the ancient Hebrew republic was the ideal society because it had been ordained by God. In this society all law, both religious and civil, had been placed into the hands of a single, law-making body, the Sanhedrin. This implied that both religious and civil law have an identical purpose, to regulate society. Since matters of personal conscience and religious belief have no bearing on the smooth running of society, the Sanhedrin, and by implication the Dutch law makers, have no jurisdiction over personal belief. Conscience and faith, argued Grotius, lie outside the law.

Up to this point he was doing little more than restating the arguments of the sixteenth-century Swiss theologian Thomas Erastus. But Grotius then moved on to cite the Talmud. He showed that that under certain circumstances the Sanhedrin had the power to suspend religious law and to punish those who 'commit a crime in sacred matters'[43] The civil court therefore had absolute jurisdiction even over religious matters. There were no grounds for a separate religious authority beyond the government of the state. The Talmud proved, to Grotius's satisfaction, that religious tolerance was axiomatic.[44]

---

[42]  Bodian, 2006.

[43]  Nelson, 2010.

[44]  For a full treatment of Grotius's arguments see Nelson, 2010, p. 97ff.

Petrus Cunaeus was a friend and colleague of Hugo Grotius. A professor of Law at Leiden University and amongst the most influential writers on the Hebrew Republic, Cunaeus pioneered a new perspective on land ownership. The Bible had decreed that the Land of Israel was to be divided equitably amongst the twelve Hebrew tribes, and that territory could not be sold in perpetuity. Cunaeus quoted Maimonides and the 'requirements of Talmudic law'[45] to show that his theories of land ownership would lead to a harmonious and equitable society.[46]

Political Hebraists, whose Protestantism was firmly wedded to the belief that the Jews had to be converted, made full use of the Talmud, but they did not flatter or lionize it. They recognized the ability of the ancient Talmudists to interpret the biblical text but in their eyes this was because of their command of the ancient Hebrew language, not due to any merit possessed by the Talmud itself. They used it to develop their political ideas but Cunaeus rejected 'its trifles', by which he meant the allegorical and non-legal material which supports Jewish tradition. Indeed, he considers the Karaites, who considered the principles of the Talmud to be worthless, and who focused only on the biblical text, to be 'more intelligent' than the Talmudists.[47] Likewise, Hugo Grotius only supported the rights of Jews to settle in Holland because he believed that the Dutch Reformed Church was the most likely to be able to convert them.[48]

## England's Protestant Chief Rabbi

The Hebraists in England were less disdainful towards the Jews than their European colleagues. They could afford to be, officially there had been no Jews in England since Edward I expelled them in 1290. They wouldn't be formally readmitted until midway through the seventeenth century, when Menasseh ben Israel, the leading rabbi in Amsterdam and a correspondent of Hugo Grotius

---

[45] See Ziskind, 1978 for the full argument. Cunaeus based his analysis on the minority view of Rabbi Yehuda in Nedarim 61a who absorbs the Jubilee year into the beginning of the subsequent seven-year cycle, rather than treating it as the outside the cycle. Usually, unless there is a good reason, the majority view in a Talmud discussion is the one that is adopted by subsequent law makers.

[46] Laplanche, 2008.

[47] Laplanche, 2008.

[48] Bodian, 1999.

and Petrus Cunaeus,[49] began to lobby Cromwell for their return.[50] It was the absence of any Jewish scholarly presence in Shakespeare's sceptred isle that made the achievements of John Selden, described by Milton as 'the chief of learned men' and by Grotius as 'the glory of the English nation',[51] so remarkable.

John Selden was a lawyer by profession. In his mid-thirties he had caused a rumpus within the Church by arguing in his book *The Historie of Tithes* that priests did not have a divine right to receive tithes from their parishioners. This had been a burning political issue for some years. Selden's book showed that there was no direct historical connection between the tithes that the Old Testament demanded for the Hebrew priests, and the voluntary system of tithing which had found its way into the Church in the early medieval period. His work threatened to deprive the clergy of a significant proportion of their income.

Selden was elected to Parliament in 1624. Five years later he found himself on the wrong side of a dispute between the king's supporters and their opponents. He insulted the king's chief spokesman in Parliament, took the side of John Rolle, an MP who was refusing to pay customs duties and commanded the Speaker of the House to put the matter to a vote, on pain of being removed from office. He was hauled before the Privy Council for his pains, and cast into the Tower of London.[52] It was from the Tower that he wrote the letter to his friend, the antiquarian scholar Sir Robert Cotton, which, according to Jason Rosenblatt, would change the course of his life and deepen his scholarship. Selden, whose enforced idleness left him with 'much time here before me', asked Robert Cotton to borrow for him a copy of the Talmud from the Westminster Abbey Library.[53]

Over the next five years Selden was in and out of the Tower. It took an apology to the king before he was granted absolute freedom. Amongst the many things he did with his imposed leisure was to study the Talmud. Unlike the Hebraists on the Continent he almost certainly had no tutor, there were no

[49] Ziskind, 1978.

[50] There almost certainly were a few Jews in England throughout the whole of this period, but in Selden's day at least there were only a handful, mainly ex-conversos with links to the Amsterdam community, and it is unlikely that he had contact with any of them.

[51] Rosenblatt, 2008, p. 105 and frontispiece.

[52] 'Selden, John (1584–1654)', Paul Christianson in *Oxford Dictionary of National Biography*, H. C. G. Matthew and Brian Harrison (eds) (Oxford, Oxford University Press, 2004).

[53] (Rosenblatt, 2008).

learned Jews that he could consult. But his depth of learning was such that for the rest of his life he studied the Bomberg edition of the Talmud that Cotton had obtained from Westminster Abbey, and composed six works of Talmudic scholarship, covering topics as diverse as natural law, divorce, inheritance, the calendar, the Karaites and his final work, a two-thousand-page study of Jewish jurisprudence.

Selden's Talmudic writings influenced a generation of British political thinkers. Jason Rosenblatt, in his masterly study, *Renaissance England's Chief Rabbi,* demonstrated how Selden's works inspired Isaac Newton, Milton, Ben Jonson and Hobbes, amongst others. The German Hebraist Johann Stephanus Rittangel, knowing full well that Selden was not a Jew, nevertheless wrote to him as 'Rabbi' Selden. Rosenblatt laments the obscurity into which his Talmudic works subsequently fell.

The Talmud has had many great and distinguished scholars during its long lifetime. But none quite like John Selden. His name deserves to rank amongst them.

# 12

# The wisdom of the Greeks

Yohanan ben Zakkai said: If you have a sapling in your hand and someone says 'the Messiah has come'; first plant the tree, then go to greet the Messiah.[1]

The Talmud's encounter with the world of Protestant scholarship was only brief. Their paths diverged in the face of new scientific discoveries, new ways of thinking and, from the Talmud's side at least, new things to worry about.

The Talmud had encountered many enemies. But even those who saw it as an object of contempt, to be destroyed and eradicated from human history, agreed with its underlying premises; that the world had been created by God who continued in some unknowable way to manage its affairs, and that the Hebrew Bible was his unmediated word. The Talmud's enemies disagreed with each and every conclusion that its compilers drew from those facts, but the facts themselves were immutable. Or they had been, up till now.

One of the incontrovertible facts of God's creation was the way in which the universe operated. The Bible stated quite clearly that Heaven and Earth were created first, with the sun, moon and stars coming into existence on the fourth day. The earth clearly stood at the centre of God's creation and any fool could see, just by looking at the sky, that the heavenly bodies orbited it. When Nicolaus Copernicus proved from his observations that the earth revolved around the sun, he was roundly denounced by Orthodox Church theologians. As for the Talmudists, most of them were so immersed in their world of study that the news never reached them. Those who did hear mention of it paid little attention. Scientific progress fell into the category of 'Greek Wisdom'. It held no interest for them.

But even in the most closed societies there are always a few who are open to new ideas. Particularly when it came to astronomy, which had always occupied

---

[1] Avot d'Rabbi Natan 31b.

a special place in the Talmudic world. The Babylonian Talmud, conceived in the ancient birthplace of astrological and astronomical study, contains a number of passages which speculate on the size of the heavens, the seasons of the zodiac and the movements of the stars.[2] Several medieval Talmudists had written astronomical treatises.[3] Many Arabic astronomical works had been translated into Hebrew.[4]

The genesis of their astronomical interest lay in a practice in ancient Jerusalem. Its high court had been required to regulate the calendar by proclaiming that the new moon had been sighted. Witnesses would appear before the court declaring they had seen the new moon, but they couldn't always be taken at their word; frequently they got it wrong. They may have mistaken the last appearance of the waning moon for the beginnings of the new one. Or they could have been misled by a patch of light from the setting sun reflecting off a cloudy sky. Gamaliel II, whom we met in the first chapter, had charts and calculations on the wall of his study showing the shape, orientation, position and size of the new moon at different times of the year. He would examine the witnesses to see if what they had seen corresponded to his astronomical charts.[5]

Nicolaus Copernicus had studied at the University of Cracow, in Poland. The city would become home to Moses Isserles, who as we've seen, had commented extensively on the *Shulchan Aruch*, Joseph Caro's definitive law code. Isserles had inherited the Talmud's interest in astronomy, he even wrote two treatises on astronomical matters. He has been cited as the founding father of Talmudic astronomy in Poland,[6] placing him at the beginning of a process in which modern technical and scientific discoveries were incorporated into Talmud study.[7] But although Isserles lived in the same city as had Copernicus and was in his teenage years when the great astronomer published his theory, he either didn't know about it or, more probably, dismissed it; in his universe the sun continued to revolve around the earth. But despite his old-world astronomical

---

[2] See, for example, Pesachim 94a–b, Eruvin 56a, Rosh Hashanah 20b–21a and 24b–25a.

[3] The best-known include Abraham ibn Ezra, Levi ben Gershom (Gersonides) and Solomon ibn Gabirol in his work *Keter Malchut*.

[4] The *Almagest* by the second century, Alexandrian astrologer Ptolemy dominated astronomical thinking throughout the medieval period. It was translated into Hebrew by Jacob Anatoli and many Hebrew commentaries written on it.

[5] Mishnah Rosh Hashanah 2.8. Gamaliel had no fear of Greek Wisdom. In Sotah 49b, his son Shimon records that his students would study Greek Wisdom in his father's house.

[6] Fishman, 1997.

[7] Ruderman, 1995.

view he did open up the subject to his Talmudic students. One in particular was profoundly influenced by what he heard.[8]

David Gans had studied the Talmud under Isserles before leaving Cracow for Prague, the seat of the Holy Roman Emperor, Rudolph II. Rudolphine Prague, as it was known, was at that time a sizzling hub of cultural, scientific and intellectual activity, a place where anyone with a creative talent or an enquiring mind wanted to be. Gans, who took a far greater interest in science than most of his Talmudic contemporaries, came into contact with some of the leading practitioners of the age, including the imperial astronomer Tyco Brahe and his assistant Johannes Kepler.

Brahe and Kepler worked out of an observatory that the Emperor had made available to them in his summer palace near Prague. On three separate occasions Gans spent five days with them in the observatory which contained, according to Gans's account, 'great and wondrous astronomical instruments, that no eye had ever beheld'.[9]

One of the astronomical passages in the Talmud discusses whether the planets revolve or are stationary.[10] The Talmud records that the 'sages of Israel' abandoned their view that the planets revolved against the backdrop of the sky, in favour of the view of the 'sages of the world', presumably Ptolemy's disciples in Alexandria,[11] who maintained that they were stationary but affixed onto a revolving sky. Gans records a conversation he had with Brahe in which the astronomer expresses astonishment that the Talmud had changed its opinion. Brahe told Gans that according his observations the rabbis of the Talmud had been right and the other sages wrong.[12]

Gans was not the first Talmudist to have questioned the retraction. One of his teachers, Yehuda Loew, known as the Maharal of Prague, legendary creator of

[8] Fishman, 1997.
[9] David Gans, *Naim v'nehmad*, Jesnitz, 1743, p. 84b.
[10] Pesahim 94b.
[11] Neher, 1986.
[12] David Gans, *Naim v'nehmad*, Jesnitz, 1743, p. 15b,

the *golem*,[13] had already expressed a similar view.[14] The Talmud doesn't explain why it had originally held a dissenting view about the rotation of the planets, nor why it reversed its opinion. Rabbi Yehuda, the author of the Mishnah, whom the Talmud cites as the person responsible for the change of opinion, probably considered the new Ptolemaic system to be scientifically correct and could see no good reason for maintaining the old position. If so his attitude to science, in the second century, was far more in the spirit of the world in which Gans aspired to move, a world in the grip of a scientific revolution, than those he had left behind in Cracow, who ignored Copernicus's discoveries.

It wasn't just in the realm of theory that the new science challenged the Talmud. New discoveries also affected Talmudic law. The Talmud believed that lice, unlike fleas, do not sexually reproduce.[15] Presumably it assumed that they spontaneously generate in the skin or fur of the animal in which they live. This belief has a legal consequence. The Talmud forbids the killing of animals on the Sabbath. But if lice do not sexually reproduce, then they are not animals. So, although it is forbidden to kill fleas, which do sexually reproduce, it's OK to kill lice.

Isaac Lampronti, the author of a Talmudic encyclopedia[16] and a 'most celebrated physician-theologian amongst the learned'[17] raised this question with his teacher Judah Briel. Since it was now recognized that lice, like all other creatures, were born through sexual reproduction, shouldn't the law allowing them to be killed on the Sabbath be abolished? Briel did not agree. One of the reasons he gave was that the rabbis of the Talmud had ultimately been proved correct about the rotation of the planets. They'd been vindicated and should never have given way. The same thing applied here, argued Briel. Modern

---

[13] The *golem* was a mythical humanoid made of clay into which its creator instilled life. The best-known *golem* is the one said to have been made by the Maharal of Prague, Yehuda Loew, a giant Frankenstein-like monster, created to protect his community from anti-Semitic attacks. Mary Shelley's Frankenstein is possibly modelled on *golem* legends. See the chapter, The Golem, the Invention of a Tradition, in *Languages of Community: The Jewish Experience in the Czech Lands*, Hillel J. Kieval (University of California Press, Berkeley, 2000).

[14] Yehuda Loew, *Kitvei HaMaharal: Be'er Hagolah* (Hoenig & Sons, London, 1964), p.109.

[15] Shabbat 107b.

[16] Only the first volume, and part of the second of *Pahad Yitzhak* appeared during Lampronti's lifetime. Publication of the entire encyclopedia was not completed until 1887, one hundred and thirty years after his death.

[17] The quote comes from a stone table affixed to the house in Ferrera, Italy, in which Lampronti used to live (Ruderman, 1995).

science had probably got this wrong, just like Ptolemy had. The Talmud's view on how lice reproduced would, said Briel, probably one day be vindicated.[18]

The scientific advances which prompted Lampronti's question would change the Talmud's world, just as it would everywhere. But the Talmud had no bone to pick with science, it may have taken it time to adjust to the new discoveries but science was nothing more than the means of understanding God's creation. A far greater challenge than science came from philosophy. The philosophy of one person in particular. He didn't particularly have the Talmud in his sights, his aim was broader than that. But the challenge was felt most keenly by the Talmud because, as befits a Talmudic paradox, it came from someone who had been reared in its orbit.

## The first secular European

Baruch Spinoza was born in Amsterdam in 1632 to a family, who like most of the city's Jews at the time, were *conversos*, recently arrived from Portugal. Most of Spinoza's biographers assume that he had received an education in Talmud but, as Edward Feld has argued, there is no reason to assume that. As a child he received a formal Jewish education and he was well versed in Bible and the Hebrew language. But rarely in his writings does he mention, let alone quote the Talmud, only six times altogether, and even then his references are offhand and careless.[19] It's odd because he is a stern critic of Maimonides's philosophy and of the belief in the divine authorship of the Bible. If he had been familiar with the Talmud one would expect him to offer a more systematic treatment of it, since it was a fundamental part of the system he was arguing against. Feld suggests that he left school at an early age, before he had graduated to the Talmud classes.[20]

Nevertheless, whether Spinoza studied Talmud or not, we do know that he was taught by people who were well versed in the discipline, and their methods of thought would certainly have influenced his. As did the Amsterdam that he lived in, a wealthy, tolerant city, enjoying the Golden Age of the new Dutch Republic, with its burgeoning worldwide trade and expanding empire. This was the city where Rembrandt was painting, where Descartes had lived, where boats

---

[18] Ruderman, 1995.
[19] Nadler, 2001.
[20] Feld, 1989.

arrived daily from Borneo, Africa, Brazil and North America carrying exotic cargoes, strange animals and precious merchandise. Amsterdam had its dark side too, the West India Company played its part in the slave trade, populating the plantations of the Caribbean with victims seized from their homes in Africa. Economically prosperous, its elegant, canal-side houses filled with art, sculpture and fine furnishings, Amsterdam was a place of merchants, bankers, artists and intellectuals. We saw how the Political Hebraists had flourished in Amsterdam; it was a city where minds were open to new ideas, and Baruch Spinoza's fertile mind, seeking to forge coherence from multiplicity, was foremost amongst them.

Spinoza was a fiercely rational philosopher who challenged religious thinking and current beliefs in the nature of God. He could not accept that there is a divine Being who created and controlled the world, but that didn't mean he denied the existence of God. For Spinoza, God and nature are one and the same. As for the Bible, he was the first to maintain that it was the product of human minds, conceived by inspired people. The Bible, according to Spinoza, is a system of law and ritual which, if followed, promises worldly happiness, but it has nothing to do with eternity.

Needless to say Spinoza's theology did not go down well with the Jewish community in Amsterdam. He was excommunicated at the age of twenty three, before he had even published anything. He spent the rest of his life developing his philosophy whilst earning a living as a lens grinder, a craft at which he excelled but which didn't bring him worldly happiness. The dust which he inhaled as he polished the glass for his lenses killed him before he was forty five.

Spinoza was a Jew and a philosopher of religion, but he wasn't a philosopher of Judaism. His ideas about God were anathema to both Jews and Christians. The Talmudic world rejected his ideas, and continues to do so today, but it was unable to escape the consequences of his life and thought. By subjecting religion to the new tools of rationalism he opened up the Talmud to a new form of investigation. That's why he is part of the Talmud's story. He separated the realms of reason and ritual and in so doing laid the foundations for nineteenth-century thinkers to construct an academic discipline in which Talmudic texts would be subjected to the same forms of analysis and criticism as any other work of classic literature.[21]

---

[21] Silverman, 1995 sees Spinoza as important in the cultural emancipation of the Jews through the *Wissenschaft des Judentums* (Scientific Study of Judaism) movement and his separation of the reason and ritual as important for the development of Reform Judaism.

From this point forward religious theorists who reflected the new ways of thinking would appropriate Spinoza to validate their ideologies.[22] In time a Jewish enlightenment would emerge, which would simultaneously enrich and challenge the Talmud. The excommunicated Spinoza, who never stopped thinking of himself as a Jew, unwittingly created the conditions for the Talmud's entrance into modernity. He marks a turning point between the medieval and the modern in Jewish religious thinking.[23]

## Away from the light

The scientific revolution didn't reach everywhere, and it didn't always survive in those places it did reach. Prague had been a centre of scientific innovation under Rudolf II. It didn't last. The devastation of the Thirty Years' War and the victory of the Counter-Reformation marked its demise. A similar decline took place in Poland; Cracow's reputation for astronomical excellence came to an end; social instability and the rise of obscurantism impeded the influx of new ideas.

The Talmudic communities of eastern Europe, in Poland and Lithuania, whose populations had swelled over the previous centuries, knew little of science, and even less of the Enlightenment that was coming in its wake. They carried on much as they had done for centuries. All that distinguished them from their Christian neighbours was their faith, their language and their various customs. Including their educational system. Education was considered to be a communal responsibility, and was administered accordingly. At its heart sat the Talmud. A communal edict in Lithuania in 1622 required every town or village which was large enough to engage a rabbi to maintain a Talmudic school, or *yeshiva*.

Boys (only boys, the modern world was still dawning) would attend *yeshiva* from the age of thirteen. Well-off families paid for their sons' education, those who could not afford it were supported from communal funds. Learning was meritorious, students were looked upon kindly in the divine realm and it was a long-established tradition that those whose work prevented them from studying could reap the same reward by providing financial support to poor students. Lodgings would be found in local homes for the pupils, the better-off

---

[22] Schwartz, 2012.
[23] Schwartz, 2012.

households would invite students from the *yeshiva* to dine at their Sabbath table, and sometimes during the week. For the rest of the time the young men were likely to go hungry. In a mainly agricultural world where most trades were forbidden to Jews, every parent's ambition for their son was that he would become, if not the Messiah himself, then at least a renowned Talmud scholar.

Life was hard but in many ways the *yeshiva* world was no different from any other cloistered, religious environment. It looked inwards and paid little attention to events beyond its borders. Until the day in 1648 when the Cossack warlord Bohdan Chmielnicki led an uprising against state and Church subjection of his people. His call to arms was to rid the land of its Jews. The horrific violence that his hoards perpetrated resulted in the slaughter at a conservative estimate of seventy five thousand and possibly up to three hundred thousand souls across a swathe of the Ukraine and Poland. It left behind nothing but a climate of despair and confusion, a populace bereft of hope. The Chmielnicki massacres helped create the conditions for the brief success of one of the strangest characters to enter the pages of Talmudic history.

## A messianic debacle

The Ottoman Empire was the dominant power in the Islamic world. Its borders took in the Balkan states, Greece, Turkey, the whole of North Africa and Arabia. But despite the vast territory it covered, economically and culturally it had long been in decline. The Golden Age of Islamic philosophy, mathematics and science was but a distant memory. The Talmudic communities in the Ottoman Empire were submerged in the same state of intellectual paralysis as everyone else. The ancient centres, where the academies had once flourished, now rarely produced Talmudists of distinction. Nor were the Ottoman lands touched by the currents of enlightenment and secularism which were beginning to flow through Europe.

Although the Talmud and the *hadith* had developed side by side, scholarly contact between the two communities had all but ceased long ago. Notwithstanding the trade links which formed part of everyday life, Jews and Muslims each lived in their own cultural silos. There was little engagement of any sort between the Talmud and its host communities.[24] The only time they

---

[24] Braude and Lewis, 1982.

came into any sort of prolonged contact was when one local ruler or another decreed an expulsion or persecution of the Jews in his land.

Nobody foresaw the maelstrom that was about to rip through the becalmed intellectual climate. Even now, with the benefit of hindsight, it appears quite unthinkable. Individuals, families and whole communities across the Ottoman Empire and Europe were caught up in one of the most phenomenal eruptions of collective delusion the world has ever witnessed. It was not the result of any external threat and yet it threatened the Talmud more than any burning, or censor's pen had ever done.

A Jewish tradition holds that the Messiah will be born on the anniversary of the Temple's destruction, the ninth day of the Hebrew month of Av. Shabbetai Tzvi, around whom this episode in the Talmud's story revolves, was born on that very anniversary, in the Turkish city of Smyrna on the Aegean coast, in 1626. His name, deriving from the Hebrew word for Sabbath suggests that he arrived in the world on a Saturday. We don't know whether the child's parents thought that the date and day of his arrival was a portent but as a young student of Talmud and *kabbalah* he gained a reputation as an 'inspired man' and attracted a circle of enthusiastic followers around him.[25]

Tzvi suffered from an extreme form of bipolar disorder. He was prone to profound fits of melancholy, and states of great elation. In 1648, when news of the Chmielnicki slaughters in Poland reached Smyrna, Tzvi heard a voice proclaiming him the saviour of Israel.[26]

Over the next few years his behaviour became increasingly erratic. He married three times, each time he refused, or was unable, to consummate the marriage and divorced his wife within a few months. He repeatedly proclaimed himself as Messiah, engaged in bizarre, pseudo-*kabbalistic* rituals and publicly pronounced the forbidden, mystical name of God, the mention of which had always been treated with the greatest gravity.[27] It had only ever been enunciated once a year, in a state of great awe and solemnity, by the High Priest in the Jerusalem Temple. Since the Temple's destruction, a millennium and a half earlier, no one had dared utter it.

---

[25] Scholem, 1973.

[26] Scholem, 1973.

[27] The importance of *kabbalah* in Shabbetai Tzvi's messianism has divided scholars. Gershom Scholem elucidates Tzvi's quasi-*kabbalistic* system in great detail (Scholem, 1973) but later scholars, particularly Moshe Idel, take issue with Scholem's view, cf. Idel, 2000.

Shabbetai Tzvi's behaviour publicly challenged the authority of the Talmud. As he ritually desecrated religious law he would utter what was to become his trademark blessing, to God 'who permits the forbidden'.[28]

By all accounts Shabbetai Tzvi, who at times was charming, charismatic and blessed with a beautiful singing voice, could be wild and frightening. As his dark moods became more frequent people stopped seeing him as a benign fool and began to regard him as dangerous. Eventually he was forced to leave Smyrna. He began a period of wandering, during which he seemed to return to a calmer frame of mind. He ended up in Jerusalem where he heard about Nathan of Gaza, a young man, who it was said, could reveal the secret root of a soul, and provide a kabbalistic formula for its cure. Shabbetai, still convinced he was the Messiah, travelled to Gaza to meet him.

When they met Nathan was quickly won over to the belief that Shabbetai Tzvi was indeed the Messiah. Shabbetai, for his part, was overwhelmed by Nathan's gift of prophecy. Within just a few months Shabbetai's personal delusions, brought to public attention by Nathan's remarkable PR skills, were to spread throughout the Jewish world. Communities in Poland and Lithuania, so recently traumatized by the slaughters perpetrated by Chmielnicki now rejoiced, the Messiah had arrived, salvation was at hand. Elsewhere in Europe, North Africa, Arabia and the Near East, where the reports of the massacres had been an ominous omen from a foreign land, people counted themselves lucky not just to have lived far from the slaughter, but to have been born in the generation when the long-awaited Messiah had arrived. They were in no doubt. Fifteen hundred years of exile and suffering were drawing to a close.

Shabbetai Tzvi's Messianic claims, the enthusiasm of his supporters and the fierce opposition he engendered, had a devastating impact. The faith of those who believed the promise of a new, utopian world would have been touching were it not so misplaced. The dismay of their friends and relatives, who saw their beloved ones succumbing to the madness, often casting aside their livelihoods and possessions to chase mere dreams and promises, turned to rage as the delusion spread. Families and communities were torn apart. Those who believed in Tzvi regarded those who did not as infidels. The Talmud was abandoned in favour of mystical practices, its laws repudiated, or reinterpreted, to meet the demands that Tzvi placed upon his followers. In many

---

[28] This is a play on the Hebrew blessing for the release of captives. By changing one letter 'he who releases the bound' becomes 'he who permits the forbidden'.

small communities and villages the Sabbatean movement swept up the entire population. In Amsterdam, one of Tzvi's most committed opponents, Jacob Sasportas, believed that the 'infidels' were in the minority, overwhelmed by those who followed Shabbetai. In the Yemen, the isolated and mistreated Jewish community gave up their trades, donated all their possessions to charity and prepared to travel to Jerusalem, for the long-awaited 'ingathering of the exiles'. Similar stories were reported from Germany, Poland, Morocco and the Papal States. Even in staid London, which was recovering from the Great Plague of 1665, the news was met with joy.[29]

Not everybody lost their heads. They didn't all believe in Shabbetai Tzvi and Nathan his prophet. This was a man who publicly profaned the law to prove his Messianism. That wasn't how it was supposed to be. Granted, the Talmud had said that the Messiah would be proclaimed by a prophet, but that prophet should have been Elijah. Even if one could stretch a point on his identity, who was to say that Nathan was a prophet? It was well known that the age of prophecy had ended long ago.

In Amsterdam, Jacob Sasportas pointed to the passages in the book of Deuteronomy which warned against false prophets.[30] A true prophet could only be known, according to biblical and Talmudic tradition, if he performed a miracle, or if he made predictions that came true. In either case a court of law had to verify the facts. Private testimonies were not enough.[31] Since no court had ever verified Nathan's prophetic ability, he didn't make the grade, and if he was no prophet then there was no evidence for Tzvi as Messiah. Indeed, Nathan had effectively admitted as much. In stark contrast to the Talmudic view, he had insisted that neither he nor the Messiah would prove themselves by performing miracles. They demanded nothing less than pure faith.[32]

Shabbetai Tzvi had first met Nathan in early 1665. At the end of that year he prepared to travel to Istanbul, capital of the Ottoman Empire. Reports had already reached Istanbul that a new king of the Jews had arisen and that his followers were preparing themselves for the advent of the messianic era. The excitement had spread beyond the Jewish population, the entire city was

[29] Scholem, 1973.
[30] Deuteronomy 13.1–6 and 18.18–22.
[31] Goldish, 2004.
[32] Scholem, 1973.

gripped by a carnival atmosphere. The imperial authorities, who were well used to putting down insurrection and revolt, opened their armouries.

Tzvi journeyed from Gaza through Syria, remaining for a few months in his home town of Smyrna before setting off for Istanbul. On his arrival in the capital, Shabbetai Tzvi was arrested and cast into the most foetid dungeon the city could offer. It could have been worse, many expected him to be sentenced to death.

Bribes were paid and eventually Tzvi was transferred to a more spacious prison where, on the eve of Passover, he sacrificed a lamb; a ritual which, as it could only be performed in the Jerusalem Temple, had long been abrogated. He made his customary blessing to 'He who permits the forbidden'.

On 16 September 1666 Shabbetai Tzvi was hauled out of jail and brought before the Sultan. He was given a choice, of death or conversion to Islam. Everyone assumed that Shabbetai would opt for martyrdom, that's what self-proclaimed messiahs were expected to do. Instead he chose to convert. The Sultan was delighted, this was a prize catch. He gave Tzvi a royal pension. His followers were thrown into utter disarray.

Reaction to Shabbetai Tzvi's apostasy was mixed. Many refused to believe what had happened, or if they believed it, saw the events as part of some great messianic plan. In Turkey and Hamburg it was believed that he had ascended to heaven and it was merely his likeness which remained behind.[33] A handful of his closest followers followed his lead and became Muslims. Their descendants make up the Donmeh sect in Turkey today.

With the benefit of hindsight we can see that the Sabbatean outbreak, hysterical as it may have been, was no more than the product of its times. Messianic expectations were rife in Europe and across the Mediterranean. In Britain, millenarian beliefs, which John Gray places at the heart of the Reformation, had by the seventeenth century spawned radical messianic groups like the Ranters and the Fifth Monarchy Men who, taking their name from the prophecies of the Book of Daniel, were preparing for the Second Coming.[34] Matt Goldish has demonstrated close parallels between the belief in Shabbetai Tzvi and the growth of utopian movements including the Quakers and the French Prophets.[35]

---

[33] Scholem, 1973.
[34] Gray, 2007.
[35] Goldish, 2004.

In time the majority of those who had been taken in by the Shabbetai delusion returned to their former lives and the Talmud resumed its place at the centre of religious life. But it wasn't the end of the story. Shabbetai Tzvi may have converted to Islam, abandoned his messianic pretensions and lost most of his supporters, but the movement he inspired didn't disappear overnight. It simply went underground, with its tentacles still protruding. Many Sabbateans disguised their affiliation, living outwardly as normal members of the community and practising their sectarian rites in secret.

# 13

# The challenge of the Enlightenment

The baptismal certificate is the admission ticket into European civilisation.

Heinrich Heine

## After the storm

Shabbetai Tzvi's death, ten years after his conversion, led to a flurry of speculation amongst some of his former fans. Traditionally the Messiah could only be a descendant of King David's royal line. But the Talmud refers in passing to another Messiah, a descendant of the Bible's multi-colour-robed Joseph, who would be slain before David's descendant could assume his role.[1] When Tzvi died, some of his former followers assumed that he must have been the Josephite Messiah and that his death was part of the great Divine, messianic plan. A further, brief flurry of utopian expectation swept through Bohemia.

Over the years the anti-Sabbatean environment turned nasty. Sabbatean prophets continued to circulate, preaching a message of ultimate redemption and Talmudic rejection.[2] The Talmudic establishment launched a counter-offensive, rooting out suspected closet Sabbateans from amongst their own number. One of the best-known, and most antagonistic, confrontations erupted between two highly regarded Talmud scholars, Jacob Emden in Germany and Jonathan Eybeschutz in Prague.

Jonathan Eybeschutz was widely regarded as one of the greatest Talmudic authorities of his generation. A child prodigy he became head of the *yeshiva* in

---

[1] Sukkah 52a. The Messiah, son of Joseph, seems to be an early theme which may first occur in the Dead Sea Scrolls (see A Dying and Rising Josephite Messiah in 4Q372, David C. Mitchell, *Journal for the Study of the Pseudepigrapha* 2009, 18: 18). The idea doesn't get fully developed until post-Talmudic times and its early origins need further research. The alleged reference in the pseudepigraphic work Testament of the Tribes (Testament of Benjamin 3.8) is almost certainly a later Christian interpolation.

[2] Goldish, 2004.

Prague and in 1725 was one of a group of rabbis who formally excommunicated the Sabbatean movement in the city. The author of many highly regarded works on Talmudic law, he was on track for a glittering career, rapidly moving from one senior rabbinic post to another. When he was accused of being a Sabbatean himself his congregants and students refused to believe it.

Eybeshutz's chief accuser was Jacob Emden. Emden's father had battled the Sabbateans in Amsterdam and his son now took up the cudgel. But Emden, an outstanding Talmudist in his own right, had also been Eybechutz's rival for the post of rabbi of the Three Communities of Hamburg, Altona and Wandsbek.

The confrontation began with a book that had appeared in 1724. The work promoted a quasi-*kabbalistic* view that was seen as heretical to traditional belief, and which accorded with Sabbatean mystical doctrine. The Sabbateans themselves claimed the work as one of theirs, and named Eybeschutz as the author. Eybeschutz denied any involvement but suspicions were not fully allayed, even when he took part in the Prague excommunication of the Sabbatean movement. Thirty years later, when Jacob Emden opened some amulets that Eybeschutz had written and found that they contained Sabbatean material, the controversy flared up anew.

The Talmudic world was divided. Accusations and counter-accusations flew. There was scarcely a Talmudist in the world who could remain neutral. There were calls to depose Eybeschutz as rabbi of the Three Communities. He was obliged to appeal to the king for support. The monarch ordered fresh elections for the rabbinic post. Eybeschutz was confirmed in his position but the question mark over whether he really was a follower of Shabbetai Tzvi never went away. His cause was certainly not helped when his son declared himself to be a Sabbatean prophet.

Jacob Emden didn't emerge from the dispute happily either. Many people blamed him for fanning the flames of a controversy that should have been left to simmer quietly.[3] He fled to Amsterdam where he spent the next few years publishing legal texts and works dedicated to denouncing Sabbatean *kabbalistic* doctrines, particularly publications which he considered to be propaganda to win over *yeshiva* students.

---

[3]  Maciejko, 2011.

## An odious redeemer

Even after all that had happened, the age of messianic pretenders was still not over. It wasn't long until a far more sinister contender emerged in the person of Jacob Frank, a follower of Shabbetai Tzvi though without the charisma. As a young man Frank had been initiated into the Sabbatean movement and had spent time with a branch of the Donmeh sect of Shabbetai Tzvi's followers in Salonika. Following a pilgrimage to the grave of Nathan of Gaza, Jacob Frank returned to his original home in Podolia, Poland, where he rounded up followers, preached a message of anarchy and thinly disguised hedonism and sought to abolish the Talmud altogether.

Jacob Frank boasted that he knew nothing of the Talmud. He described himself as an unlearned man. But it is clear from his letters that he was familiar with the Bible and *kabbalah*.[4] He may even have known a little of the Talmud.

On one occasion a group of Sabbateans under Jacob Frank's direction were discovered holding a secret ritual, an interpretation of a mystical Sabbatean ritual of human marriage with the Torah.[5] They danced unclothed around a naked woman adorned with the ornaments of a Torah scroll. The villagers who stumbled across them at the climax of their rite were horrified. They informed the Polish authorities, the participants were arrested, Jacob Frank fled and his followers were put in prison.

Now that they had been outed as Sabbateans, Jacob Frank's followers began to hold their rituals publicly, hoping to win recruits from the mainstream Jewish community. The local rabbis asked Jacob Emden, who, as a result of his publications and his battle with Jonathan Eybeschutz had gained a reputation as an anti-Sabbatean activist, what they should do. He suggested that, since new religions were forbidden in Poland, the rabbis should ask for help from the Church to curtail the Sabbatean activities. But Jacob Frank was no fool. He outflanked the rabbis. Twenty one of his followers prepared a manifesto in Latin, a language well understood within the Church but wholly alien to most Talmudists. The manifesto alleged that the Talmud was blasphemous, contrary to reason and against the Divine commandments. They submitted

---

[4] Wacholder, 1982.
[5] Maciejko, 2011.

their pamphlet to the bishop, called themselves contra-Talmudists and claimed that they had been persecuted, excommunicated and falsely accused.[6]

The Church saw a two-pronged opportunity. Potentially, the Frankists could be a valuable weapon in the Church's centuries old crusade against the Jews. And, handled properly, there seemed to be a good chance that Frank's followers might be converted to the Christian faith.

The Frankists petitioned the Church to order the rabbis to attend a disputation. A key topic would be the validity of the Talmud. The rabbis, aware of the Talmud's history, had a pretty good idea where this would end up. They managed to resist for a full year. Finally, after extreme pressure from the bishop they gave in. They turned up to the debate in Kamienic where they were horrified to be confronted by a Frankist contingent containing several of their own colleagues, who, it turned out, had always harboured secret Sabbatean beliefs.

On 17 October 1757 the bishop decided that the Frankists had won the debate. He ordered Jewish homes to be searched and all copies of the Talmud confiscated and burnt.

The burnings took place in November 1757. On the ninth of that month the bishop was suddenly taken ill and died. Everybody, Frankists, Churchmen and rabbis saw it as an omen. The burnings ceased, the Frankists took fright and Jacob Frank fled with many of his followers to Turkey where, following Shabbetai Tzvi's example, he converted to Islam.

Meanwhile those of his followers who had remained in Poland turned back to the Church. They reminded the ecclesiastical authorities of the promises of protection the deceased bishop had given them. After some discussion the king issued a decree of royal protection. When Jacob Frank heard of it he shrugged off his conversion to Islam and returned home.

Now that they were able to live openly, Jacob Frank told his followers that it was time to follow a new path. This would involve rejecting all forms of law but only in secret. Outwardly they were to convert to Christianity. He provided a mystical justification for all this then tried to make a deal with the Church. He would present himself and all his followers for baptism, but only on condition that they could continue to live as a separate sect with their own rituals. He also demanded a further opportunity to debate as contra-Talmudists with the rabbis. One of the themes was to be the old charge of the blood libel,

---

[6] Maciejko, 2011.

the accusation that the Talmud demands that Jews use the blood of Christian children for ritual purposes.

The blood libel had been undergoing something of a revival. The number of trials of Jews accused of ritual murder in Poland had been on the rise since the Counter-Reformation in the 1560s. In 1710, Jan Serafinowicz, a Jewish convert to Christianity, had published a book in which he claimed that the Talmud instructs Jews to desecrate the Host, the sacred bread used in the Mass, to deface Christian images and to use Christian blood in their rituals.

But Serafinowcz's book didn't have the effect he desired. The blood libel trials had begun to attract attention, the wrong kind of attention, in Rome and in Protestant Europe. The Middle Ages were over, Church leaders no longer believed the myth of the blood libel and there was little sympathy for Jacob Frank's attempts to revive the charge. As far as the Church was concerned, the man was becoming an inconvenience.

The dispute Frank asked for did eventually take place, but nothing much came of it. In 1759 Jacob Frank, who had been born a Jew, had converted to Islam, rescinded his conversion and then founded his own religion, was baptised, along with thousands of his followers, into the Christian faith. The Talmud was to hear no more of him.

## A free spirit

Many in the rabbinic camp saw the conversion of Frank and his followers as a tremendous victory. One man deeply regretted it. He may even have died of pain because of it.[7] He was no Frankist and he was certainly no enemy of the Talmud. But he saw Jacob Frank and his followers as part of the mystical body of Israel, and their apostasy as the equivalent of the amputation of a limb. His name was Israel Ba'al Shem Tov, meaning the Master of The Good Name. He is usually referred to by his initials, the *Besht*. He is known as the founder of the deeply spiritual Hasidic movement.[8] He is one of three men born in the early

---

[7] Maciejko, 2011.

[8] Scholars now believe that the Baal Shem Tov is credited with founding a movement which already existed (Doktor, 2011). There were small groups of mystical pietists in Poland before the *Besht* but it was his charisma and the legends that grew up around him that propelled Hasidism into a mass movement. It is for this reason that it is reasonable to refer to him as the movement's founder.

eighteenth century, each with radically different world views, each of whom would have a seminal and enduring influence on the story of the Talmud.

The Ba'al Shem Tov was born into a world in which magical events regularly occurred and wonder-working rabbis, Masters of the Name, travelled from village to village. They were able to heal the sick, write amulets and exorcise demons. But whilst the Ba'al Shem Tov was capable of this, and much more besides, he was no ordinary miracle-working mystic. Yes, he could prophesy the future, reveal to people their previous incarnations and understand the healing nature of plants. But what set him apart from all other wonder-working rabbis was his ability to touch souls, to bind himself up, inextricably, in the needs of others. It was his charisma, rather than any seemingly supernatural powers, which drew people to him, which created a circle of followers around him, which resulted in a hagiography of stories, legends and fables, reverently passed down amongst his acolytes.[9]

The Ba'al Shem Tov inspired the mystical, life-affirming movement that became known as Hasidism. It wasn't the first deeply spiritual movement to emerge in the Jewish world but it took hold like no other. It still flourishes today, three hundred years after the *Besht*, perhaps even stronger than ever.

The *Besht* was a man of the people. This comes across clearly in the many tales in which he is found talking to innkeepers, travelling with wagon drivers, wandering through the markets, drinking and swapping stories with a group of companions in the forests. It was this simplicity which attracted followers to him. It also brought him and the first generations of his followers into conflict with those Talmudists who were not drawn to the lifestyle he advocated.

One of the fiercest critics of Hasidism, David of Makow, who married in the year that the Baal Shem Tov died, described him as 'an ignoramus, a writer of amulets, who didn't learn because he wasn't able to learn, who walked through the streets and markets with a stick, pipe and tobacco'.[10] We shouldn't read too much into these words, David of Makov was a polemicist and couches his criticism of Hasidism in extreme terms, even appearing to find something shameful about sticks, pipes and tobacco. But his description of the *Besht* illustrates the depth of resentment that developed between the Hasidim and the mainstream.

---

[9] One of the most comprehensive and best-told collections of Besht stories is by Yitzhak Buxbaum Buxbaum, 2005.
[10] Cited in Wilensky, 1956, p. 147.

Whatever David of Makow said, the Baal Shem Tov and his followers were deeply religious people and they held fast to all the basic principles of their faith, including the virtue of study. But the way they studied was not the way it was done in the Talmudic colleges. The Talmudists studied the Talmud as a duty and an intellectual exercise, analyzing and challenging its arguments, peering beneath its many layers to determine the theoretical roots and practical application of religious law. The Hasidim saw something else in Talmudic study. Their ultimate goal was to elevate the soul to a mystic state of union with God. This could be achieved through complex spiritual exercises, but also through simple, joyous activities like dance, song and study. As one of the *Besht's* followers puts it:

> When they learn Gemara (=Talmud) they clothe themselves in great fear, trembling, terror and awe of the Holy one. Their Torah (=learning) lights up their faces. When they mention the name of a tanna or any of the Talmudic authorities they imagine that person standing alive in front of them, illuminated by the heavenly chariot … . When they emerge from their learning, miracles and wonders happen to them, just as in earlier generations, they heal the sick and bring down benevolence upon all Israel.[11]

The traditional Talmudists, many of whom were not averse to mysticism themselves, had little interest in this sort of approach. They wouldn't have denied that studying the Talmud was a religious activity that brought spiritual reward. But their prime motivation was to understand the law, not to become mystically enriched.

Hasidism emerged and expanded rapidly in those parts of Poland which were home to the dissenting Raskol community, which had broken away from the Orthodox Church half a century earlier. Yaffa Eliach believes that the *Besht* was heavily influenced by this community and may even have spent his formative years amongst them. She sees parallels between their rituals and those of the early Hasidim, for which they were roundly condemned by their opponents. These included dressing in white, whirling, dervish-like dances in which they waved white handkerchiefs, feasting on the anniversary of a parent's death and allegiance to a deeply spiritual leader.[12]

---

[11] *Iggeret HaKodesh*, printed at the back of *Noam Elimelech*, published 1798 by Elimelech of Lizhensk (1717–86), reprinted and retypeset Jerusalem 1995.
[12] Eliach, 1968.

There is no doubt that some of the early Hasidic practices were very alien to traditional Talmudists. It seems that they even worried some of the Hasidic leaders themselves. A nineteenth-century Hasidic leader, Menahem Mendel of Lubavitch, paid tribute to those Talmudists who had fought bitterly against the early manifestations of the movement. Had it not been for those battles, he claimed, the Talmud would have been scorched 'by the fire of Kaballah'.[13] Practical observance would have become worthless in the face of the intense fire of mystical introspection. In particular he singled out one man, Elijah of Vilna, the fiercest of all their opponents and without doubt the greatest Talmudist for many generations, for particular thanks.

## The *Gaon* of Vilna

The title *gaon* hadn't been used much since the days of Baghdad. But it had not disappeared altogether. It was still applied occasionally, to people of such sharp intellect that the designation rabbi, which means teacher, did them no justice at all.

Elijah of Vilna, or Vilnius, in Lithuania was one such man. He wasn't a community rabbi, he didn't head up a college, he didn't even really have any students in the usual sense of the word; the only people who studied under him were mature, respected scholars in their own right. He'd been a child prodigy, delivered a sermon in the local synagogue at the age of six and answered probing questions on it. He spent his life in endless study, shut away from the world, rarely sleeping for more than half an hour at a time and for no more than two hours in total during a night. It is said that he spent his nights in an unheated room with his feet in a bowl of cold water so that he would stay awake. He had an unrivalled command of the Talmud, its associated literature and of *kaballah*. They called him the Vilna *Gaon*.

The enthusiasm which greeted Hasidism in its heartlands, in Polish Ukraine, wasn't repeated in Vilna. It was a populous city, regarded as the intellectual centre of the Lithuanian Empire. Its university was one of Europe's most respected institutions of learning. The majority of its inhabitants were Jews, and even though they were excluded from the university, they shared the city's

---

[13] *Mekor Baruch* Baruch Halevi Epstein, 2:619 cited in *Torah Lishma*, Norman Lamm (Ktav Publishing House, New York, 1989).

temperament for culture and scholarship.[14] They regarded the mystical exercises of the rural Hasidim as frivolous. That's not to say they ridiculed mysticism, the Vilna *Gaon* was as immersed in *kabbalah* as he was in Talmud. But for them mysticism was a route towards intellectual understanding, not to spiritual ecstasy.[15]

Elijah was an implacable opponent of the Hasidim. He saw the Hasidim as a deviant, heretical sect. As far as he was concerned their panentheistic belief that God was in everything conflicted with the traditional view of both the Talmud and *the kabbalah*.

Elijah condemned the Hasidim for their attitude to Talmud study and its place in religious life. The highest of all virtues, for Elijah and his followers, who became known as the *misnegdim* or opponents, was a life devoted to Talmud study and the lifestyle it demanded. The Hasidim didn't deny the value of Talmud study. But it was just one of several potential routes to mystical ecstasy, alongside prayer, joy and devotion. The dispute between the Hasidim and the Vilna *Gaon* hinged on which was the correct form of religious worship, study of the Talmud or prayer.[16]

This might seem trivial to modern, secular minds. But all organized religions have had divisions at some point in their history, some have had them through the whole of their history. Often starting with apparently minor matters these disputes can escalate to a magnitude that is unfathomable to anyone not caught up in them. Religions are conservative institutions and in a conservative world all change has the power to threaten. The traditionalists had not forgotten the Sabbatean and Frankist affairs. They had no wish for anything else that disturbed their time-hallowed world view.

When Elijah was born, Vilnius was recovering from war. Its wooden dwellings had been ravaged by fire and its population decimated by plague. As a young man he would have fretted with the other Jews as the citizens of the town petitioned to have them expelled, a consequence of the king's gift to them of trading rights. But by the time he reached middle age the city was recovering economically, low infant mortality was boosting the population of both the Jewish and Catholic communities and a new spirit of tolerance abounded, brought about by the encroaching Enlightenment. The Church, under the

---

[14] Stern, 2011.

[15] Etkes, 2002.

[16] Etkes, 2002.

leadership of Bishop Massalski, stopped seeking converts, and even drove away those who sought voluntary apostasy.[17] Vilna's Jewish community became large, thriving and confident. The vast majority were opposed to the Hasidim. In the city they had the numbers, and the civic autonomy, to do something about it.

In 1772 they launched a fierce and uncompromising campaign against the Hasidim. Hasidic leaders were arrested, imprisoned and excommunicated, their writings seized and burned, Hasidic gatherings were prohibited. The *Besht* was dead by now but two of his most prominent followers, Schneur Zalman of Liady and Menahem Mendel of Vitebsk, travelled to meet the Vilna *Gaon*. They wanted to explain Hasidism to him, to defuse the conflict. The *Gaon* refused to see them. Not only was he unwilling to compromise, he didn't even want to give the impression that he was open to dialogue.

The leaders of the Vilna community recognized that in Elijah they had a rare and valuable treasure in their midst. They took it upon themselves to support him. They paid him a stipend that far exceeded that of the communal doctor, and was nearly as much as that paid to the judge.[18] Some people objected. Communal funds came from taxation, and many felt that they were already being taxed too heavily without taking on the support of a reclusive scholar. Complaints began to be hurled at the leaders of the community, and in particular one man, Abba Wolf, a staunch supporter of the *Gaon*. In 1787, Abba Wolf's son, Hirsch, walked into the local monastery and asked to convert to Christianity. The monastery took him in, notwithstanding Bishop Massalski's strictures. His father was distraught.

Abba Wolf went to see the *Gaon* Elijah. Together they concocted a plan. They bribed another convert to Christianity to befriend Hirsch in the monastery. They gave him a large sum of money and asked him to win Hirsch's trust. Eventually, when Hirsch was confident in his new friend, they went for a walk together. Hirsch's brothers were waiting outside. They grabbed him, dressed him in women's clothing, threw him into a carriage and smuggled him out of the city.

Five days later the local authorities arrested Elijah and Abba. Elijah refused to answer any of their questions and was sentenced to twelve weeks in gaol. He was in prison for the festival of Sukkot, when Jews leave their homes and live in a temporary dwelling, as a reminder of the Israelites' wanderings in the

---

[17]  Stern, 2013.
[18]  Stern, 2013.

wilderness. Being in prison Elijah could not fulfil the obligation of sleeping in the temporary hut. Those incarcerated alongside him reported that for the whole week of the festival he paced up and down his cell, holding his eyes open, so as not to be guilty of the offence of sleeping in the wrong place.[19]

Elijah of Vilna's legacy was not his battle against Hasidism. That was merely something he felt he had to do. His personal contribution to the life of the Talmud was intellectual, and his influence was most keenly felt in the world of Talmudic education. He had an encyclopedic command, not just of the Talmud itself but of all the sources that lay behind it, and of the commentaries and law codes that had emerged from it. Unlike those earlier Talmudists who had rejected the 'wisdom of the Greeks', Elijah of Vilna saw the value of science and mathematics, albeit as a way of gaining a better understanding of the Talmud. He even encouraged one of his students to translate Euclid, the classical master of geometry, into Hebrew. All in all his system of study was far more methodical and analytical than his forerunners. He laid the foundations for a new, rigorous approach to Talmud study, one which would be developed further by his outstanding disciple, Hayyim of Volozhin.

From the point of view of both the Hasidim and their opponents, the struggle had not been good for the Talmud. It had become neglected, a victim of all the quarrelling and invective. Hayyim of Volozhin bewailed the fact that in the villages the communal study houses were full of books devoted to ethical conduct but rarely contained a full edition of the Talmud.[20] The focus of education had shifted from theory to behaviour, to how, not why.

The remedy lay, Hayyim believed, in reforming the educational system. The old *yeshiva* structure had fallen into decline. Its reliance on the charitable support of local communities had been humiliating for the students, whose subsistence had depended upon the goodwill of strangers. It had been obsessed with a technique known as *pilpul*, meaning sharp, or peppery. This was characterized by a search for ingenious but obscure ways of comparing and dissecting two or more pieces of text, or for setting and solving clever but irrelevant problems. In the early eighteenth century Jacob Hagiz[21] had poked fun at this trend. He asked his students: 'According to the law a mourner must not cut his hair until his friends complain about his unkempt appearance. But what is the

---

[19] Stern, 2013.

[20] *Nefesh Hahayyim* by R. Hayyim of Volozhin, various editions, Chapter 4, Section 1.

[21] *Halakhot Ketanot*, Venice 1704, Part 1, p. 113, cited in Jacobs, 2004.

law where a person has no friends?' Two hundred years earlier Jacob Landau
had published a book of Talmudic riddles. He'd asked how two people could
each be the other's uncle, without any incest having been involved?[22]

Many people agreed that this approach, often described as hair-splitting,
denigrated the Talmud; it was a way for students to show off their sharp
wittedness, but it wasn't the substance of serious learning. Hayyim wanted
something better. He raised funds from people who supported his efforts and
established a *yeshiva* in his hometown of Volozhin that would be financially
independent. He abandoned the hair-splitting methods of Talmud study and
introduced the techniques which characterized Elijah of Vilna's approach, in
which analysing the text and understanding its plain meaning were paramount.
He created a round-the-clock system of study, so that when one group went to
bed another group arose. His educational system laid the foundations for the
modern Talmudic college.

In time the struggle between the Hasidim and the 'opponents' played itself
out. As we saw earlier, Menahem Mendel of Lubavitch acknowledged that
Hasidism had been saved from its own excesses by the strictures of the Vilna
*Gaon* and his allies. A modus vivendi was achieved. There were bigger battles
looming, the winds of enlightenment were starting to blow in from the west.
This was no time for the two camps to irrevocably fall out. Particularly as they
were about to face a new and, to the religious mind, far more insidious threat,
albeit as yet unacknowledged. It was the threat of secularism.

## The seeds of emancipation

The Jews were a confident, secure majority in Catholic Vilnius. Not so, five
hundred miles away, in the Protestant city of Berlin. Not that they were persecuted to any great degree, after all Berlin was the heartland of the religiously
tolerant Enlightenment. Indeed, full emancipation was on offer to the Jews.
All they had to do was convert to the Lutheran Church. They weren't under

---

[22] *Sefer Hahazon* in *Sefer Ha'Agur Hashalem*, ed. Yaakov Baruch Landau, reprinted by Menoreh Institute,
New York, 1959. The solution to the first problem is that someone with no friends is regarded as dead and
the law does not apply to dead people. In the second one, Jacob has a daughter Dinah. Dinah marries David.
They have a son, Reuben. David has a daughter, Rachel from a previous marriage. Jacob marries Rachel. They
have a son, Simon. Simon is Dinah's (Reuben's mother's) brother. He is therefore Reuben's uncle. Reuben is
Rachel's (Simon's mother's) brother. He is therefore Simon's uncle.

pressure to do so, nobody was burning their Talmuds. But who would choose to remain in a tiny minority, just 3 per cent of the population, with few political and civil rights, when they could become fully emancipated into a tolerant, reasonable, enlightened majority? Conversion, so the Lutherans reasoned, was a small price to pay.

Such reasoning didn't go down well with Moses Mendelssohn. As a young man he had studied the Talmud, German literature, philosophy, the classics and modern languages. He'd made a name for himself as a philosopher. Unusually for a Jew, he had many friends in the German literary world and was accepted into the cultural salons frequented by Berlin's Protestant intelligentsia.

As a philosopher Mendelssohn owed a debt to Spinoza.[23] Culturally, Spinoza had helped create the conditions that spawned Mendelssohn's thought and allowed it to propagate. Religiously however, Spinoza caused him a problem. He tried to divorce Spinoza's philosophy from his attitudes to religion. He admired Spinoza the philosopher, felt sorry for the fate of Spinoza the religious heretic and condemned those who had hated him.[24]

For many years Mendelssohn concentrated on his philosophy, writing in both German and Hebrew, albeit for different audiences. His reputation grew and grew. He became known as the German Socrates. He kept away from religious disputes. Until the day in 1769 when he was confronted by a Lutheran clergyman, Johann Caspar Lavater who had translated a philosophical, Calvinist work into German. Believing that this work made out an irrefutable case for Christianity, Lavater challenged Mendelssohn either to publicly refute the work or else do what 'Socrates would have done if faced with an irrefutable truth', in other words concede the argument and convert.

Mendelssohn was far from convinced by the arguments in the book Lavater had translated and was deeply hurt by the personal attacks hurled at him, which intensified as the argument continued. He realized that, as the Yiddish proverb put it, he could no longer 'dance with one backside at two weddings'. The Protestant intelligentsia would never fully accept him as an accultured German philosopher whilst he simultaneously remained intellectually wedded to Talmudic tradition. The Jews would always remain suspicious of his loyalties

---

[23] *Spinoza's Modernity: Mendelssohn, Lessing, and Heine*, Willi Goetschel (University of Wisconsin Press, Madison, WI, 2004).

[24] Feiner, 2010.

while he held himself aloof and supped in Berlin's coffee houses. Mendelssohn knew he had to reconcile his two positions.

His response was twofold. He began to involve himself in the growing calls for the political emancipation of his people, arguing for a pluralistic society, for minorities to have full rights and an equal voice in German society.[25] And he looked for ways to encourage the Jews, who for the main part still lived outside the city in rural, Yiddish-speaking communities, to appreciate the value of secular German culture, to speak its language and absorb its literature.

He wrote a translation of the Hebrew Bible into German, which he based on the Talmud's interpretations. He wanted to offer Jewish students a literary, German alternative to the rather wooden, Yiddish renderings that they had used up to now, an alternative which was more substantial than the current Christian translations which, by ignoring Talmudic interpretations, failed in his view to draw out the full meaning of the text.[26]

Mendelssohn's Bible translation was based on Talmudic interpretations but was far more than just that. He tried to create a synthesis between traditional, religious faith and modern, scientific reason. He wanted to harmonize contemporary science and philosophy with traditional Talmud and Bible scholarship.[27]

His German translation was originally published using Hebrew characters but was very quickly reprinted in German script. It became hugely popular amongst both Lutherans and Jews. Subscribers to the first edition included professors, pastors and nobles. A subscription was even taken out in the name of the King of Denmark. Mendelssohn's use of Talmudic tradition exposed his German readers to new ways of understanding the Old Testament and it showed his Jewish readers that they had nothing to fear from examining their own heritage in the German language.

Mendelssohn is a key figure in the *Haskalah*, or religious enlightenment movement, an important aspect of which was to integrate traditional Talmudic and religious thought with modernity, as part of a process of cultural fusion and political emancipation. Not everyone approved of it, many traditional scholars railed against what they saw as an assault on their time honoured way of life. Mendelssohn and his colleagues had as many opponents amongst their own people as they had amongst proselytizing Churchmen.

---

[25] Sorkin, 1994.

[26] Stern, 2011.

[27] Sorkin, 1992.

But for every thinker who disapproved of his agenda, there was another who eulogized him. When he died, at the age of fifty six, after a life of ill health, over a thousand people, Christians and Jews, crowded into the tiny cemetery. Shops in Berlin closed out of respect. Newspapers discussed his final illness, his doctor held a press conference, his friends swapped tales about him and quoted his best-known sayings.[28]

Friend and foe alike saw him as a giant on the historical stage, either a hero or a villain.[29] He either saved the Jews from medieval obscurity or dangled them over the yawning chasm of secularization and assimilation. It all depended upon your point of view. All his admirers wanted a piece of him; he became, in Shmuel Feiner's words 'a pawn to the partisans of various agendas, each waving him like a banner and adopting him for their world view'.[30] Which, if nothing else, must be a testament to his greatness.

Moses Mendelssohn wasn't Spinoza's disciple but they do have something in common. They each stand at important crossroads along the same road in the Talmud's encounter with modernity.

Of the three eighteenth-century figures who brought the Talmud into the modern world, the impact of the *Besht* and the Vilna *Gaon* is readily discernible, even if today the boundaries between their respective groups of followers has become somewhat blurred, at least from the outside. Each in their own way ensured the continuity and vibrancy of Talmudic life. The picture with Moses Mendelssohn is more complex. In many ways he took on a far greater challenge. The *Besht* and the *Gaon*, in their very different ways, inspired their followers. Mendelssohn sought to put in place a huge cultural shift. He didn't wholly succeed, some of his children converted to Christianity, including his son Abraham, father of the composer Felix Mendelssohn. He became, as David Sorkin put it, a legend in his own lifetime and a symbol thereafter.

---

[28] Feiner, 2010, p. 13.
[29] Sorkin, 1994.
[30] Feiner, 2010.

# 14

# The problem with emancipation

When we were young we were treated as men, now that we have grown old we are looked upon as babies.[1]

## Pioneers

The origins of the Jewish community in Charleston, South Carolina date back to 1695. It is the oldest in North America. In the early nineteenth century it was also the largest, the most sophisticated and the most comfortable. Its members lived alongside their neighbours in a state of happy emancipation. The Talmud had never been much on their minds, most of them had probably never even seen a copy. There were no rabbis, as far as anyone knows, in America at this time; it was a country of pioneers, attracting only the most adventurous souls. Traditionalists tended to stay back in Europe, where they were used to the way things were done.[2]

But although they weren't thinking about the Talmud, the inhabitants of Charleston were by no means cut off from their co-religionists in Europe. They had heard about reforming currents that were beginning to circulate in Germany. Continuing emancipation and the new ways of thinking which Moses Mendelssohn had encouraged were bringing fresh ideas to the fore. Traditionalism was under threat in Europe, and post-revolutionary America was certainly no place for musty conservatism, particularly if it stood in the way of social and economic advancement. The old ways were changing and, even though in Charleston the connection to the old ways was already tenuous, a formal commitment to progress felt like a good thing.

---

[1] Bava Kamma 92b.
[2] Tarshish, 1985.

In 1824 a group of Charleston Jews established the Reformed Society of Israelites. Their aim was to reform the synagogue service, to make it more intelligible to the English speaker and to expunge 'the erroneous doctrines of the Rabbins'.[3] They weren't particularly motivated by a disregard for, or a dislike of, the Talmud; it's just that they felt that their prayer service was in need of modernization. But their desire to change the prayer service was the practical consequence of an ideological struggle that was taking place back in Europe, particularly in Hamburg, where the seeds of the Charleston campaign had been sown.[4] And in Hamburg, indeed across most of Germany, the Talmud sat at the heart of the conflict.

## A time to change

The Reform movement began, as these things do, not as a formal enterprise but as a result of a small number of innovations, largely uncoordinated but all heading in the same general direction. The French and American revolutions of the eighteenth century had created the conditions for the political emancipation of the Jews, a gradual process which unfolded throughout the latter part of the eighteenth century and most of the nineteenth. As part of this process Moses Mendlessohn, despite his steadfast commitment to traditional Jewish practice, had unbarred the gates which had kept the Jews far from world culture and learning. His translation of the Bible into German was a deliberate strategy to encourage the people of the Talmud to learn the language of those amongst whom they lived. It gave them the tools to explore the great literary heritage of Germany, and that in turn had a stirring effect upon their outlook.

From the late eighteenth century there was a growing feeling amongst more worldly, socially acculturated Jewish circles that their religious practices were archaic, out of step with the spirit of the age. This was most immediately noticeable in the synagogue service, which was unintelligible to those without a grasp of Hebrew, and which lacked the decorum and musical solemnity of the great churches. Here and there, in Amsterdam, in Seesen and Cassel in

---

[3] Tarshish, 1985.
[4] Editor's preface to *The Sabbath Service and Miscellaneous Prayers*, adopted by the Reformed Society of Israelites, founded in Charleston, SC, 21 November 1825, ed. Barnett A. Elzas (Bloch Publishing Company, New York, 1916).

northern Germany, and ultimately in Hamburg, congregations were established which did things differently. The practices they instituted did not conform to the traditions of the Talmud, but nor were they, in the early days, intended as anti-Talmud. Indeed the Reformers aspired to demonstrate the Talmud's support for their innovations. They even engaged a Talmudic scholar to champion their cause.[5]

The Reform movement grew quickly. By the 1840s congregations across Germany, France, Hungary and Austria were experimenting with innovation. They introduced prayers in German into the synagogue service, brought in organs and instituted sermons. They modified stringencies around Sabbath observation and the dietary laws. They appointed a different type of rabbi, men with secular education who had spent little or no time in the *yeshivot*.

At a conference at Brunswick in 1844, Samuel Holdheim, one of the leading intellectual lights of the movement, poured scorn on the earlier attempts in Hamburg to use the Talmud to justify their innovations. The Talmud, he argued, had only enjoyed legitimacy in its own time, these days it was no longer authoritative. A schism was in the making.

## A time to refrain from changing

Traditional Talmudists did not sit idly by as the Reform movement grew in popularity. The rabbinic council in Hamburg, traditionalists to a man, wrote to the leading light of their generation, Moses Sofer, asking for his support in their campaign against the innovations in the Hamburg Temple.

Moses Sofer believed passionately in the intrinsic worth of every aspect of Talmudic life. His conservatism was not driven by fear of change. Rather it was a deep commitment to the values of tradition, encapsulated in his motto 'innovation is forbidden by the Torah'; a pun on the Talmudic injunction that the 'new [grain harvest] is forbidden by the Torah', before an offering is brought to the Temple.[6]

Sofer applauded the ban that the traditionalists had imposed upon the use of Reform prayer books and musical instruments in the synagogue.[7] He then

---

[5] Mendes-Flohr and Reinharz, 1995.
[6] Mishnah Orlah 3.9.
[7] Mendes-Flohr and Reinharz, 1995.

embarked on an unrelenting, strategic campaign against the Reform movement and the religious enlightenment. He mustered rabbis of every temperament, not just the most conservative rabbis, to contribute to a collection of letters arguing against Reform.[8] He appealed to the nationalist aspirations of the masses in condemning the Reform movement's abolition of Hebrew as the language of prayer.[9] He strengthened the traditionalists' ties with the Hapsburg authorities, established the largest *yeshiva* in Europe in his adopted home town of Pressburg, and whenever a prestigious rabbinic post fell vacant he tried to install one of his best and brightest pupils. In his ethical will he condemned Mendlessohn's work and warned his students never to yield to the pressure to change their traditional language, clothes or names.

Sofer's defence of the old Talmudic ways was unyielding. But it didn't suit everyone in the traditional camp. There were many who were receptive to the changing world, but not to the same extent as the Reformers. They didn't want to be part of a movement heading towards a rejection of the Talmud. Reform was too radical for them, and Moses Sofer's traditional Orthodoxy was too unyielding. They didn't know it yet, but they were waiting for a new champion to come along.

## Duelling friends

In 1829 two young men met at the University of Bonn. They'd previously been introduced to each other in Frankfurt. Now they began to strike up a close friendship through their university activities.[10]

Both men shared a passion for igniting the religious commitment of those German Jews who were drifting away from their faith, seduced by a new and exciting, modern world. But each man would set about it in a fundamentally different way. The older of the two, Samson Raphael Hirsch dreamed of inspiring new ways of approaching the Talmud that would draw on all the benefits that a secular education could offer. The younger, Abraham Geiger, was convinced that the Talmud simply reflected a moment in history. It was part of the ongoing

---

[8] Schreiber, 2002–3. The collection, *Eleh Divrei HaBrit* included praise for Moses Mendelssohn, against whose approach Moses Sofer was firmly opposed.

[9] Samet, 1988.

[10] Heinemann, 1951.

development of Jewish law and practice, not an unchanging expression of the will of Heaven.[11]

In 1835 Hirsch laid out plans for a book which would interpret the Bible's teaching on human destiny, and explain the underlying, moral purpose of Talmudic law. One of his friends showed the book's outline to a German publisher who said that he wasn't sure there would be a market for such a lofty volume; perhaps the author could try out his ideas in something smaller first. If that sold well then he was sure that he would be able to find a publisher to take on the whole project.

So Hirsch wrote a book in the shape of a fictional correspondence between a student and young rabbi, in which the student set out the religious issues that were troubling him, and the rabbi responded. He wrote it under a pseudonym and called it the *Nineteen Letters*. It was an instant hit. Hirsch had put his finger on exactly the questions that were bothering people, not just religious questions, but social and national issues too. The book struck a chord because Hirsch provided modern, ethical reasons for the things the Talmud expected them to do. He didn't treat the laws as the outcomes of faded discussions in ancient, oriental academies, but as a means of making sense of life in modern, nineteenth-century Europe.[12]

The success of the *Nineteen Letters* enabled Hirsch to write the book that he had originally planned, and over the course of his life, many more besides. By explaining what he saw as the reasons that underpinned religious practice he was able to remove the artificial barriers that time had erected between the Talmud and the wider world. In Hirsch's system the fully rounded student of Talmud is a student of life, willing and able to investigate and respond to all branches of human knowledge.

Hirsch was not just driven by an ideological passion. He was deliberately trying to stem the tide of reform. His slogan, 'Torah with worldly involvement'[13] became the motto for generations of secularly educated, culturally assimilated, religiously observant Talmud students.

Hirsch didn't achieve his goal of eliminating the Reform movement. But he did provide a platform for those who wished to integrate a traditional lifestyle with the modern world. The reason he didn't halt the Reform movement in its

---

[11] Meyer, 1988.

[12] Grunfeld, 1962.

[13] Hirsch's slogan, *Torah im derech eretz*, is taken from Mishnah Avot 2.2.

tracks is due in no small part to Abraham Geiger, the friend of his youth, with whom he was to fall out so badly.

Geiger's response to the *Nineteen Letters* was severe. He attacked the 'doglike obedience' of those who observe the Talmudic commandments, likening it to idolatry.[14] It was the end of his friendship with Hirsch.

Small, with long, straight, shoulder-length hair tucked behind his ears, two-inch sideburns and wire-framed glasses, Abraham Geiger cut a striking pose. He had grown up in a strictly observant household and had delivered a Talmudic discourse at the age of thirteen but, according to one of his biographers, shortly after his father's death he became 'utterly disgusted with the Talmud'.[15] Unfortunately the biographer does not speculate on why this may have been and whether it was connected with his father's passing.

Hirsch was interested in the thought and philosophy that underpinned his faith. Geiger was concerned with its development and history. Intellectually he should have been destined for a university chair but such positions were not open to Jews in nineteenth-century Germany and he was left with little choice other than to become a rabbi. This decision cast him straight into the bear pit of religious conflict; his first application for a rabbinic post was vetoed by traditionalists in Breslau who, aware of his anti-Talmudic leanings, accused him of being a Karaite or Sadducee. His early rabbinic career was dogged by lack of advancement due to the efforts of more traditional colleagues.[16]

The Reform movement that Geiger conceived was more than a reaction to overlong, unintelligible synagogue services and seemingly petty restrictions. He strove to develop a coherent theology of Reform. He argued that centuries of studying the Talmud in enclosed, monastic, ghetto communities had led to an excessive legalism in Jewish practice. The only way to rediscover the ethical underpinnings of the faith was to return to a time before the Talmud, to the liberalizing, democratic spirit of the early Pharisees.

But, at this stage in his life Geiger worked as a rabbi, not an as academic. And like all men of the cloth, he wasn't able to spend enough time on intellectual pursuits. Real life gets in the way. In Abraham Geiger's case real life was an event

---

[14] Heinemann, 1951; Shreiber, 1892.

[15] Shreiber, 1892.

[16] The main impediment to Geiger's rabbinic career was Solomon Tiktin, the traditionalist chief rabbi of Breslau who tried his best first not to have Geiger appointed and then, when he was in post, to remove him. When Tiktin died in 1843, however, Geiger was appointed chief rabbi.

half a world away, in a city he had never visited. It threw him off his guard, just as he was taking up his first rabbinic post.


## The Damascus Affair

In 1840 Padre Tommaso, an elderly Italian monk and his servant disappeared in Damascus. He had visited the Jewish quarter of the city on the day he vanished. Rumours began to spread in the Christian district that he had been ritually murdered by the Jews.

The authorities arrested twelve Jews and tortured them to gain a confession. Four suspects died as a result of the torture, one converted to Islam and the remainder were incarcerated, awaiting execution.

The case was unusual for several reasons. Accusations of ritual murder against the Jews in Muslim countries were relatively rare. Even on those few occasions when Christians in the Ottoman Empire had stirred up the old blood libel charge against the Jews, the authorities refused to pursue it.[17] But Syria was no ordinary Ottoman country. Its government was in revolt against the Empire and was manoeuvring to win European allies, particularly France, through the support of its Christian subjects.

The French consul got involved and the affair was picked up by the European media. It became something of a cause célèbre. It dominated the headlines in Europe for weeks. In a show of solidarity with the captives, the Jewish communities of England and France sent Sir Moses Montefiore and Adolphe Crémieux, two high-profile, well-connected, community leaders to Syria. Meetings were held and within a month the surviving Jewish prisoners were released. Neither Padre Tommaso, his servant, nor their abductors were ever found.

The incident was the catalyst for an outpouring of anti-Jewish feeling in the European media. The influential *Leipziger Allgemeine Zeitung* dramatically announced that three rabbis had been imprisoned with orders to translate the Talmud so that the secrets of the Jewish religion could be discovered.[18] *The Times* in London devoted large amounts of space to discussions of whether the Talmud prescribed ritual murder.[19] A pernicious but unsigned piece in *The*

---

[17] Frankel, 1997a.
[18] Frankel, 1997a.
[19] Frankel, 1997b.

*Times*, purporting to be written by a convert from Judaism, repeated the old charges of ritual murder and laid the blame squarely at the feet of the Talmud.[20] It was not tolerant, post-enlightenment Europe's finest hour.

Abraham Geiger was unwilling to get caught up in the reverberations of the Damascus Affair. On 22 May 1840 the *Leipziger Allgemeine Zeitung* carried an advertisement signed by 'prominent Jewish businessmen' calling on 'the most dauntless hero of our faith, Dr Geiger' to respond to the attacks on the Talmud. It was not a friendly call, the sarcastic tone of the advertisement indicated that it had been placed by people who had it in for Geiger, and who wanted to embarrass him. Unfortunately Geiger didn't let them down. He condemned the charges of murder in Damascus as laughable but he couldn't help having a go at the Talmud itself. He declared that the views of the Talmud did not carry any divine authority and wondered why the men who had placed the advertisement had appealed to him, rather than the venerable rabbis who saw salvation in the Talmud and yet would not raise their voices to save its honour.[21]

## The academic Talmud

In his final years Abraham Geiger managed to obtain an academic post, as the head of a new rabbinic college in Berlin. It was a fitting appointment. For he wasn't just the leading theologian of the German Reform movement. He was also one of the leading lights in a new secular enterprise, inspired by the religious enlightenment and the work of men like Moses Mendelssohn. It was known as *Wissenschaft des Judentums*, the Scientific Study of Judaism. It would lead, a century later, to the establishment of Jewish Studies faculties at universities throughout the world.

The *Wissenschaft* movement was both the product of the *Haskalah*, the religious enlightenment movement and a reaction to it. It was the product of the Enlightenment, inasmuch as it treated Judaism as any other cultural phenomenon, using scientific methodology to investigate its history, culture and development. It was a reaction to it, because growing acculturation was creating a new kind of Jew, one with little or no interest in their religious heritage. *Wissenschaft*, which separated scholarship from belief had, in theory,

---

[20] *The Times*, London, 25 June 1840.
[21] Frankel, 1997a.

no religious axe to grind. It provided a means for assimilated Jews to reconnect with their cultural heritage.[22]

The new science subjected the Talmud to detailed, critical scholarship. As Marc Shapiro points out, traditional Talmud scholars had always tried to resolve difficulties in the Talmud text by referring to, or even proposing alternative readings.[23] But the new critical scholars went far further than this; they actively collected and compared as many variant sources as possible, assessed the Talmud's language against other ancient Semitic tongues, and re-evaluated its understanding of history, medicine and the natural world.

Even its relation with the Mishnah was challenged. It may have been the core text, upon which the Talmud was a commentary, but in 1861 Hirsch Mendel Pineles challenged the fundamental principle that it was the authentic interpretation of the Mishnah. His book claimed to defend the Mishnah, against the many misinterpretations that he sought to demonstrate had been made by the Talmud.[24]

Even Czar Nicholas I of Russia, who hated the Jews, was caught up in the *Wissenschaft* endeavour, though not as he had intended. During his reign Nicholas had made life as difficult as possible for his Jewish subjects, expelling them from their homes, forcibly drafting young boys into the army from the age of twelve, keeping them there for a minimum of twenty five years; frequently snatching them from the streets or kidnapping them from their homes. He passed legislation banning them from the major cities and herded them into villages in the Pale of Settlement, a strip of land running from the Baltic to the Black Sea, taking in large chunks of Lithuania, Poland and Ukraine.[25] He set up a network of schools with the avowed aim of bringing them 'nearer to the Christians and to uproot their harmful beliefs which are influenced by the Talmud'.[26]

In 1841 Nicholas commissioned a report which concluded that the Talmud was the reason the Jews refused to assimilate into Russian society. He decided

---

[22] The leading lights of the *Wissenschaft* movement were not wholly impartial to religion. There was a connection to the Reform conception of a dynamic, historically evolving religion (Kohler, 2012).

[23] Shapiro, 2006.

[24] Shapiro, 2006. Pineles's work, *Darkah shel Torah* was of course considered heretical by many traditionalists.

[25] This is the origin of the phrase 'beyond the pale'. It applied to those who tried to live outside the Pale of Settlement.

[26] Kniesmeyer and Brecher, 1995.

that the only way to expose the Talmud was to have it translated, so that people could see what it really was. He offered large sums of money to anyone who could translate it.

In Germany, Ephraim Moses Pinner had already drawn up plans to translate the Talmud into German. He wanted to make it accessible to German-speaking Jews, and to counter the accusations of its opponents. He applied to Nicholas for funding for his project, and Nicholas assented, assuming that Pinner would provide the condemnation of the Talmud that he sought.

In 1842 the first volume appeared. Nicholas purchased one hundred copies. The kings of Prussia, Holland, Belgium and Denmark also bought copies. When Nicholas discovered that Pinner had produced a direct translation, which didn't seek to distort or polemicize against the Talmud, he was furious. He withdrew his funding. No further volumes appeared.[27]

Hirsch Mendel Pineles's defence of the Mishnah and Pinner's desire to make the Talmud accessible to those who couldn't understand the original were just two of the many endeavours in the growing field of academic Talmud scholarship. Over the course of the nineteenth century new tools appeared, all designed to facilitate critical scholarship. Amongst the most important were Raphael Rabbinowicz's 1867 comprehensive listing of all the variant readings contained in known Talmudic manuscripts and printed versions, and Marcus Jastrow's *Dictionary*.

Jastrow wasn't the first to try his hand at writing a dictionary. The German scholar Wilhelm Gesenius had produced a Latin lexicon in 1815 that was subsequently translated into English. But Jastrow's work, which gives Talmudic examples for each word, remains the standard study aid for English-speaking Talmud students even today.

Academic Talmudic scholarship wasn't confined to Jews. It attracted the attention of the missionary Protestant, Franz Delitzsch, and his students. Delitzsch was a Lutheran Bible commentator with a profound knowledge of, and a keen interest in rabbinic literature.[28] His knowledge proved to be the downfall of August Rohling, a priest and professor of Hebrew Literature at Charles University in Prague.

In 1871 Rohling published *The Talmud Jew*, an annotated collection of quotations allegedly from the Talmud. Unfortunately he made all the quotations up,

---

[27] Mintz, 2006.
[28] For a comprehensive evaluation of missionary Protestantism's engagement with Jewish studies see Gerdmar, 2009.

and it was quite clear that his intention was nothing other than scurrilous. Rohling compounded his stupidity when, called as a witness in a blood libel trial, he came out with the old calumny that the Talmud instructed Jews to use Christian blood in their rituals. Joseph Bloch, a young rabbi, soon to become a member of the Austrian parliament, called Rohling a fraud and offered to pay him three thousand florins if he could translate a page of the Talmud. Rohling, who wasn't up to the task, tried to avoid the challenge by suing for libel. Bloch called upon Franz Delitzsch, who comprehensively refuted Rohling's polemic. Rohling dropped the case before it came to court, was forced to pay costs and was suspended from his university chair.[29]

In 1878 August Wunsche, a student of Delitszch, translated passages from the Talmud. And in 1887 Hermann Strack, a Protestant missionary and professor of the Old Testament at Berlin University published his Introduction to the Talmud. Strack's book has been enlarged and reprinted several times. It remains a classic work for academic Talmud scholars today.

Rohling was also indirectly responsible for the first full German translation of the Talmud. Not content with one downfall, August Rohling had sought another by commissioning a converted Jew to write a book proving that the Talmud demanded ritual murder. The author of the book was convicted of defamation. Lazarus Goldschmidt, an expert in Semitic languages living in Leipzig was urged by his non-Jewish landlord to write a translation of the Talmud, to put accusations like this to rest.[30]

## The end of the old ways

The old ways were also changing in Poland and Russia. So much was happening to destabilize the established patterns of life. By the middle of the nineteenth century a three-way, cultural struggle was taking place between the Hasidim, their traditionalist opponents and those committed to the *Haskala*. At any time and in nearly any place two of the factions would be engaged in joint enterprise against the third, dividing families and communities and causing social upheaval.[31]

---

[29] Levy, 2005.
[30] Mintz, 2006.
[31] Dawidowicz, 1967.

At the same time, gradual emancipation was making people more politically aware, active and organized. Karl Marx's writings were being discussed, workers' groups were meeting, and agitating. Zionism was on the agenda, news of pioneers who were rebuilding the homeland was firing imaginations, particularly amongst the young. If that wasn't distraction enough, there were economic pressures, industrialization, urbanization and ever-growing waves of emigration to the utopias of America and northern Europe. Set against a background of anti-Semitic legislation, persecutions and pogroms, it's little wonder that the long-established, Talmud-based system of education was crumbling.

In the *yeshivot*, traditionally and exclusively dedicated to Talmud study, students were becoming politically aware, often without the knowledge and approval of the teachers. Many *yeshivot* themselves were changing; a new impetus towards ethical education was gaining ground, eating into the long hours that were once dedicated solely to the Talmud. Known as the *Musar* movement, founded by the saintly Israel Salanter, its goal was moral improvement through introspection and the study of inspirational, ethical literature. The influential, elite *yeshiva* at Volozhin, and those which had been founded in its image, frowned upon *musar*. For them the proper study of Talmud, and Talmud alone, provided all the character-building a student would ever need.

By the beginning of the twentieth century the once, seemingly monolithic, eastern European communities were fragmenting into a mosaic of differing sects, movements, parties and factions. Each with their own perspective on the Talmud, or none. Meanwhile the USA was setting a different pace.

## A seafood banquet

In 1883 the Reform movement's college in Cincinnati held a banquet to celebrate their first-ever graduation ceremony. By this time the number of Jews in the USA had swelled considerably. The Reform movement was still dominant but it now catered for many tastes, from out-and-out rejectionists of the Talmud on one wing, to traditionalists on the other. Neil Gillman describes it as the 'American Reform coalition'.[32]

---

[32] Gillman, 1993, p. 25.

The college invited the movement's leading lights to the banquet. As the first diners took their seats some could be seen shaking their heads in disbelief, turning and murmuring discontentedly to their neighbours. As more diners filed into the room the murmur turned into a hubbub. Finally a good number of red-faced, furious-looking people stormed out of the room. One man waved the menu card in the air, yelling 'This is a disgrace'.

The printed menu for the nine-course banquet had been on the tables when they entered the room. On it were clams, crabs and shrimp, all of which are specifically prohibited in the book of Leviticus.[33] The main course was beef and the desert, cheese and ice cream, a combination of meat and milk dishes the prohibition of which was so ancient that even the Talmud is aware of it.[34]

The walkout in Cincinnati was when the Talmud in the USA started to fight back. The fight intensified a few years later when a conference of Reform rabbis in Pittsburgh declared allegiance only to the moral laws of Judaism, rejecting Talmudic legislation as apt 'to obstruct, rather than further, modern spiritual elevation.'[35]

In a deliberate secession from the Reform movement, the traditionalists announced the creation of a new rabbinical seminary in New York, based on 'conservative' principles. Known as the Jewish Theological Seminary, its constitution declared its commitment to 'historical Judaism' as expounded in 'Biblical and Talmudic writings'.[36] The curriculum was to combine traditional Talmud study with *Wissenschaft* subjects including Jewish philosophy, history and literature.

In 1901 the Seminary's governors persuaded Solomon Schechter to leave the hallowed tranquillity of Cambridge University in England, to take up the position of president. Born into a Hasidic family in Romania, Shechter had been brought up in a traditional, eastern European *yeshiva* before moving to Berlin where he was drawn to the *Wissenschaft* school. Academically orientated and traditional in outlook, he attracted a circle of similarly minded scholars to the Seminary, many of them recent immigrants from Europe. He laid the foundations for the Seminary to become one of the world's leading centres of

---

[33] Leviticus 11.10–12.
[34] M. Hullin 8, 1.
[35] Mendes-Flohr and Reinharz, 1995, p. 469.
[36] Gillman, 1993.

Talmudic research and study for most of the twentieth century. But the scene of his greatest achievement was not Romania, Berlin, Cambridge or New York. It was the back alleys of Cairo.

## The Cairo Genizah

In 1896 Mrs Agnes Smith Lewis and Mrs Margaret Dunlop Gibson, twin sisters, now widowed, travelled to Egypt. They'd been there before. Both women were accomplished scholars, able to read Greek, Syriac, Arabic and Hebrew. On a previous visit to the Middle East they had discovered a fifth-century Syriac gospel, the leaves of which were being used as butter dishes in the refectory of St Catherine's monastery on Mount Sinai.[37]

On this trip they were in a Cairo market when a vendor offered them some pages from a Hebrew manuscript. On their return to England they showed them to Solomon Schechter. He realized they must have been torn from a Hebrew version of the book of Ecclesiasticus, or Ben Sira, which previously had only been known in Syrian or Greek translation.

Ancient Hebrew documents had been circulating in Cairo for a number of years. Several had made their way back to the USA and England. It was known that they were being filched from an ancient storeroom, or *genizah*, in the old synagogue in Fostat, where worn-out, sacred documents were deposited. Schechter, realizing that there may be many more valuable treasures to be found, organized a trip to Cairo and negotiated with the synagogue authorities to buy the entire contents of the store.

The storeroom had no windows or doors. To enter Schechter had to climb a ladder and crawl through a hole in the wall. He was amazed at what he found. The Cairo *Genizah* turned out to contain nineteen thousand documents, some sacred, but many just the ordinary ephemera of community life: legal contracts, letters and school books. Amongst them were lost fragments and manuscripts of the Talmud dating back to 870 CE.

Schechter brought the contents of the *Genizah* back to Cambridge. Over a century later its manuscripts are still being analysed. They have helped to

---

[37] The Taylor-Schechter Genizah Research Unit, 2002.

explain many obscure or corrupted Talmudic passages and have thrown light on life and conditions in ancient Egyptian communities.

When he arrived in New York Schechter would have encountered people who reminded him of the family he had left behind in Romania. Waves of immigration from eastern Europe had brought many strictly observant families to the city. Their style was very different from those with a cultured German or English background. They'd come from rural towns and villages where traditional Talmud study had been the norm, and the new ways of thinking an oddity. In New York they found that the reverse held true. They couldn't make any sense of Reform at all. Even Schechter's Jewish Theological Seminary seemed too radical.

But this was America and even the most traditional methods of Talmud study couldn't completely avoid change. The immigrants set up their own seminary, on the Lower East Side, and adopted the latest method of study, which had been developed in the Lithuanian tradition once pioneered by the Volozhin *yeshiva*. The method, even more analytical than its predecessors, had met with considerable opposition when first introduced in Europe by Hayyim of Brisk.

Whereas traditionalists were interested in studying the Talmud to determine practical law, the Brisker method was focused purely on analysis of the argument. Students tended only to study those volumes of the Talmud where the keenest argumentation was found. On one occasion Hayyim of Brisk was grappling with a difficult legal problem. He wrote to Isaac Elchanan Spektor, after whom the New York *yeshiva* would be named, gave him all the facts and asked for his ruling. But he insisted that Spektor was not to tell him his reasons. He was happy to defer to a practical decision but he didn't want to know the reasoning behind it. In case he was tempted to review it, and reach a different conclusion.[38]

The Talmud was now well and truly embedded in America. As events unfolded it became clear that it had crossed the Atlantic just in time. Events in Germany were about to put an end to its thousand-year sojourn in Europe. For the next half century America was to be its most important home. But Europe still had one major contribution to make.

---

[38] Jacobs, 1984.

## A page a day

A young man stood up at a conference of traditional rabbis in Vienna, in 1923. Meir Shapiro was a highly accomplished orator, he sat in the Polish parliament and was the rabbi of a smallish town in south-east Poland. He had won acclaim in parliament for a detailed plan he submitted to reform the Polish economy[39] but his abiding passion was education, particularly its improvement and reform. He would soon found a Talmud academy in Lublin that would become renowned not just for its rigorous curriculum but also for its inspiring physical environment, which he felt was essential for successful study.

Meir Shapiro told the conference that he was concerned about two aspects of contemporary Talmud study. One, that it was accessible only to an elite, who had the opportunity and educational background to enrol in a *yeshiva* and spend years studying there. The other, that only a small number of volumes were studied, notably those which lent themselves to detailed analytical investigation.

Shapiro's suggestion was brilliant in its simplicity, and far-reaching in its outlook.[40] He proposed setting up study groups for lay people in which one page of Talmud would be studied each day. The two thousand seven hundred pages of Talmud would take nearly seven and half years to complete and would involve a commitment from participants of around an hour a day. It was a significant commitment but it was achievable. It would bring the Talmud to a much wider audience and bind its world together, the same page would be studied on the same day everywhere; travellers would be able to continue their studies wherever they went.

Shapiro's plan didn't go down well with everyone. His namesake, the ultra-conservative Hayyim Eleazar Shapira, a Hasidic leader in the Transylvanian town of Munkacz, opposed it on the grounds that it was a deviation from traditional methods of learning, that in any case topics did not end neatly at the bottom of each page and, perhaps most pertinently, it was an initiative of those who supported the Zionist cause, to which the Munkacz Hasidim were firmly opposed.[41]

---

[39] Letter by R. Daniel Lowy in *Tradition*, 10(3) (Spring 1969), p. 114.

[40] But see Marc Shapiro's note 23 in (Shapiro, 2006) in which he points out that Meir Shapiro was not the first to have the idea.

[41] Shapiro, 2006; Nadler, 1994.

But Meir Shapiro's proposal was agreed by the conference and in 1924 the first cycle of what became known as the *daf yomi* or 'daily page' programme began. It was to become perhaps the most significant, and certainly the most democratising, Talmud initiative of all time. But that wouldn't happen until long after the rise, and downfall, of Nazi Germany.

# 15

# A new world in the making

Hillel said: If I am not for me, who will be for me? When I am for me, what am I? And if not now, when?[1]

## Destruction

The problems began even before the Nazis came to power in 1933 but accelerated sharply thereafter. Nazi bans on the ritual slaughter of meat, the forcible closure of Jewish shops and other measures designed to deny the Jews a livelihood led to profound dilemmas for Talmudists whose entire world view was founded on strict religious observance. Could the laws restricting work on the Sabbath, or regarding the slaughter of meat be modified and, even if they could, would this be desirable, or would it lead to an unleashing of the flood gates, an increasing destruction of religious life, handing the Nazis the victory they wanted?

The Rabbinic Seminary in Berlin, which prided itself in producing Talmudic scholars who had also received a general education, was condemned when it made plans to relocate with its students to Tel Aviv. Esriel Hildesheimer, the inspiration behind the college, was accused of abandoning his people; the Seminary existed to produce rabbis for the German community, and now, in their darkest hour, it was threatening to leave. He was also strongly criticized by conservative eastern European rabbinic leaders. They had only tolerated the college's embrace of secular studies as a bulwark against German Reform. They strongly disapproved of his taking what they saw as a fundamentally heretical curriculum to Israel, where there was no Reform presence. Hildesheimer,

---

[1] M. Avot 1.14.

although not answerable in any way to the conservatives, revoked his plans; the Talmud remained in Berlin.[2]

As conditions worsened, Leo Baeck, the great philosophically minded leader of German Reform predicted the end of a thousand years of Jewish life on German soil. Nevertheless he refused to leave Germany, electing to stay with his people until at the last he was deported to the Theresienstadt concentration camp. The Talmudist Jehiel Jacob Weinberg didn't agree with Baeck's prediction.[3] The Talmud knows nothing of finality, there are many ways of addressing a problem. Seventy years on we can see they were both right. It was indeed the end of Jewish life on German soil. Until the fall of the Soviet Union in 1991 marked the beginning of an astonishing revival.

The rise of Nazism led to a bout of soul searching for those who held firm to Samson Raphael Hirsch's approach of including secular study alongside a Talmudic education. Many German Jews could no longer see anything of value in a culture which could spawn the evil of Nazism.

In the end events took control. On 7 November 1938, Herzl Grynspan, a seventeen-year-old Polish Jew, who had just heard that his parents had been expelled from Germany, shot a German diplomat in the Paris embassy. On 9 November a co-ordinated action by Nazi storm troopers and Hitler Youth across Germany destroyed close to three hundred synagogues, shattered the windows of seven and a half thousand Jewish commercial properties, looted the buildings, slaughtered ninety one people and transported thirty thousand people to concentration camps. It became known as *Kristellnacht,* the night of broken glass. The Berlin Seminary never opened its doors again.

Eleven million people were slaughtered by fanatic, ruthless Germanic efficiency. Six million of them were Jews, rounded up and herded into death camps. Their possessions, books and, in many cases, all records of their existence were destroyed along with them. Two thirds of the entire Jewish population of Europe were slaughtered.

Amongst the most heart-rending accounts of Talmudic life from that time, one of the few textual witnesses to survive, is Rabbi Ephraim Oshry's remarkable record. He was one of twenty five thousand souls who were driven into the tiny ghetto in Kovno, Lithuania, when the Nazis invaded in 1941. The

---

[2] Shapiro, 1999.
[3] Leo Baeck survived Theresienstadt. His is one of many stories of inspirational courage and heroic survival. At the end of the war, he moved to London.

ghetto was liquidated in 1944 when, with the advancing Russian army breathing down their necks, the fleeing Nazis transported as many of its inhabitants as they could to death camps, and murdered most of the remainder on the spot. Rabbi Oshry survived. His wife and children did not.

Oshry served as a spiritual guide to those in the ghetto. People would approach him daily with their problems, and questions. He tore scraps of paper from wherever he could to record everything they asked, and all his responses. He hid the scraps. Following the war he published five volumes of his record.[4] Among the questions he was asked was whether it was permissible to pressurize someone to try to save another person's life, knowing that they may not succeed and may be risking their own life in doing so. He turned to a Talmudic discussion to help him formulate his answer. The Talmud had wanted to know how one should act if commanded by a tyrant to slay someone or be slain themselves. The Talmud asked 'Who can say your blood is redder than his'?[5] In other words there is no way to value one life more highly than another. Saving life is the highest of all priorities, but not if it means taking another life.[6]

Following the war, and the liberation of the death camps, Europe was studded with refugees, of every nationality, faith and political conviction. The victorious Allied Forces were overwhelmed, they had never confronted human suffering on such a scale before. Penniless, homeless and traumatized, the refugees were placed into displaced persons camps, whilst the authorities agonized over how to resettle them all. The DP camps, as they were called, were miserable places, often little better than the concentration camps. Some were even set up on the site of former Nazi camps.

The refugees incarcerated in the DP camps struggled to rebuild their lives. For the Jews, education, as ever, was a priority; the younger children had never been to school, their older siblings had been torn away from their studies. They needed books of all types. Including copies of the Talmud. There were none to be found.

A group of rabbis approached the Commander of the American Zone in Germany and asked for the US Army's help in obtaining copies of the Talmud. A survivor of the Dachau Camp and former chief rabbi of the Lithuanian

---

[4] Oshry, 1983.
[5] B. Sanhedrin 74a and elsewhere.
[6] Levine, 2011. Of course there are situations when it is permissible to kill in order to save a life, most obviously when a murderer is trying to kill an innocent person.

Army, Rabbi Samuel E. Snaig, suggested that copies be printed in Germany. The American Joint Distribution Committee sent two copies from the USA and the US Army commandeered an old German printing plant in Heidelberg. One hundred copies of what became known as the Survivor's Talmud were printed. On presses that the Nazis had used to print their propaganda. It was a small but welcome irony, the people of the Talmud printing their ancient tome on presses belonging to the villains who had tried to destroy them. It was a pity the architect of their destruction was no longer alive to witness the humiliation.

## A new beginning

The Talmud hadn't been destroyed but its environment would never be the same again. The European *yeshivot* and seminaries were gone. With eastern Europe under Soviet control there was neither the will nor the opportunity to rebuild them. The teachers and students who had survived were traumatized and broken, they could see no future.

From one tiny corner of the globe a ray of hope glimmered. The United Nations had voted to grant independence to the state of Israel. It wasn't an easy birth, war broke out with its Arab neighbours on the day the state was founded, and a further population upheaval began as communities in the Arab-speaking world overnight found themselves unwelcome in the lands where their families had lived for generations.

In 1941, just before the Nazis arrived, students from the *yeshiva* in the Polish town of Mir had managed to obtain exit visas from the Soviet occupiers. Unable to flee westwards into Nazi-dominated Europe, they had enlisted the aid of the Japanese and Dutch consuls in Kovno, who managed to get them entry visas to the Caribbean island of Curacao. Four hundred of them travelled across Russian by the Trans-Siberian railway to Japan. They never made it to Curacao. The Japanese, who were fighting alongside the Germans, moved them to Shanghai and in 1943 forced them into a ghetto. But they did survive, unharmed. In 1946, when travel became possible again, they left, arriving first in the USA and finally re-establishing themselves in Israel.[7]

---

[7] Yad VaShem, 2013.

A few other old European *yeshivot* were also reincarnated in Israel or the USA. These countries became the centres of the new Talmudic universe; with a sprinkling of outposts in other English-speaking lands. Fortunately the Talmud was no stranger to the English language. Nor to the scholars who spoke it.

In 1933 the Reverend Herbert Danby, canon at the Anglican Cathedral of St George in Jerusalem, had published his translation of the Mishnah into English. He was the last big name in a short but notable line of English-speaking, Christian Hebraist clergymen. Whereas their sixteenth-century predecessors had ostensibly studied the Talmud to help them construct a better case against Judaism, or to gain a better understanding of Christianity, the twentieth-century scholars had no qualms about admitting their admiration for the Talmud, its sages and the rabbinic system that underpins it.

In his introduction Danby, who would end his career as Regius Professor of Hebrew at Oxford University, noted that his translation and notes followed traditional Jewish interpretation. To neglect the centuries of extensive study of the Mishnah and Talmud would, he wrote, 'be as presumptuous as it is precarious'.[8]

Thirty years earlier R. Travers Herford, a Unitarian minister in Manchester had published *Christianity in Talmud and Midrash*. He judged the Talmud to be 'a consistent and logical endeavour to work out a complete guide to the living of a perfect life'.[9] He trawled the Talmud and associated rabbinic literature, seeking out every reference to Jesus and Christianity and finding many more than there actually are. Although his work appears today to be a little over-eager and uncritical, the scholarship which he applied, in an age when a two-million-word text could not be searched digitally, is formidable.

Herford's passion, and the subject of his major works, was the literature and outlook of the early Talmudic, Pharisaic period. His slightly older contemporary, George Foot Moore, a Presbyterian pastor and Professor of the History of Religion at Harvard concentrated on the Bible and on the origins and theology of religion. He wrote a three-volume work on Judaism during the period that the Talmud was gestating.[10] Many of his works are studded with Talmudic references.

---

[8] Danby, 1933.
[9] Herford, 1903, p. 8.
[10] *Judaism in the First Three Centuries of the Christian Era: The Age of Tannaim*, 3 volumes, George Foot Moore (Harvard University Press, Cambridge, MA, 1927).

In London, two years after Danby's Mishnah appeared, a small group of Jewish scholars headed by Isidore Epstein undertook a project to translate the Talmud into English. The work was interrupted by the war and not completed until 1952. It wasn't the first such project, a highly unsatisfactory, late nineteenth-century, English translation had been made by Michael Rodkinson who had moved to the USA after being accused of various misdemeanours, including support for the anti-Talmud polemicist August Rohling.[11] His translation leaves out passages that he felt were irrelevant or of no interest, and he failed to grasp the sense of much that he was translating.[12] This is not surprising since he spoke very little English, he translated the Talmud into Yiddish and then got schoolchildren to render it in English. Kauffmann Kohler, a leading Reform scholar complained that 'the vandalism perpetrated against the text is unparalleled'.[13]

Epstein and his team were of a far different calibre. Their scholarly translation appeared in thirty five volumes, each with an introduction and concise, explanatory notes. The translation was published by the Soncino Press, named after the famous fifteenth-century Italian family of printers.[14]

Although its language appears a little archaic now, and its notes can sometimes be as impenetrable as the text they are trying to explain, the Soncino translation functioned for many years as the main study aid for English-speaking Talmud students.

## The Westminster Talmud

Henry VIII's Talmud had lain virtually untouched in Westminster Abbey for over four centuries. At lest that's what the few who knew about it thought. In 1956 it was put on display at the Victoria and Albert Museum in London. Jack

---

[11] Heller, 2013.

[12] Rodkinson's *New Edition of the Babylonian Talmud: Original Text Edited, Corrected, Formulated, and Translated into English* was published between 1896 and 1903 by Boston New Talmud Publishing Company in New York. Its title is reminiscent of the Yiddish version of Hamlet staged in New York in the 1890s by Boris Tomashevsky and billed as *Hamlet, Schauspeil Von Shakespeare, Verandert Undt Verbessert (Hamlet, a Play by Shakespeare, Changed and Improved)*. For criticisms of Rodkinson's work see Mintz, 2006.

[13] Quoted in Heller, 2013, pp. 214, 239.

[14] Epstein, 1935–52.

Lunzer, a collector of ancient manuscripts saw it and tried to acquire it. But the Abbey would not sell.

Twenty five years later Lunzer managed to acquire a medieval copy of Westminster Abbey's founding charter that was on sale in the USA. He had already agreed with the Abbey that if he could acquire the charter they would swap it for the Talmud. The nine-volume edition, printed by Daniel Bomberg between 1522 and 1538 is now in the Valmadonna collection in New York. But it now transpires the copy in the Abbey may not have belonged to Henry. Each volume has the owner's initials, RB, stamped on it. It was assumed that this stood for either *Rex Brittanicus*, King of Britain or *Regio Bibliotheca*, the King's Library. But a letter to *The Times* from the Reverend Edward Carpenter, Dean of Westminster poured cold water on this idea.[15] He pointed out that there was no surviving binding from the Royal Library that bore these initials. According to the Dean, Henry VIII's copy was almost certainly donated by the Old Royal Library to the British Museum in 1757 and is now in the British Library.[16] Subsequent research, confirmed by the Valmadonna Trust catalogue, is that the volume acquired by Lunzer belonged to Richard Bruarne, who was Regius Professor of Hebrew at Oxford.[17]

## The new Rashi

The last few decades of the twentieth century saw the beginnings of an explosion in Talmud learning. More people now studying it than at any other time in history. But it didn't happen overnight. Many reasons have been put forward for the phenomenon, but it wouldn't have happened without a few key people and institutions that were instrumental in making the Talmud accessible to everyone. Adin Steinsaltz is one such man.

Born in Jerusalem in 1937, Steinsaltz was brought up in a secular home. He studied science at university before embarking on a rabbinic career. His website refers to him as a 'teacher, philosopher, social critic and prolific author.'[18] He's

---

[15] *The Times*, London, 8 July 1980.

[16] The British Library, in private correspondence, have to date been unable to confirm the provenance of the Bomberg Talmud in their possession.

[17] Samuel, 1978–80.

[18] https://www.steinsaltz.org/Biography.php

certainly prolific, he has written over sixty books. But his most significant achievement is his new edition of the Talmud, which he began working on when he was just twenty seven.

The problem that Steinsaltz was trying to solve when he decided on a new edition of the Talmud was that the traditional volumes are all based on the late-nineteenth-century edition printed in Vilna by the wonderfully named Widow and Brothers Romm. This, in turn, was based on Bomberg's edition. The text is unpointed, meaning it has no punctuation or vowels; in Hebrew and Aramaic vowels are not part of the alphabet; they can be added as marks above or below the letters but texts for native readers are generally printed without any indication of what the vowels should be. In addition, as befits a nineteenth-century text, the typography, although perfectly legible, is not as easy on the eye as a modern reader is used to. And the commentaries that surround the main text, are those of Rashi and the *tosafot*, which, although integral to traditional study, are centuries old and difficult for many people to comprehend.

Steinsaltz's edition addressed all these problems. He reset the type in a modern format and translated the text into either modern Hebrew or English, depending on the edition, weaving his own running commentary into the translation. In addition to the traditional commentaries of Rashi and *tosafot*, he explained unusual or difficult words and provided illustrations and scientific explanations where these would be helpful. His printers used twelve different typefaces to help the reader distinguish between the different types of material.

A 1988 article in *Time* magazine described Adin Steinsaltz as a modern Maimonides or Rashi.[19] Over a million copies of his Hebrew edition have been sold. A new format of his English edition has recently been produced by Koren publishers to which they have appended the traditional Vilna page.

In Steinsaltz's view the Talmud is the central pillar of Jewish life, more so than the Bible. If he had his way, rather than teaching the Bible as the key text in Israeli schools, they would teach the Talmud. His opinion carries credibility; he was the youngest ever principal of an Israeli high school, at the age of twenty three.

Steinsaltz pioneered the popularization of the Talmud. Some felt he had been too radical; that he had produced an edition of the Talmud for reading, rather than for learning. That was certainly the view of the editors of the next major project to

---

[19] Ostling, 1988.

make the Talmud accessible to a wider audience. The ArtScroll Talmud reverted to the traditional Hebrew layout but the facing page included a clear, comprehensible English translation, interwoven with a running commentary, and detailed notes.

When they began to produce their edition of the Talmud, ArtScroll was already a well-established publishing house, specializing in elegantly produced, ideologically certain, religious texts. The success of their Talmud edition is due in part to its visual appeal but mainly to the clarity with which it communicates and explains the discussion. Apocryphal stories circulate of ArtScroll readers who cannot understand Hebrew but can study the Talmud perfectly well using only the English translation.

Artscroll is much more traditional in its outlook than the Steinsaltz edition, belonging more to the *yeshiva* than to the university. Consequently it is far more welcome in strictly religious circles. Its use of English is less dense than that of the Soncino translators and it is far more dogmatic in its conclusions; it both confuses and challenges its readers less. It excels as a study aid. Its translations are now available in modern Hebrew, English and French.

## The secular Talmud

Printed books are only one of the reasons for the growth in the Talmud's popularity. A revival of religious interest, coupled with the worldwide, gap-year phenomenon has led to a remarkable increase in the number of people studying the Talmud at Israel *yeshivot* and seminaries. Many school leavers now spend one, two or even three years studying, before going to university, or embarking on a career.

Even a casual search on the internet shows just how widespread *yeshiva* study has become. Hundreds, possibly thousands, of sites offer resources for Talmud study. Some contain online lectures, or pages of study notes. Others are dedicated to intense Talmudic conversation between students, conducted in a patois virtually unintelligible to outsiders. Known as *yeshivish*, it even has its own dictionary. Chaim Weiser, who compiled the dictionary, describes it as an infusion into English of a lexicon of words from different languages, which are then subjected to the rules of English grammar.[20] *Yeshivish* is the Creole of the modern Talmud student.

---

[20]  Weiser, 1995.

But the Talmud is no longer the exclusive property of the religious. Nor does it just belong to men. The old cultural assumption that education is only for men was set aside generations ago, and even though it is still felt in some circles that the Talmud is a closed book for women, that view is changing fast. There are now many women Talmudic scholars.

One of the most striking things about the Talmud, which sets it apart from almost every other religious text, is that one does not have to be a believer in order to study it. It helps of course to be familiar with the Bible and religious concepts, but the Talmud is fundamentally an exercise in interpretation and logic. It assumes, but doesn't demand, belief.

Academics have long recognized this. Dozens of universities around the world now have departments devoted to Jewish Studies. Talmud is high on the list of subjects they research and teach. Directly descended from the nineteenth-century *Wissenschaft* movement, the field has broadened considerably. Academic Talmud study today explores the structure, style and content of the literary units that make up the text; researches parallel sources both within the Talmud and beyond, seeks to clarify the discussions and sets them within their historical and cultural context. It is no different in form from academic study of any other ancient text.[21]

Secular Talmud study isn't just happening in universities. It makes perfect sense to us that someone, irrespective of their religious commitment would want to study the texts that make up their cultural heritage. But it's hard to know what the old, narrowly focused Talmud scholars of the Middle Ages would have made of the most recent development in the Talmudic world.

In the mid-1990s small groups of irreligious Jews, primarily in Israel but also in the USA, began to gather together to study Talmud from a cultural perspective. In part this was a quest for identity in a pluralistic world, but for many it was simply for the enjoyment of coming to grips with a complex, challenging text that they had heard so much about. Since they are not studying in a traditional institution they are able to be far more creative about the way they engage with the text. Elul, an Israeli organization dedicated to secular

---

[21] The list of distinguished academics who have researched the Talmud is long and growing daily. Some, but by no means all, are noted in the Bibliography at the back of the book. The omission of a scholar's writings from the Bibliography is not a reflection upon their work, but a consequence of the vastness of the subject.

study of the Talmud and other ancient texts, uses storytelling, music, art and creative literature as part of its instructional method.[22]

In 2013 Ruth Caldron, the head of a secular Talmud study centre, was elected to the Knesset, the Israeli parliament. In her maiden speech she delivered a lecture from the Talmud. She took a moving passage about a woman waiting for her husband to come home, gradually coming to terms with the fact of his death. She turned it into a plea for diversity and mutual respect. Her fellow Knesset members included ultra-religious men who had never heard Talmud taught from a secular perspective, and certainly not from a woman. Her speech became an internet phenomenon.

Today tens of thousands of people attend secular Talmud study groups. In fact, secular Talmud study programmes engage more people worldwide than almost any other structured programme. The exception is *daf yomi*, the page-a-day programme that Meir Shapiro set up in 1924.

## The thirteenth cycle

On 1 August 2012, ninety three thousand men packed into the Metlife stadium in New Jersey. They had come to mark the conclusion of the twelfth cycle of *daf yomi*. It had run continuously since its inauguration. Tens of thousands of men and women attended similar events across the world. The following day the thirteenth cycle began. There is no let up in the *daf yomi* schedule.

Typically, participants in the *daf yomi* programme study together in small groups, making time outside of their working day to meet. There are even groups who meet daily on trains, as they commute to work. Some sessions take the form of a lecture, others are made up of people with a similar level of knowledge, who work through the text together, often using printed or internet resources to help them. Its popularity belies its gruelling schedule.

The scale of *daf yomi's* reception is intriguing. For its first half century it was a fringe activity, only the most committed took part. In 1975 the conclusion ceremony in New York attracted around five thousand participants, by 1990 it was twenty thousand and in 2013 ninety three thousand. Haym Soloveitchik sees this as emblematic of a contemporary quest for identity; in today's world

---

[22] http://www.elul.org.il

our religious or cultural identity is no longer inevitable, we all make cultural choices.[23] Turning to the Talmud as part of an identity quest is one such choice.

But it's not just a matter of identity. There's little doubt that technology has helped fuel the popularity of the *daf yomi* programme. In the days before the internet, *daf yomi* lectures were recorded on cassette or delivered through telephone help lines. When the internet came along its programmes were amongst the first experiments in e-learning. Today, when the *daf yomi* participant goes online, she can choose from hundreds of websites containing texts and study guides; listen to, or watch, any one of dozens of experts delivering a lecture and download apps providing every conceivable form of assistance. And when she picks up a volume of her tastefully formatted ArtScroll or Koren edition, the traditional burden of 'labouring in the Talmud' is made so much easier.

## The future

The diversity of those interacting with the Talmud today reflects the pluralist, multi-cultural world in which we live. What is counter-intuitive however is that, although the content of the Talmud is ancient, it can be construed as anticipating modernity, intrinsically suited to the twenty-first century.

Like the internet, the Talmud is a multi-dimensional, non-linear text in which nearly every line links to content on other pages, creating a web of connections and multiple paths for the reader to explore.[24] The core text, which equates to the home page of a website, links to a hierarchy of on-the-page commentaries, these connect to a second tier at the back of each volume exploring the commentaries themselves, and infinitely expanding tertiary and subsequent levels are contained in separate publications on the Talmudist's bookshelves. Unlike the internet, however, the links are not highlighted or underlined on the page. The Talmud's hyperlinks are fluid, responsive to the reader's imagination, analytical skills and subject of interest, not to the page designer's commercial or creative agenda.

It's not just the internet. Some Talmudic calculations caused headaches for medieval commentators, who struggled to explain the thinking behind them.

---

[23] Soloveitchik, 1994.

[24] See the section Talmud and Internet in (Alexenberg, 2006) and Jonathan Rosen's personal memoir Rosen, 2001.

Mathematicians are now discovering that at least some of the solutions lie in game theory.[25]

There's also an aspect of Talmudic decision making which is reminiscent of quantum theory. Science knows that sub-atomic particles do not occupy a definite state, until they are observed. It is the fact of observation which fixes them. There is a category of problem in the Talmud which draws on a similar concept. Its solution is known to be one of two possibilities, but each is equally probable. In most cases the problem can be resolved by reference to an actual case; if the editors of the Talmud have a record of an earlier authority deciding in a particular way, then this becomes the solution to the problem. But sometimes there is no authority who has already ruled on the problem. In this case the Talmud remains undecided, the solution exists in two states simultaneously until the end time when, traditionally, the prophet Elijah will solve it. The Talmud calls this suspended solution *teyku,* which means let it stand.

A well-known, somewhat extreme illustration of this is the case of a house from which all bread has been removed, as required for the Passover festival. The house is in a state of 'no longer needing to be cleaned'. Then a mouse is seen running in to the house with a piece of bread in its mouth. A few moments later a mouse is seen running out of the house with a piece of bread in its mouth. What is the state of the house now? Do we assume that the same mouse ran in and ran out, with the same piece of bread in its mouth and the house remains in its state of 'no longer needing to be cleaned'? Or do we assume that a different mouse ran out with a different piece of bread, the original mouse and its bread still being in the house, so that it is now in a state of 'needing to be cleaned'?[26] Each case is equally probable. (The problem was posed long before there was any forensic way of testing whether two different mice had been in the house.) The Talmud declares *teyku*; let the problem remain undecided. Technically the house now exists in two different states simultaneously; it will only assume a final state of 'needing to be cleaned' or 'not needing to be cleaned' when Elijah observes it. Just as an unobserved sub-atomic particle will only have its state fixed when someone observes it.[27]

---

[25] For a detailed treatment of the problem in Mishnah Ketubot 10.3 see Aumann, 2002.

[26] Note that the question is not whether or not the bread is in the house; that can be discovered by a simple search. The question is whether or not the search is necessary.

[27] B. Pesahim 10b. For a full discussion of this problem (of which only an abridged version has been given here) and for an analysis of the whole Teyku question see Jacobs, 1981.

Of the many cultures with which the Talmud has come into contact in its fifteen-hundred-year history, perhaps the most unusual has been the experience in South Korea. There, the Talmud has been adopted as a primary school text.

When news first emerged that South Korean children were studying the Talmud, and that every Korean home has a copy, it was greeted with disbelief. It had to be a spoof, after all adults struggle to understand the Talmud, let alone children, and most Jewish homes don't have a copy, so why should all Korean families possess one?

As befits a Talmudic narrative, the reports are both true, and false. It all depends on how you understand them. Korean children are studying the Talmud, and there are apparently copies in every home. But it's not the multi-volume, two-million-word, densely argued version. It's a highly abridged version, containing some of the stories and ethical teachings from the Talmud. Aspirational Koreans appreciate that Talmud study is an effective way of training the mind in problem solving. Combing its cut–and-thrust method of debate with the more rigid Confucian methods of teaching gives Korean students a multi-dimensional, educational experience that is unheard of anywhere else in the world.

It's nearly two thousand years since the first discussions in the Babylonian academies. The Talmud's history has been long and eventful. There's no knowing what will come next. There's no doubt that it will continue to be studied, and if the trends of the last half century are anything to go by, the number of people poring through its tomes will continue to increase for some while yet. And it will continue to reach new audiences, particularly if the South Korean experience is anything to go by.

We can't know for certain where the Talmud can go, but, for now at least, it is no longer the exclusive property of the *yeshiva,* even though that is where it will continue to challenge minds and provoke discussion the most.

The people who created the Talmud conquered no empires, nor did they build fine palaces to display their grandeur. Those who nurtured it and preserved it from the flames were not honoured by kings and princes, nobody wrote ballads in their name,[28] they received neither estates nor wealth for their trouble. The students whose eyes grew dim through long hours, days and nights of study did not do so for the sake of personal gain; not in this world at any rate.

---

[28] Robert Browning did write *Rabbi Ben Ezra,* a poem in honour of Abraham Ibn Ezra, but he was a Bible commentator, astronomer and poet, not a Talmudist.

But between them all they created a pillar of world literature, a testament to the power of the human mind. Not everyone will consider it sacred literature. Most will find it too dense to spend much time with. But it stands amongst the great classics of scholarly endeavour. It has had its fill of suffering but its world view is optimistic. Its story still has a long way to run.

# Glossary

| | |
|---|---|
| *aggada* | The non-legal material in the Talmud, including commentaries on biblical verses, ethical and religious ideas or attempts to explain the workings of the natural or spiritual worlds. More or less synonymous with *Midrash*. |
| *amora* pl. *amoraim* | a) A Talmudic scholar who lived during the period of composition of the Talmud; b) The assistant to the head of the *yeshiva*, who would proclaim his words to the students in front of him. |
| *baraita* pl. *baraitot* | Material from the period of the Mishnah which was not included in the Mishnah and which may, but doesn't necessarily, occur in another work from the Mishnaic period. |
| *conversos* | Jews who converted to Christianity as a result of the Spanish and Portuguese inquisition. |
| *daf yomi* | The programme of daily study of a page of Talmud inaugurated in 1923 by Rabbi Meir Shapiro. |
| *dina malchuta dina* | 'The law of the kingdom is the law,' Subordination of all Talmudic monetary and contractual law to the law of the land in which people live. |
| *gaon* pl. *geonim* | Literally 'Excellency'. Originally the head of the Academy in Babylon in the immediate post-Talmudic period, later a term applied to a rabbi of outstanding distinction. |

| | |
|---|---|
| *gemara* | 'Teaching' synonymous and interchangeable with Talmud. Used in the Talmud text to indicate the end of passage from the Mishnah and the beginning of a passage from the Talmud. |
| *genizah* | A storeroom where worn out Hebrew and religious documents are kept. The best known was the Cairo *Genizah*. |
| *golem* | A robotic humanoid created using mystical techniques. |
| *haberim* | Zoroastrian priests. Not to be confused with the Hebrew *haverim*, literally friends, a term used to describe members of the rabbinic circle. |
| *halacha* | 'Pathway' or 'way to go'. a) The body of Jewish religious law; b) A single religious law. |
| *Haskalah* | The Jewish religious enlightenment, part of the European Enlightenment. |
| Hasid, pl. Hasidim | Followers of Hasidism. |
| Hasidism | The mystical-joyous religious sect founded by the Ba'al Shem Tov or *Besht*. |
| *kabbalah* | Jewish mysticism. |
| *kallah* | Month-long public study sessions held twice yearly in the Babylonian academies. |
| Karaites | A Jewish sect who take the Bible literally and do not accept the Oral Law. |
| *maggid* | An itinerant preacher, also a supernatural guide or mentor. |
| *Midrash* | Literally 'exposition'. a) Homilies drawn from biblical verses. Often interchangeable with *aggada*; b) Books containing these homilies. |
| *misnegdim* | Literally 'opponents'. Those who resisted and opposed Hasidism |
| Mishnah | The first codification of the Oral Law, completed 200–220 CE. |
| *musar* | Ethical teachings, instruction in correct personal behaviour. |
| *nasi* | The leader of the Jewish community in Israel under Roman occupation. |

| | |
|---|---|
| Pharisees | Plebian, social-religious sect prior to the destruction of the Jerusalem Temple, forerunners of the rabbis. |
| *pilpul* | Literally 'sharp' or 'peppery'. Casuistic, hair-splitting analysis of Talmudic texts or Talmudic problems. |
| Sadducees | Patrician social-religious sect during the period of the Roman occupation of Israel, opponents of the Pharisees. |
| *Shema* | Declaration of faith from the Torah, read twice daily by observant Jews. |
| *tanna* | a) Rabbi of the period of the Mishnah; b) Memory man who recited the Mishnah to students in the Babylonian academies. |
| *Taska* | A tax similar to ground rent, paid on agricultural land, to the Sassanian authorities. |
| *teshuva*, pl. *teshuvot* | A written rabbinic responsum to a legal question. |
| *teyku* | Literally 'let it stand'. An unsolved Talmudic problem. |
| Torah | The Five Books of Moses, also known as the Pentateuch. The first and, to the Jews the most sacred, books of the Old Testament. |
| *tosafist* | Talmudic commentator of the twelfth–fourteenth-century French school. |
| *Tosafot.* | Compilation of commentaries by the *tosafists*. |
| *Tosefta* | Collection of rabbinic material from the period of the Mishnah which was not included in the Mishnah. |
| *Wissenschaft des Judentums* | 'Science of Judaism.' Academic analysis of Jewish thought, texts and history. |
| *yeshiva*, pl. *yeshivot* | A college for the study of the Talmud. |
| *Zohar* | The principal text of *kabbalah*. |

# Bibliography

Abramson, S., 1987. Mi-torato shel Rav Shmuel HaNagid mi-Sefarad. *Sinai*, Volume 100, pp. 22–3.

Abun-Nasr, J. M., 1987. *A History of the Maghrib in the Islamic Period.* Cambridge: Cambridge University Press.

Adler, J., 2000. The Jewish Kingdom of Himyar (Yemen): Its Rise and Fall. *Midstream*, 46(4).

Adler, M. N., 1907. *The Itinerary of Benjamin of Tudela: Critical Text, Translation and Commentary.* New York: Phillip Feldheim, Inc.

Ahren, R., 2012. *Never mind the Bible, it's the sanity of the Talmud you need to understand the world and yourself.* [Online] Available at: http://www. timesofisrael.com/never-mind-the-bible-its-the-sanity-of-the-talmud-you-need-to-understand-the-world-and-yourself-adin-steinsaltz [accessed 24 April 2013].

Alexander, E. S., 1999. The Fixing of the Oral Mishnah and the Displacement of Meaning. *Oral Tradition*, 14(1), pp. 100–39.

Alexander-Frizer, T., 1991. *The Pious Sinner: Ethics and Aesthetics in Medieval Hasidic Narrative.* Tubingen: Mohr Siebeck.

Alexenberg, M., 2006. *The Future of Art in a Digital Age: From Hellenistic to Hebraic Consciousness.* Bristol: Intellect Books.

Altmann, A., 1973. *Moses Mendelssohn: A Biographical Study.* London: Routledge & Kegan Paul.

Aumann, R. J., 2002. *Game Theory in the Talmud,* Ramat Gan: Research Center on Jewish Law and Economics, Department of Economics, Bar Ilan University.

Baer, Y., 1961. *A History of the Jews in Christian Spain.* Philadelphia: Jewish Publication Society.

Bamberger, J., 2009. *The Jewish Pope.* Ramat Gan: Bar Ilan University Press.

Baron, S. W., 1928. Ghetto and Emancipation: Shall We Revise the Traditional View? *Menorah*, 14, p. 526.

Bartolucci, G., 2007. The Influence of Carlo Sigonio's 'De Republica Hebraeorum' on Hugo Grotius' 'De Republica Emendanda'. *Hebraic Political Studies*, 2(2), pp. 193–210.

Benayahu, M., 1971. *Copyright, Authorization & Imprimatour for Hebrew Books*. Israel: Ben Zvi Institute.

Ben Sasson, H. H. ed., 1967. *A History of the Jewish People*. Cambridge, MA: Harvard University Press.

Bernstein, J. A., 2001. *Print Culture and Music in Sixteenth-Century Venice*. Oxford: Oxford University Press.

Bodian, M., 1999. *Hebrews of the Portuguese Nation: Conversos and Community in Early Modern Amsterdam*. Bloomington: Indiana University Press.

—2006. The Biblical 'Jewish Republic' and the Dutch 'New Israel' in Seventeenth-Century Dutch Thought. *Hebraic Political Studies*, 1(2), pp. 186–202.

Braude, B. and Lewis, B., 1982. *Christians And Jews In The Ottoman Empire: The Functioning of a Plural Society*. New York: Holmes and Meier.

Brenner, M., Caron, V. and Kaufman, U. R., 2003. *Jewish Emancipation Reconsidered: The French & German Models*. Tubingen: Mohr Siebeck.

Brody, R., 1994. *Teshuvot of Rav Natronai bar Hilai Gaon (Hebrew)*. Jerusalem: Friedberg Library.

Brook, K. A., 2006. *The Jews of Khazaria*. 2nd edn. Lanham, MD: Rowman & Littlefield.

Brown, H. F., 1891. *The Venetian Printing Press: An Historical Study Based for the Most Part on Documents Hitherto Unpublished*. New York: G. P. Putnam's Sons.

Burnett, S. G., 1998. The Regulation of Hebrew Printing in Germany, 1555–1630: Confessional Politics and the Limits of Jewish Toleration. In: M. Reinhart and T. Robisheaux (eds). *Infinite Boundaries: Order, Disorder, and Reorder in Early Modern German Culture*. Kirksville, MO: Truman State University Press, pp. 329–48.

—2005. Christian Aramaism: The Birth and Growth of Aramaic Scholarship in the Sixteenth Century. In R. L. Troxel, K. G. Friebel eds. *Seeking Out the Wisdom of the Ancients Essays Offered to Honor Michael V. Fox on the Occasion of His Sixty-Fifth Birthday*. Winona Lake, IN: Eisenbrauns.

—2012. *Christian Hebraism in the Reformation Era (1500–1660)*. Leiden: Brill.

Buxbaum, Y., 2005. *The Light and Fire of the Baal Shem Tov*. New York: Continuum International Publishing Group, 2006.

Carlebach, E., 2006. The Status of the Talmud in Early Modern Europe. In *Printing the Talmud: From Bomberg to Schottstein*. New York: Yeshiva University Museum, pp. 79–89.

Chavel, C. B., 1983. *The Disputation at Barcelona*. New York: Shilo.

Chazan, R., 1977. The Barcelona 'Disputation' of 1263: Christian Missionizing and Jewish Response. *Speculum*, 52(4), pp. 824–42.

—2005. Christian Condemnation, Censorship, and Exploitation of the Talmud. In: *Printing the Talmud; From Bomberg to Schottstein*. New York: Yeshiva University Museum, pp. 54–60.

—1994. 'Turpitudinem uxoris fratris tui non revelavit': John Stokesley and the Divorce Question. *The Sixteenth Century Journal*, 25(2), pp. 287–387.

—1997. *Henry VIII's Conservative Scholar: Bishop John Stokesley and the Divorce, Royal Supremacy and Doctrinal Reform*. Berne: Peter Lang.

Cohen, J., 1982. *The Friars and the Jews: The Evolution of Medieval Anti-Judaism*. New York: Cornell University Press.

—1999. *Living Letters of the Law: Ideas of the Jew in Medieval Christianity*. Berkeley: University of California Press.

Cohen, M. R., 1994. *Under Crescent & Cross – The Jews in the Middle Ages*. Princeton, NJ: Princeton University Press.

Cowley, A., 1906. Bodleian Geniza Fragments. *The Jewish Quarterly Review*, 18(3), pp. 399–405.

Daiches, S., 1913. *Babylonian Oil Magic in the Talmud and in the Later Jewish Literature*, London: Jews' College.

—1921. *The Study of the Talmud in Spain*. London: J. Mazin.

Dan, J., 1999. *The 'Unique Cherub' Circle: A School of Mystics and Esoterics in Medieval Germany*. Tubingen: Mohr Siebeck.

Danby, H., 1933. *The Mishnah; Tanslated from the Hebrew with Introduction and Brief Explanatory Notes*. Oxford: Oxford University Press.

Dawidowicz, L. S., 1967. *The Golden Tradition: Jewish life and Thought in Eastern Europe*. Syracuse: Syracuse University Press,.

Doktor, J., 2011. The Beginnings of Beshtian Hasidism in Poland. *Shofar: An Interdisciplinary Journal of Jewish Studies*, 29(3), pp. 41–54.

Dunlop, D. M., 1954. *The History of the Jewish Khazars*. Princeton, NJ: Princeton University Press.

Efron, N. J., 1997. Irenism and Natural Philosophy in Rudolfine Prague: The Case of David Gans. *Science in Context*, 10(4), pp. 627–49.

Eisenberg, S. R., 2008. Reading Medieval Religious Disputation: The
    1240 'Debate' Between Rabbi Yehiel of Paris and Friar Nicholas Donin.
    University of Michigan PhD Dissertation.

Elazar, D. J. and Cohen, S. A., 1985. *The Jewish Polity: Jewish Political
    Organization from Biblical Times to the Present.* Bloomington: Indiana
    University Press.

Eliach, Y., 1968. The Russian Dissenting Sects and Their Influence on Israel
    Baal Shem Tov, Founder of Hassidism. *Proceedings of the American
    Academy for Jewish Research,* Volume 36, pp. 57–83.

Elior, R., 2004. *The Three Temples – on the Emergence of Jewish Mysticism.*
    Oxford: Littman Library of Jewish Civilisation.

Ellman, Y., 1999. Orality and the Redaction of the Babylonian Talmud. *Oral
    Tradition,* 14(1), pp. 52–99.

—2007a. The Socioeconomics of Babylonian Heresy. In: A. Gray and B.
    Jackson (eds). *Jewish Law Association Studies XVII: Studies in the Mediaeval
    Halakhah in Honor of Stephen M. Passamaneck.* 2007d, pp. 80–126.

—2007b. Middle Persian Culture and Babylonian Sages. In: C.E. Fonrobert
    and M. S. Jaffee (eds). *The Cambridge Companion to the Talmud.*
    Cambridge: Cambridge University Press, pp. 165–97.

Elukin, J., 2007. *Living Together, Living Apart: Rethinking Jewish-Christian
    Relations in the Middle Ages.* Princeton, NJ: Princeton University Press.

Epstein, I., ed., 1935–1952. *The Babylonian Talmud.* London: The Soncino
    Press.

Epstein, J. N., 1935. Remainders of She'ilthoth: 1. Oxford Fragments (in
    Hebrew). *Tarbiz,* 6(4), pp. 460–97.

—1948. מבוא לנוסח המשנה (Introduction to the Text of the Mishnah). Jerusalem:
    Magnes Press.

Etkes, I., 2002. *The Gaon of Vilna: The Man and His Image.* Berkeley:
    University of California Press.

Feiner, S., 2010. *Moses Mendelssohn: Sage of Modernity.* Yale: Yale University Press.

Feld, E., 1989. Spinoza the Jew. *Modern Judaism,* 9(1), pp. 101–19.

Finkelstein, L., 1936. *Akiba: Scholar, Saint and Martyr.* New York: Jason
    Aronson Inc.

—1944. *Rab Saadia Gaon: Studies in His Honour.* New York: Jewish
    Theological Seminary.

Fishman, D. E., 1997. Rabbi Moshe Isserles and the Study of Science among
    Polish Rabbis. *Science in Context,* 10(4), pp. 571–88.

Fishman, T., 2011. *Becoming the People of the Talmud: Oral Torah as Written Tradition in Medieval Jewish Cultures.* Philadelphia: University of Pennsylvania Press.

Francesconi, F., 2012. 'This passage can also be read differently' How Jews and Christians censored Hebrew texts in early modern Modena. *Jewish History,* 26(1–2), pp. 139–60.

Frankel, J., 1997a. *The Damascus Affair: 'Ritual Murder', Politics, and the Jews in 1840.* Cambridge: Cambridge University Press.

—1997b. 'Ritual Murder' in the Modern Era: The Damascus Affair of 1840. *Jewish Social Studies,* 3(2), pp. 1–16.

Freedman, H., 2009. *The Gospels' Veiled Agenda, Revolution, Priesthood and the Holy Grail.* Winchester: O-Books.

Friedlaender, I., 1912. Jewish-Arabic Studies. I. Shiitic Elements in Jewish Sectarianism. *The Jewish Quarterly Review,* 3(2), pp. 235–300.

Friedman, J., 1987. Jewish Conversion, The Spanish Pure Blood Laws and Reformation. A Revisionist View of Racial and Religious Antisemitism. *The Sixteenth Century Journal,* 18(1), pp. 3–30.

Friedman, S., 2004. A Good Story Deserves Retelling – The Unfolding of the Akiva Legend. *Jewish Studies, an Internet Journal,* Volume 3, pp. 55–93.

Gafni, I., 1990. *The Jews of Babylonia in the Talmudic Era – A Social and Cultural History.* Jerusalem: Yale University Press.

Gafni, I. M., 1986. Talmudic Chronology in the Iggeret of R. Sherira Gaon. *Zion,* Volume 52, pp. 1–24.

—2006. The Political, Social and Economic History of Babylonian Jewry 224–638 CE. In S. T. Katz, ed. *The Late Roman-Rabbinic Period.* Cambridge: Cambridge Universty Press.

Gerdmar, A., 2009. *Roots of Theological Anti-Semitism: German Biblical Interpretation and the Jews, from Herder and Semler to Kittel and Bultmann.* Leiden: Brill.

Gil, M., 1995. The Exilarchate. In: *The Jews of Medieval Islam: Community, Society, and Identity: Proceedings of an International Conference Held by the Institute of Jewish Studies, University College London, 1992.* Leiden: Brill.

—2003. The Origins of the Karaites. In: M. Polliack, ed. *Karaite Judaism, a Guide to its History and Literary Sources.* Leiden: Brill.

—2004. *Jews in Islamic Countries in the Middle Ages.* Leiden: Brill.

Gillman, N., 1993. *Conservative Judaism.* West Orange, NJ: Behrman House.

Ginzberg, L., 1909. *Geonica, The Geonim and Their Halakic Writings*. New York: The Jewish Theological Seminary of America.

Godman, P., 2000. *The Saint as Censor: Robert Bellarmine between Inquisition and Index*. Leiden: Brill.

Goitein, S., 1952. Who Were Mohammed's Jewish Teachers?. *Tarbiz*, Volume 23, pp. 146–59.

—1999. *A Mediterranean Society – An Abridgment in One Volume*. Berkeley: University of California Press.

—2005. *Jews and Arabs: A Concise History of Their Social and Cultural Relations*. Mineola: Dover Publications.

—1967. *A Mediterranean Society*. Berkeley: University of California Press.

Golb, N. and Pritsak, O., 1982. *Khazarian Hebrew Documents of the Tenth Century*. Ithaca, NY: Cornell University Press.

Goldblatt, D. M., 1975. *Rabbinic Instruction in Sassanian Babylon*. Leiden: Brill.

Goldish, M., 2004. *The Sabbatean Prophets*. Cambridge, MA: Harvard University Press.

Graetz, H., 1919. *Popular History of the Jews*. New York: Hebrew Publishing Co.

Gray, J., 2007. *Black Mass: Apocalyptic Religion and the Death of Utopia*. London: Allen Lane.

Grossman, A., 1988. Background to Family Ordinances – R. Gershom Me'or ha-Golah. In: A. Rapoport-Albert and S. J. Zipperstein (eds). *Jewish History: Essays in Honour of Chimen Abramsky*. London: Peter Halban.

—2004. *Pious and Rebellious: Jewish Women in Medieval Europe*. Lebanon, NH: Brandeis University Press.

—2011. *Hachmei Ashkenaz haRishonim*. Jerusalem: Magnes Press.

Grunfeld, I., 1962. Introduction to Horeb. In: *Horeb*. London: Soncino.

Guandan, P., 1984. Jews in Ancient China, A Historical Survey. In: S. Shapiro, ed. *Jews in Old China*. New York: Hippocrene Books, pp. 46–102.

Halperin, D. J. and Newby, G. D., 1982. Two Castrated Bulls: A Study in the Haggadah of K'ab al-Ahbar. *Journal of the American Oriental Society*, 102(4), pp. 631–8.

Heinemann, I., 1951. Samson, Raphael Hirsch; The Formative Years of the Leader of Modern Orthodoxy. *Historia Judaica*, 13(1), pp. 29–54.

Heller, B., 1934. Ginzberg's Legends of the Jews (Continued). *The Jewish Quarterly Review*, 24(4), pp. 393–418.

Heller, M. J., 2006. Earliest Printings of the Talmud. In: *Printing the Talmud: From Bomberg To Schottenstein*. New York: Yeshiva Univ Museum, pp. 62–79.

—2013. *Further Studies in the Making of the Early Hebrew Book*. Leiden: Brill.

Herford, R. T., 1903. *Talmud in Christianity and Midrash*. London: Williams and Norgate.

Herman, G., 2008. The Story of Rav Kahana (BT Baba Qamma 117I–b) in Light of Armeno-Persian Sources. *Irano Judaica*, Volume VI, pp. 52–86.

Hirschberg, H., 1974. *A History of the Jews in North Africa – From Antiquity to the Sixteenth Century*. Leiden: Brill.

Idel, M., 2000. *Messianic Mystics*. Yale, CT: Yale University Press.

Jacobs, L., 1957. The Economic Conditions of the Jews in Babylon in Talmudic Times Compared with Babylon. *Journal of Semitic Studies*, 2(4).

—1973. The Talmudic Sugya as a Literary Unit: An Analysis Of Baba Kamma 2a–3b. *Journal of Jewish Studies*, 24(2).

—1981. *Teyku: The Unsolved Problem in the Babylonian Talmud*. London: Cornwall Books.

—1984. *A Tree of Life; Diversity, Flexibility and Creativity in Jewish Law*. Oxford: Littman Library.

—1995. *The Jewish Religion, A Companion*. Oxford: Oxford University Press.

—2004. The Rabbinic Riddle. In: *Beyond the Letter of the Law: Essays on Diversity in the Halakhah in Honor of Moshe Zemer*. Pittsburgh, PA: Solomon B. Freehof Institute of Progressive Halakhah.

—2005. *Rabbinic Thought in the Talmud*. London: Valentine Mitchell.

—2005. The Relevance and Irrelevance of Hasidism. In: *Judaism and Theology, Essays of the Jewish Religion*. London: Vallentine Mitchell, pp. 134–43.

Jestice, P. G., 2007. A Great Jewish Conspiracy?. In: M. Frassetto, ed. *Christian Attitudes Toward the Jews in the Middle Ages: A Casebook*. New York: Routledge, pp. 25–42.

Jokisch, B., 2007. *From Islamic Imperial Law: Harun–Al-Rashid's Codification Project*. Berlin: Walter de Gruyter.

Kalmin, R., 2006a. *Jewish Babylonia between Persia and Roman Palestine*. New York: Oxford University Press.

—2006b. The Formation and Character of the Babylonian Talmud. In: S. Katz, ed. *Cambridge History of Judaism*. Cambridge: Cambridge University Press.

Kaplan, A., 1997. *Sefer Yetzira*. San Francisco: Weiser.

Karnafogel, E., 2000. Progress and Tradition in Medieval Ashkenaz. *Jewish History,* Volume 14, pp. 287–316.

—2006. What Do They Study in Your Yeshiva? – The Scope of Talmudic Commentary in Europe during the High Middle Ages. In: S. L. Mintz and G. M. Goldstein (eds). *Printing the Talmud: From Bomberg to Schottenstein.* New York: Yeshiva University Museum.

Katz, D. S., 1994. *The Jews In the History of England 1485–1850.* Oxford: Clarendon.

Katz, J., 1961. *Exclusiveness and Tolerance: Studies in Jewish-Gentile Relations in Medieval & Modern Times.* Oxford: Oxford University Press.

Katz, S. T., 2006. *The Cambridge History of Judaism: Volume 4, The Late Roman-Rabbinic Period.* Cambridge: Cambridge University Press.

Kniesmeyer, J. and Brecher, D. C., 1995. *Beyond the Pale – The History of the Jews in Russia.* [Online] Available at: http://www.friends-partners.org/partners/beyond-the-pale/english/31.html [accessed 18 April 2013].

Koestler, A., 1976. *The Thirteenth Tribe – The Khazar Empire and Its Heritage.* London: Hutchinson.

Kohler, G. Y., 2012. Judaism Buried or Revitalised? Wissenschaft des Judentums in Nineteenth-Century Germany – Impact, Actuality, and Applicability Today. In: D. J. Lasker, ed. *Jewish Thought and Jewish Belief.* Beer-Sheva: Ben Gurion University of the Negev Press, pp. 27–63.

Kraemer, D., 1990. *The Mind of the Talmud.* New York: Oxford University Press.

Langmuir, G. I., 1990. *Toward a Definition of Antisemitism.* Berkeley: University of California Press.

Laplanche, F., 2008. Christian Erudition in the Sixteenth and Seventeenth Centuries and the Hebrew State. *Hebraic Political Studies,* 3(1), pp. 5–18.

Lassner, J., 2012. *Jews, Christians and the Abode of Islam: Modern Scholarship, Medieval Realities.* Chicago: Chicago University Press.

Leslie, D. D., 1972. *The Survival of the Chinese Jews – The Jewish Community of Kaifeng.* Leiden: Brill.

Levenson, A. T. and Klein, R. C., 2006. *Introduction to Modern Jewish Thinkers: From Spinoza to Soloveitchik.* Lanham: Rowman & Littlefield.

Levine, S. J., 2011. Jewish Law from out of the Depths: Tragic Choices in the Holocaust. *Washington University Global Studies Law Review,* 10(1).

Levy, R. S., 2005. *Antisemitism.* Santa Barbara: ABC-CLIO.

Lewin, B., 1930–1. Misaridei HaGenizah. *Tarbiz,* 2(4), pp. 385–410.

—ed., 1921. *Letter of Sherira Gaon*. Haifa: Itzkovsky.

Libson, G., 1995. Halakah and Reality in the Geonic Period; Taqqanah, Minhag, Tradition and Consensus: Some Observations. In: *The Jews of Medieval Islam: Community, Society, and Identity: Proceedings of an International Conference Held by the Institute of Jewish Studies, University College London, 1992*. Leiden: Brill.

Libson, G., 2003. *Jewish and Islamic Law: A Comparative Study of Custom during the Geonic Period*. Cambridge, MA: Harvard University Press.

Liebeschutz, H., 1961. The Significance of Judaism in Peter Abelard's Dialogus. *Journal of Jewish Studies*, Volume 12, pp. 1–18.

Lower, M., 2004. Negotiating Interfaith Relations in Eastern Christendom: Pope Gregory IX, Bela IV of Hungary, and the Latin Empire. *Essays in Medieval Studies*, Volume 21, pp. 49–62.

Maciejko, P., 2011. *The Mixed Multitude: Jacob Frank and the Frankist Movement, 1755–1816*. Philadephia: University of Pennsylvania Press.

Malkiel, D., 2003. Jewish-Christian Relations in Europe, 840–1096. *Journal of Medieval History*, 29(1), pp. 55–83.

—2008. *Reconstructing Ashkenaz: The Human Face of Franco-German Jewry, 1000–1250*. Stanford, CA: Stanford University Press.

Malter, H., 1921. *Saadia Gaon*. Philadephia: Jewish Publication Society of America.

Mann, J., 1917. The Responsa of the Babylonian Geonim as a Source of Jewish History I. *Jewish Quarterly Review*, 7(4), pp. 457–90.

—1919. The Responsa of the Babylonian Geonim as a Source of Jewish History: II. The Political Status of the Jews. *The Jewish Quarterly Review*, 10(1), pp. 121–51.

Marcus, I. G., 1982. From Politics to Martyrdom. *Prooftexts*, 2(1), pp. 40–52.

Marcus, J. R. and Saperstein, M. (eds), 1999. *The Jew in the Medieval World: A Source Book, 315–1791*. New York: Hebrew Union College Press.

Marenbon, J. and Orlandi, G., 2001. *Peter Abelard Collationes ed.* Oxford: Oxford University Press.

Margaliot, M., 1962. *Sefer Hilchot Hanagid*. Jerusalem: Y. L. & M. Epstein.

Mattern, F., 2009. *Milton and Christian Hebraism*. Heidelberg: Universitätsverlag Winter.

Mendes-Flohr, P. R. and Reinharz, J., 1995. *The Jew in the Modern World: A Documentary History*. New York: Oxford University Press.

Meyer, M. A., 1988. *Response to Modernity: A History of the Reform Movement in Judaism*. New York: Oxford University Press.

Mintz, A., 2006. The Talmud in Translation. In: *Printing the Talmud*. New York: Yeshiva University Museum, pp. 121–41.

Nadler, A., 1997. *The Faith of the Mithnagdim: Rabbinic Responses to Hasidic Rapture*. Baltimore, MD: Johns Hopkins University Press.

Nadler, A. L., 1994. The War on Modernity of R. Hayyim Elazar Shapira of Munkacz. *Modern Judaism*, 14(3), pp. 233–64.

Nadler, S., 2001. *Spinoza: A Life*. Cambridge: Cambridge University Press.

Neher, A., 1986. *Jewish Thought and the Scientific Revolution of the Sixteenth Century; David Gans (1541–1613) and His Times*. Oxford: Littman Library.

Nelson, E., 2010. *The Hebrew Republic: Jewish Sources and the Transformation of European Political Thought*. Cambridge, MA: Harvard University Press.

Nemoy, L., 1930. Al-Qirqisani's Account of the Jewish Sects. In: *Hebrew Union College Annual Vol. 7*. New York: Ktav, pp. 317–98.

Neubauer, A., 1888. *Seder Hahachamim Vekorot Haitim*. Clarendon edn. Oxford: Clarendon Press.

—1889. Where Are the Ten Tribes? II. Eldad the Danite. *Jewish Quarterly Review*, 1(2), pp. 95–114.

Neuman, K., 2005. Political Hebraism and the Early Modern 'Respublica Hebraeorum': On Defining the Field. *Hebraic Political Studies*, 1(1), pp. 57–70.

Newman, J., 1932. *The Agricultural Life of the Jews in Babylonia between the years 200 C.E. and 500 C.E.* London: Oxord University Press.

Oppenheimer, A., 1983. *Babylonia Judaica in the Talmudic Period*. Wiesbaden: Ludwig Reichert.

—2005. *Between Rome and Babylon: Studies in Jewish Leadership and Society*. Tubingen: Mohr Siebeck.

Oshry, E., 1983. *Responsa from the Holocaust*. New York: Judaica Press.

Ostling, R. N., 1988. Religion: Giving the Talmud to the Jews. *Time*, 18 January.

Parry, M., 1928. *L'epithèt Traditionnelle dans Homère*. Paris: Société d'éditions.

Patai, R., 1986. *The Seed of Abraham*. Utah: University of Utah Press.

Pearl, C., 1988. *Rashi*. London: Peter Halban.

Peters, E., 1995. Jewish History and Gentile Memory: The Expulsion of 1492. *Jewish History*, 9(1), pp. 9–34.

Popper, W., 1969. *The Censorship of Hebrew Books; Introduction by Moshe Carmilly-Weinberger*. New York: Ktav.

Rapaport-Albert, A. and Kwasman, T., 2006. Late Aramaic: The Literary and Linguistic Context of the Zohar. *Aramaic Studies*, 4(1), pp. 5–19.

Ravid, B., 1987. The Legal Status of the Jews in Venice to 1509. *Proceedings of the American Academy for Jewish Research*, Volume 54, pp. 169–202.

Raz-Krakotzkin, A., 2004. Censorship, Editing and the Reshaping of Jewish Identity: The Catholic Church and Hebrew Literature in the Sixteenth Century. In: A. P. Coudert and J. S. Shoulson (eds) *Hebraica Veritas?* Philadelphia: University of Pennsylvania Press.

—2007. *The Censor, the Editor and the Text: The Catholic Church and the Shaping of the Jewish Canon in the Sixteenth Century (Jewish Culture & Contexts)*. Philadelphia: University of Pennsylvania Press.

Rodkinson, M., 1903. *The History of the Talmud*. New York: Naby Press.

van Rooden, P., 2001. The Jews and Religious Toleration in the Dutch Republic. In: R. Po-chia Hsia and H. van Nierop (eds). *Calvinism and Religious Toleration in the Dutch Golden Age*. Cambridge: Cambridge University Press, pp. 132–7.

Rosenblatt, J. P., 2008. *Renaissance England's Chief Rabbi: John Selden*. Oxford: Oxford University Press.

Rosen, J., 2001. *The Talmud, The Internet*. London: Continuum.

Roth, N., 1995. *Conversos, Inquisition and the Expulsion of Jews from Spain*. Madison: University of Wisconsin Press.

Ruderman, D. B., 1995. *Jewish Thought and Scientific Discovery in Early Modern Europe*. New Haven, CT: Yale University Pres.

Rummel, E., 2002. *The Case against Johann Reuchlin: Religious and Social Controversy in Sixteenth-century Germany*. Toronto: University of Toronto Press.

Rustow, M., 2008. *Heresy and the Politics of Community; The Jews of the Fatimid Caliphate*. Ithaca, NY: Cornell University Press.

Samet, M., 1988. The Beginnings of Orthodoxy. *Modern Judaism*, 8(3), pp. 249–69.

Samuel, E., 1978–1980. The Provenance of the Westminster Talmud. *Transactions & Miscellanies (Jewish Historical Society of England)*, Volume 27, pp. 148–50.

Sand, S., 2009. *The Invention of the Jewish People*. London: Verso.

Schmidt-Biggemann, W., 2006. Political Theology in Renaissance Christian Kabbala: Petrus Galatinus and Guillaume Postel. *Hebraic Political Studies*, 1(3), pp. 286–309.

Scholem, G., 1973. *Sabbetai Sevi, The Mystical Messiah*. Princeton, NJ: Princeton University Press.

Schreiber, A. M., 2002–3. The Hatam Sofer's Nuanced Attitude towards Secular Learning, Maskilim and Reformers. *The Torah U-Madda Journal*, Volume 11, pp. 123–73.

Schur, N., 1995. *The Karaite Encyclopedia.* Frankfurt: Peter Lang.

Schwartz, D. B., 2012. *The First Modern Jew.* Princeton, NJ: Princeton University Press.

Schwartz, S., 2007. The Political Geography of Rabbinic Texts. In C. Fonrobert and M. Jaffee, (eds). *The Cambridge Companon to the Talmud.* Cambridge: Cambridge University Press, pp. 75–96.

Schwarzfuchs, S. R., 1967. The Expulsion of the Jews from France (1306). *Jewish Quarterly Review*, Volume 57, pp. 482–9.

Segal, Eliezer. http://people.ucalgary.ca/~elsegal/TalmudPage.html

Shäfer, P., 2007. *Jesus in the Talmud.* Princeton, NJ: Princeton University Press.

Shakir, A. M., 1956. *Umdah at-Tafsir 'an al-Hafiz Ibn Kathir.* Cairo: Dar al-Ma'arif.

Shapiro, M. B., 1999. *Between the Yeshiva World and Modern Orthodoxy; The Life and Works of Rabbi Jehiel Jacob Weinberg 1884–1966.* London: The Littman Library.

—2006. Talmud Study in the Modern Era: From Wissenschaft and Brisk to Daf Yomi. In: *Printing the Talmud: From Bomberg to Schottenstein.* New York: Yeshiva University Museum, pp. 103–10.

Shreiber, E., 1892. *Abraham Geiger, the Greatest Reform Rabbi of the Nineteenth Century.* Spokane: Spokane Printing Company.

Silver, D. J., 1965. *Maimonidean Criticism and the Maimonidean Controversy 1180–1240.* Leiden: Brill.

Silverman, R. M., 1995. *Baruch Spinoza: Outcast Jew, Universal Sage.* Northwood (Middlesex): Symposium Press.

Smalley, B., 1952. *The Study of the Bible in the Middle Ages.* Oxford: Blackwell.

Soloveitchik, H., 1994. Rupture and Reconstruction: The Transformation of Contemporary Orthodoxy. *Tradition*, 28(4), pp. 64–130.

—2006. The Printed Page of the Talmud: The Commentaries and their Authors. In: S. L. Mintz and G. M. Goldstein (eds). *Printing the Talmud: From Bomberg to Schottenstein.* New York: Yeshiva University Museum.

Sonne, I., 1943. *Expurgation of Hebrew Books -- the Work of Jewish Scholars: A Contribution to the History of the Censorship of Hebrew Books in Italy in the Sixteenth Century.* New York: New York Public Library.

Sorkin, D., 1992. Jews, the Enlightenment and Religious Toleration; Some Reflections. *Leo Baeck Institute Yearbook*, 37(1), pp. 3–16.

—1994. The Case for Comparison: Moses Mendlessohn and Religious Enlightenment. *Modern Judaism*, 14(2), pp. 121–38.

Sperber, D., 1994. *Magic and Folklore in Rabbinic Literature*. Ramat Gan: Bar Illan University Press.

Starr-LeBeau, G. D., 2003. *In The Shadow of the Virgin*. Princeton, NJ: Princeton University Press.

Steinsaltz, A., 1989. *The Talmud, The Steinsaltz Edition: A Reference Guide*. New York: Random House.

—2009. *The Essential Talmud*. New York: Basic Books.

Stern, E., 2011. Genius and Demographics in Modern Jewish History. *Jewish Quarterly Review*, 101(3), pp. 347–82.

—2013. *The Genius: Elijah of Vilna and the Making of Modern Judaism*. Yale, CT: Yale University Press.

Stern, S., 2001. *Calendar and Community; A History of the Jewish Calendar 2nd Century BCE to 10th Century CE*. Oxford: Oxford University Press.

Stillman, N., 1991. *The Jews of Arab Lands in Modern Times*. Philadelphia, PA: Jewish Publication Society.

—2012. The Jews in the Medieval Arab Speaking World. In: A. Levenson, ed. *The Wiley-Blackwell History of Jews and Judaism*. Malden, MA: Blackwell, pp. 207–23.

Stow, K. R., 1987. The Jewish Family in the Rhineland in the High Middle Ages: Form and Function. *The American Historical Review*, 92(5), pp. 1085–110.

Strack, H. L., Sternberger, G. S., 1991. *Introduction to the Talmud and Midrash*. Edinburgh: Fortress Press.

Tarshish, A., 1985. *Dawn in the West*. New York: Lanham.

Ta Shma, Y., 1999. *Hasifrut Haparshanit B'eropa U'vzfon Africa, 2 Vols*. Jerusalem: Magnes Press.

The Taylor-Schechter Genizah Research Unit, 2002. *Mrs Lewis & Mrs Gibson*. [Online] Available at: http://www.lib.cam.ac.uk/Taylor-Schechter/lewis-and-gibson.html [accessed 17 April 2013].

Urbach, E., 1968. *Ba'alei HaTosefot – Toldoteihem, Hiburreihem V Shitatam*. Jerusalem: Bialik Institute.

Wacholder, B., 1982. Jacob Frank and the Frankists' Hebrew Zoharist Letter. *Offprint from Hebrew Union College Annual*, Volume 53, pp. 265–93.

Weiser, C. M., 1995. *Frumspeak: The First Dictionary of Yeshivish*. Lanham, MD: Rowman & Littlefield.

Weiss Halivni, D., 1986. *Midrash, Mishnah and Gemara.* Cambridge, MA: Harvard University Press.

Wiersma, S., 2009. The Dynamic of Religious Polemics: The Case of Raymond Martin. In: *Interaction between Judaism and Christianity in Religion, Art and Literature.* Leiden: Koninklijke Brill, pp. 201–17.

Wilensky, M. L., 1956. The Polemic of Rabbi David of Makow against Hasidism. *Proceedings of the American Academy for Jewish Research,* Volume 25, pp. 137–56.

Wisch, B., 2003. Vested Interest: Redressing Jews on Michelangelo's Sistine Ceiling. *Artibus et Historiae,* 24(48), pp. 143–72.

Yad VaShem, 2013. *The Story of the Jewish Community in Mir.* [Online] Available at: http://www.yadvashem.org/yv/en/exhibitions/communities/mir/rescue_yeshiva.asp [accessed 23 April 2013].

Zeitlin, S., 1974. *Studies in the Early History of Judaism Vol II.* New York: Ktav Publishing House.

Ziskind, J. R., 1978. Petrus Cunaeus on Theocracy, Jubilee and the Latifundia. *The Jewish Quarterly Review,* 68(4), pp. 235–54.

# Acknowledgements

*I have acquired knowledge from all my teachers.* So wrote the author of Psalm 119, who people say was King David. I owe a debt of gratitude to all my teachers, the sages who lived in ages past, the scholars and academics whom I have never met but whose works I have encountered and of course those whose words I heard from their own mouths. (I would like to have said, as a student of earlier generations might, 'at whose feet I sat' but of course we don't sit at our teachers' feet these days.) The knowledge is theirs, any errors only mine.

More particularly I would like to thank my agent, Sheila Ableman, for her unbounded enthusiasm for the book and for her ongoing support. To Robin Baird-Smith for his positivity, energy and for believing in the idea, to Joel Simons for his adept managing of the project, and his patience even when I was at my most trying, and to Anya Rosenberg, Helen Flood and the rest of the team at Bloomsbury. Grateful thanks too to Kim Storry for project managing the prepress, and to Sue Cope for her diligent copy editing and for being prepared to work all hours to meet the deadline.

Thanks also to Professor Jerry Gotel for reading the manuscript, to Dayan Ivan Binstock for the conversations which taught me so much, to Paul Summer for solving the Jacob Landau riddle, to Ivor Jacobs for helping me lay my hands on vital out-of-print texts and to my brother Jeremy Freedman for explaining how Henry VIII's Talmudic investigations influenced English divorce law. Particular thanks must go to my parents Joan and Louis Freedman who made sure that I received an education which enabled me to read and understand the Talmud, to my children Josh and Mollie whose continual interest and probing questions obliged me to sharpen my wits and to my wife Karen for her unflagging support and encouragement. Finally, words can never adequately acknowledge just how much I owe to the greatest of all my Talmud teachers, Rabbi Dr Louis Jacobs, whose scholarship, wit, breadth of knowledge and profound humanity turned the Talmud from a dusty tome to a source of inspiration for so many people. May his memory be for a blessing.

# Index